Iggy Pop Life Class

by Jeremy Deller

Edited by Sharon Matt Atkins

Brooklyn Museum in association with Heni Publishing

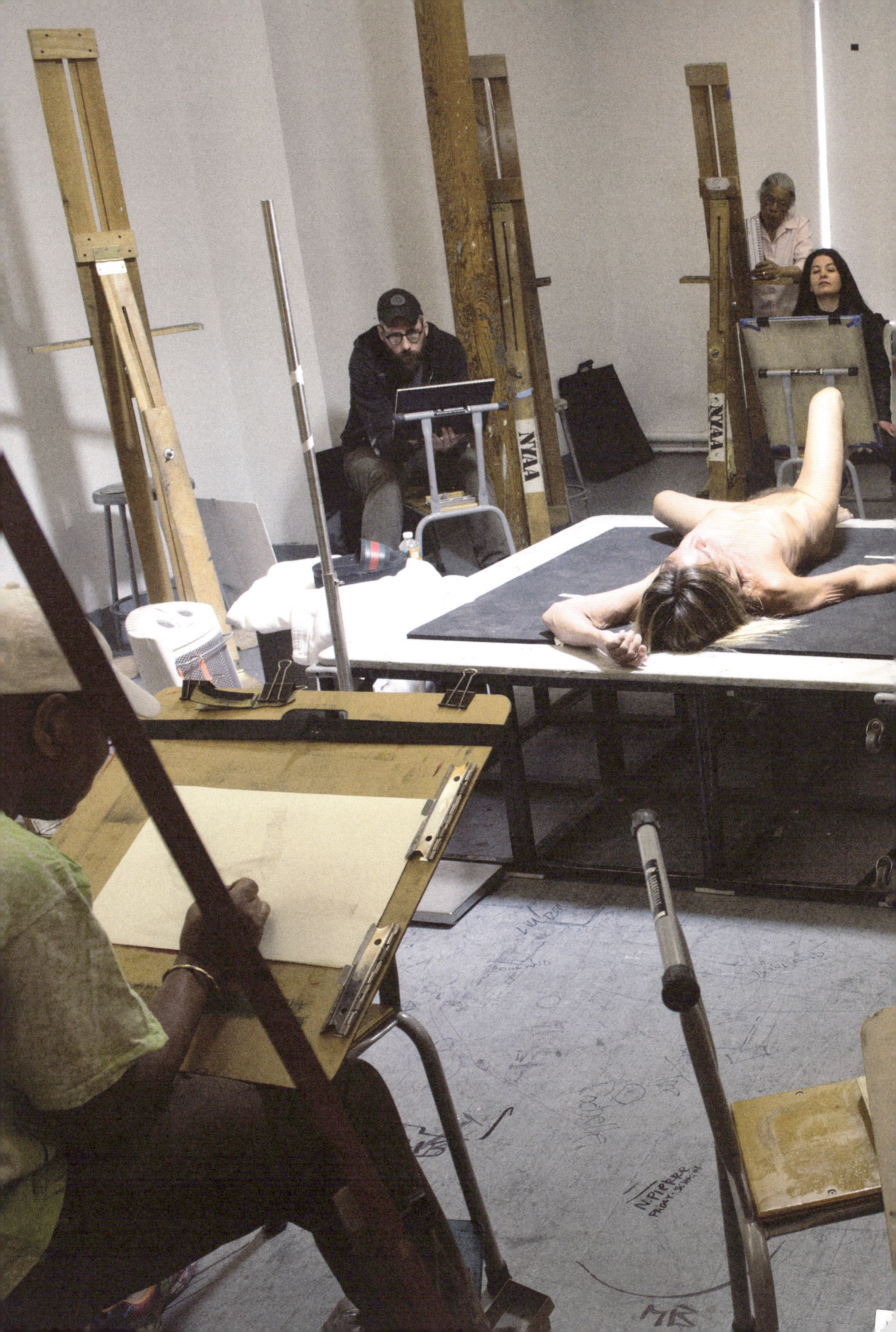
NYAA
NYAA

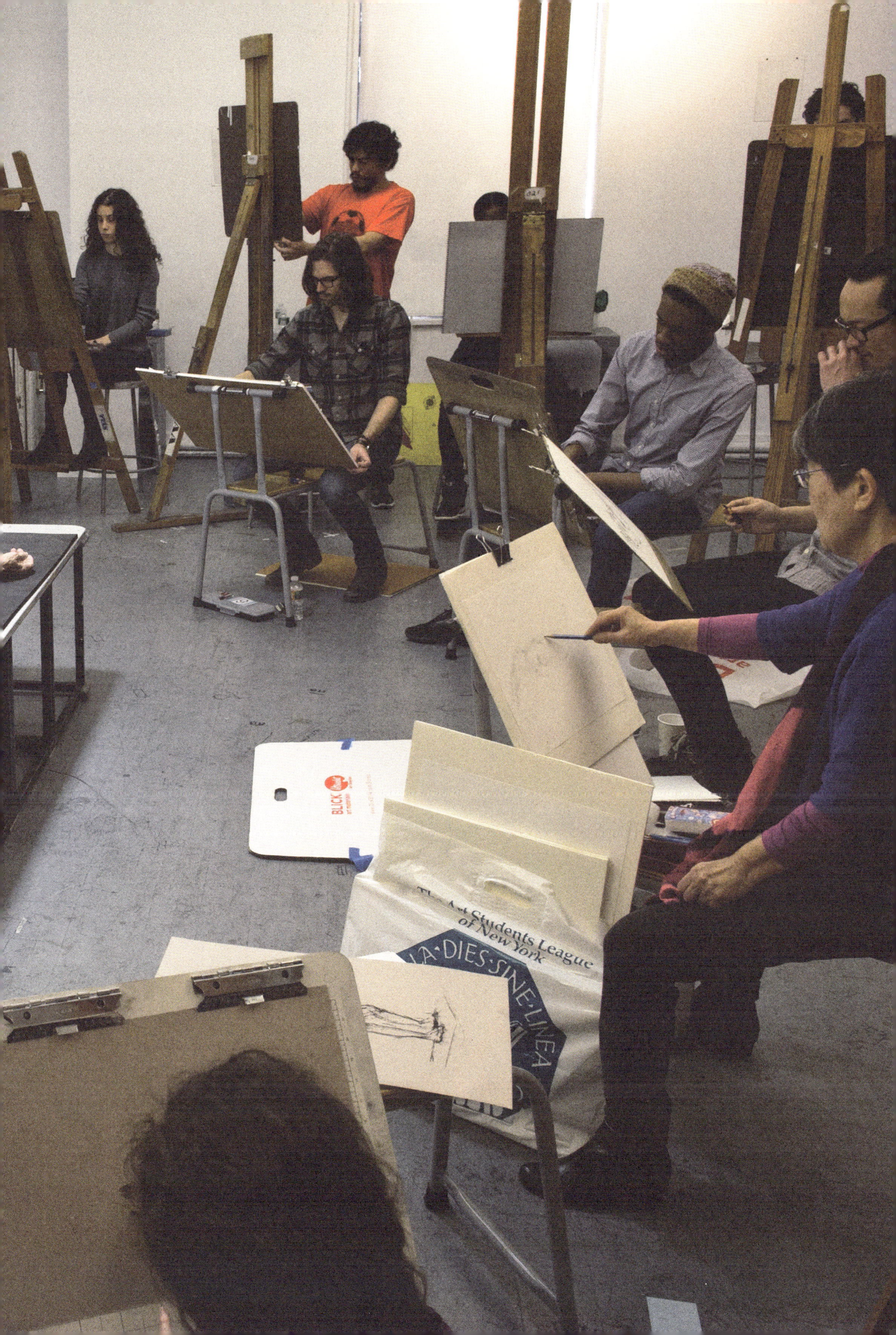
BLICK
The Art Students League of New York
LA·DIES·SINE·LINEA

Published on the occasion of
the exhibition *Iggy Pop Life Class*
at the Brooklyn Museum,
November 4, 2016 – March 26, 2017.

Iggy Pop Life Class is organized
by Sharon Matt Atkins, Vice Director,
Exhibitions and Collections
Management, Brooklyn Museum.

Generous support for this exhibition
is provided by Cristina Enriquez-Bocobo
and the FUNd.

The accompanying book is published
by the Brooklyn Museum in association
with Heni Publishing, London. This
publication is supported by the FUNd.

Iggy Pop Life Class is part of *A Year of Yes: Reimagining Feminism at the Brooklyn Museum*,
for which leadership support is provided
by Elizabeth A. Sackler, an anonymous
donor, the Stavros Niarchos Foundation,
the Calvin Klein Family Foundation,
and Mary Jo and Ted Shen. Generous
support is also provided by the Taylor
Foundation, the Antonia and Vladimer
Kulaev Cultural Heritage Fund, and
The Cowles Charitable Trust.

First published in 2016 by the Brooklyn
Museum and Heni Publishing

Brooklyn Museum
200 Eastern Parkway
Brooklyn, NY 11238-6052
United States
www.brooklynmuseum.org

Heni Publishing
2nd Floor
6–10 Lexington Street
London W1F OLB
United Kingdom
www.henipublishing.com

ISBN: 978-0-9933161-3-5

For the Brooklyn Museum
Project editors: James Leggio
with Anya Szykitka
Collection photography: Sarah DeSantis
Image and rights acquisition: Jessica Palinski
Photographs of the Life Class in progress:
Elena Olivo

For Heni Publishing
Designer: Fraser Muggeridge studio
Production manager: Phoebe Adler
Printed in Belgium

← Iggy Pop Life Class in progress, February 21, 2016,
New York Academy of Art

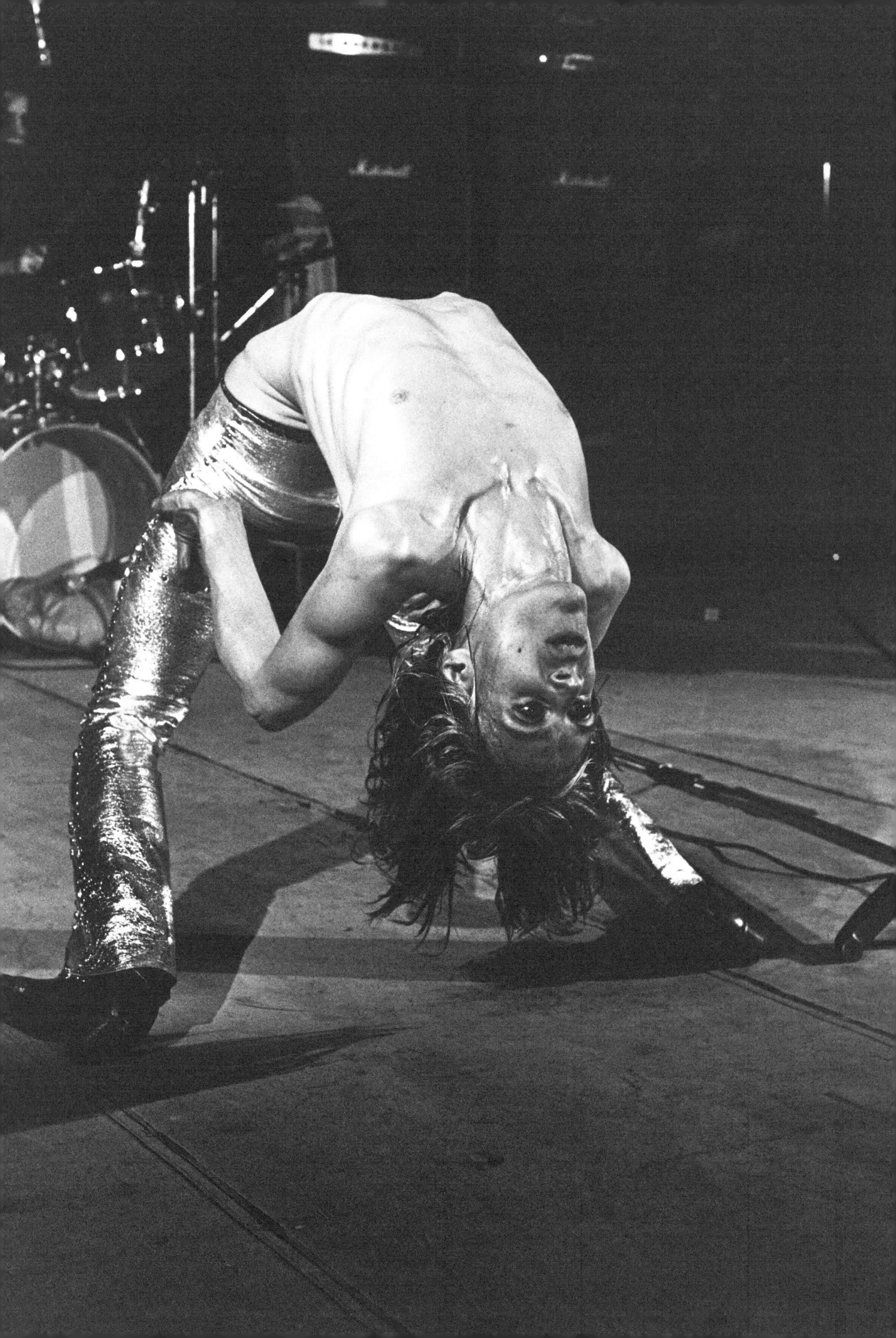

Introduction

Iggy Pop has one of the most recognizable bodies in popular culture. A body that is key to an understanding of rock music, and that has been paraded, celebrated, and scrutinized through the years in a way that is unusual for a man. It is also fair to say that it has witnessed a lot. It was for these reasons that I wanted him to sit for a life class.

Even though his body has been photographed and reproduced in print and online millions of times, I felt it could only be properly understood and appreciated by being drawn—a process in which you give the subject the attention it deserves. I am the first to admit there is a degree of absurdity in the idea of convincing someone, who is known for his dynamic stage presence, to be still for four hours.

The idea for the class occurred to me when wandering through the Louvre in 2006. There, I came upon a Mike Kelley installation, *Profondeurs Vertes* (Green Depths), that responded to six paintings from the Detroit Institute of Arts, a museum Pop knows well. Kelley has been such an influential artist to me for so many reasons, not least in his willingness to take popular culture seriously. In this installation, I thought to myself, "What would be the most outrageously 'Mike Kelley' artwork that I could make?" Almost immediately the idea of this life class occurred, more or less fully formed as you see it in this book and exhibition.

It was important to me too that the drawings would then be given to a museum where they would reside alongside artifacts from world history and cultures. This seemed appropriate when considering the roots of rock music. The idea is often the easy part though; Anne Pasternak's enthusiasm translated into a genuine commitment to making this happen, and of course our model's agreement to be looked at and documented in this way was essential. I thank them both for saying yes.

Jeremy Deller

← Mick Rock, *Iggy Pop Backbend*, 1972

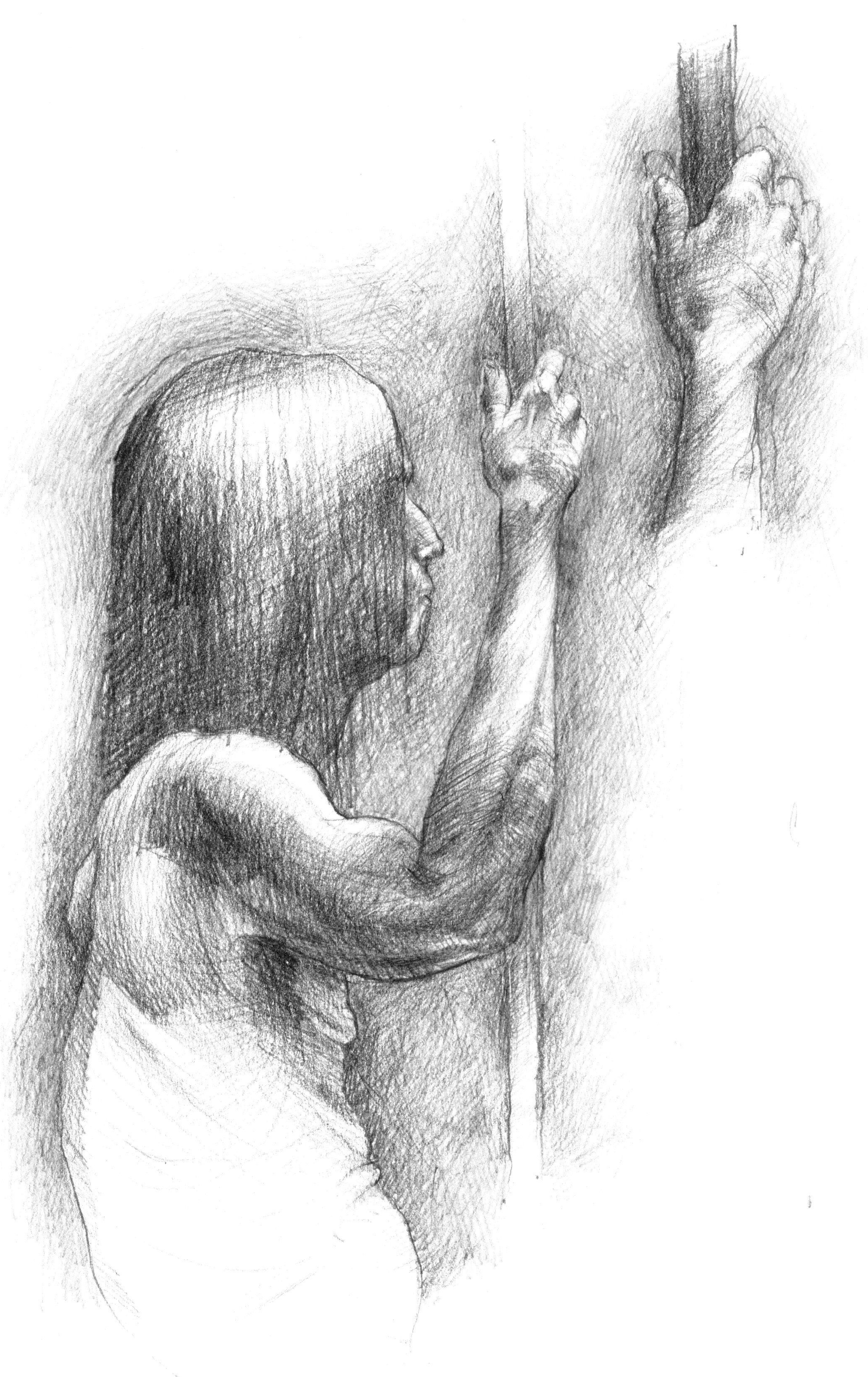

Foreword

When Jeremy Deller first approached me with his concept for *Iggy Pop Life Class*, I knew it was a perfect partnership for the Brooklyn Museum. His idea speaks to the broad impact of music on contemporary culture as well as to issues of gender, sexuality, and the representation of the iconic male body through the ages and across continents.

Iggy Pop, the model for the class, is central to the concept. As Deller notes, "His body has witnessed much and should be documented." A pioneering singer, songwriter, musician, and actor, Pop began performing in the 1960s and became known for radical, unpredictable stage performances: highly physical events where he was known to bare all, and which often left his body battered. In the process, Pop confronted taboos of male sexuality. Since Deller believes the best way to understand something is to study it, he invited twenty-two artists to study Pop's body in a life drawing class. The outcome was 107 drawings—intimate representations of his form that allow us to reconsider masculinity at a time of gender fluidity.

The resulting exhibition presents fifty-three of the drawings of the performer's naked body, alongside selected art objects from the Brooklyn Museum's historical collections that also focus on the male body, as a way to consider a more pluralistic male sexual identity.

The exhibition is presented as part of the initiative *A Year of Yes: Reimagining Feminism at the Brooklyn Museum*, extending from October 2016 to early 2018. *Iggy Pop Life Class* opens out this critical discussion by addressing how masculinity is defined, and enacted, in contemporary culture.

Many people deserve our thanks in helping to realize this exhibition and book. First and foremost, this exhibition would not have been possible without Jeremy Deller's vision or Iggy Pop's sincere generosity and willingness to participate. We are indebted to them both for making this unusual endeavor a reality. Sharon Matt Atkins, Vice Director, Exhibitions and Collections Management, organized the project with efficiency and aplomb. We are also fortunate that art historian Frances Borzello and curator, writer, and artist Mark Beasley have made important contributions to this publication, placing the life drawing within the contexts of art history and contemporary performance, respectively.

We greatly appreciate the generous support for this exhibition provided by Cristina Enriquez-Bocobo and by the FUNd.

For the ongoing support of the Museum's Trustees, I extend special gratitude to Barbara M. Vogelstein, Chair, and to every member of our Board. Without their confidence and active engagement, we would not be able to initiate and maintain the high level of exhibition and publication programming exemplified by *Iggy Pop Life Class*.

Anne Pasternak
Shelby White and Leon Levy Director
Brooklyn Museum

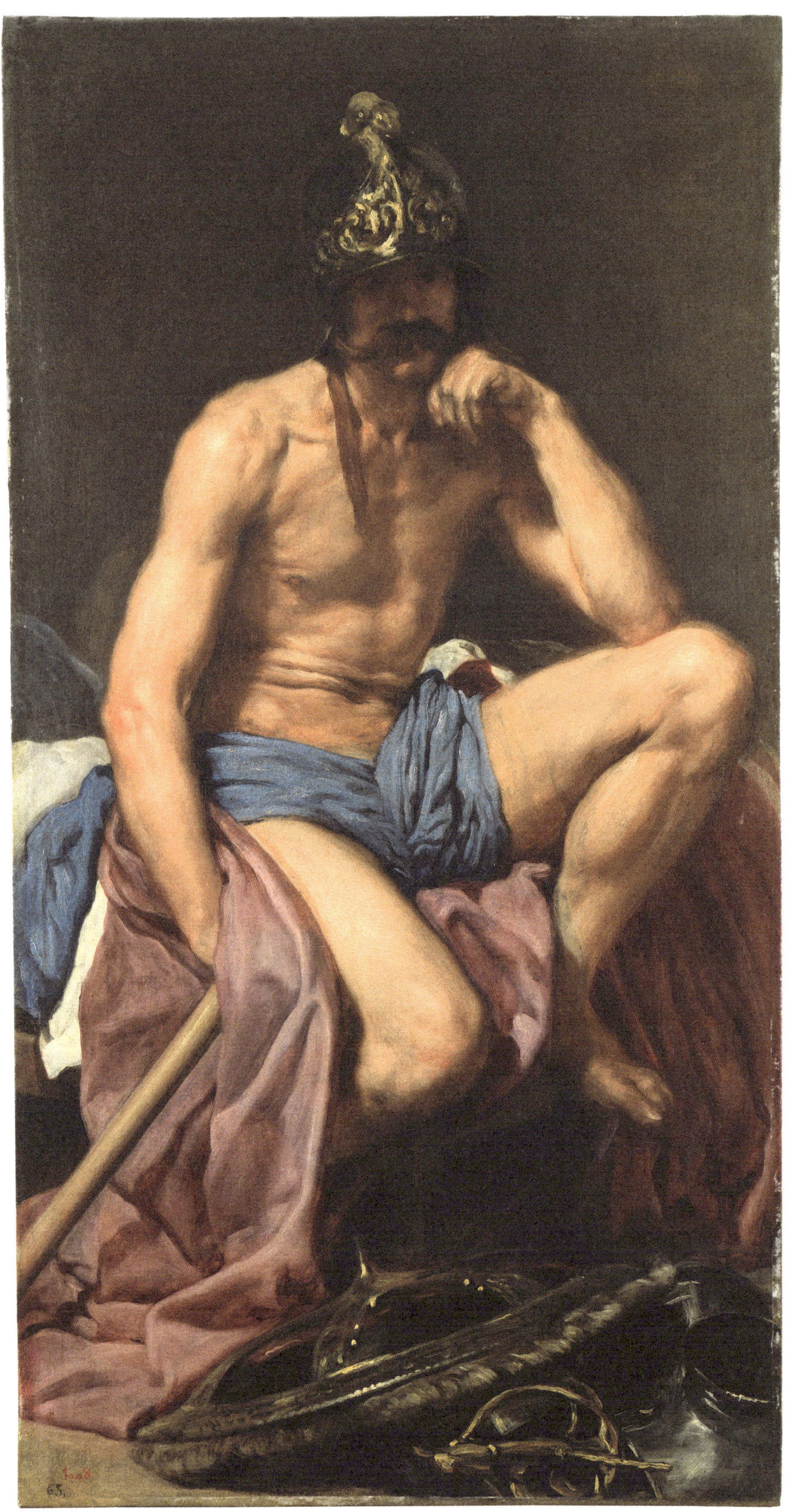

Diego Velázquez, *Mars*, circa 1638. Museo del Prado, Madrid

An Interview with Iggy Pop

Jeremy Deller and Sharon Matt Atkins

The interview took place on April 26, 2016.

Iggy Pop:

The drawings are wow. I'm going to mention unbidden that after I did the seated pose, it reminded me of something that was driving me nuts, so I was home for a few days last week, and there's a Velázquez in the Prado. It's a painting of Mars (opposite page). Do you know that painting? He's got a pole or some sort of a weapon. It's not quite the same, but it's close; he's not a young Mars. Yeah, he's been doing it for a while.

Jeremy Deller:

Yes, I know that painting. I remember when I approached you about ten years ago about doing this project and you declined. And then I approached you again last year, and very quickly you seemed keen. So I was wondering, what changed in the intervening decade?

Iggy: My initial response was like, "Red alert. Caution." Various things were going through my mind. I think one of the big problems was that you presented it to me as something that was going to be offered to a public institution, as "a gift to the Nation," and I thought, "Well, what if it's rejected?" It was very important to me that it be accepted. I'm a human being, damn it. And so that was part of it.

And then the other part of it was, I think, ten years ago I was a little too young. I just didn't have the weight yet that I felt would carry this well, away from my music career, which involves commerce, celebrity, and basically all the waste of the modern hurly-burly, all that horrible stuff that goes around—the actual buying and selling of my works and my presence. And I didn't want all that to cast a wave into this [drawing] project.

A lot of it was because Anne [Pasternak] was willing to stick the drawings in the Brooklyn Museum. I knew what that museum meant. I'm from a working-class area in Detroit, and the Detroit Institute of Arts also has a comprehensive collection, but back then, not really a very cosmopolitan audience; and I grew up near a state university, the University of Michigan, where I was lucky that I could go wander among mummies and Japanese screens and Balinese musical instruments, really with almost no fanfare, when I was nineteen or twenty years old. I don't even think you could do that now. So basically I was just apprehensive about the whole thing, and I was a little too young. So I just thought I didn't have the weight, and now I kind of feel like a lot has happened with and to my body.

So now I felt pretty confident, and I wanted to go the next step. For some reason it felt important to me that I could just stand naked for a group of human beings and have an exchange, basically that was the thing. And then I definitely didn't want to do it as a performance ... There was gonna be performance involved, but I didn't want it billed as a performance. When you look at the depiction of the male nude through history, the ways those artists framed the performances of the people in their works are at least as telling as mine, you know? There are a lot of different emotions and things that they saw.

Jeremy: Absolutely, and they all saw something different, in a way.

Iggy: Yes!

Jeremy: And I was interested in the cross section of people that we had in the life class, and it was like America looking at you, in a way; to me that is quite moving.

Iggy: I did a few nudes when I was very young and first came to New York City. I intuited, "OK, this is what you do. You come to the big city and you get recorded and multiplied and they have a look at you." And this is something I have to offer. I did a very good session with Bill King for Vogue. I did a Richard Bernstein (page 14). I did a Peter Hujar (page 15). But they all had agendas.

The one that really came across is the one done by Gerard Malanga (opposite page), who was also known as Gerard "Whips" in the Warhol entourage. He was like a lot of those people; he was what I would call a lapsed Ivy Leaguer. He had the look and the bearing, the education of a young, privileged, mid-Atlantic person, but he was out there with that group. And that photo was done in an empty penthouse ... it was just me, him, and what was probably a stolen Marilyn silkscreen that was sitting there for some reason in that place—no furniture. And, he took a very cold, hard, human look at me. And I was able to stand up to that look, that gaze, and I saw this life class as sort of the other end of that rainbow, for me.

Jeremy: The life drawing class was four hours long, and it felt at times like you were really being looked at and inspected, almost. Were you nervous or intimidated by this, or were you quite free?

Iggy: Nervous? No. I was wondering, going into it, "Well, how am I gonna stand still for so long?" That was solved very quickly, because we did a couple of standing shots or poses, which I thought were good. And then, given that I'm a lazy musician, I laid down on my back and you said, "There's one," which is fair game as a response, you know? And then with the seated pose I realized right away, "Well, this is not a flattering pose," and yet the pictures are damned flattering, a lot of them. It's kinda my favorite. And, you see, I'm sixty-nine years old; you see the girth all kinda goes toward the middle. But, I still look like I could hurt you with that thing.

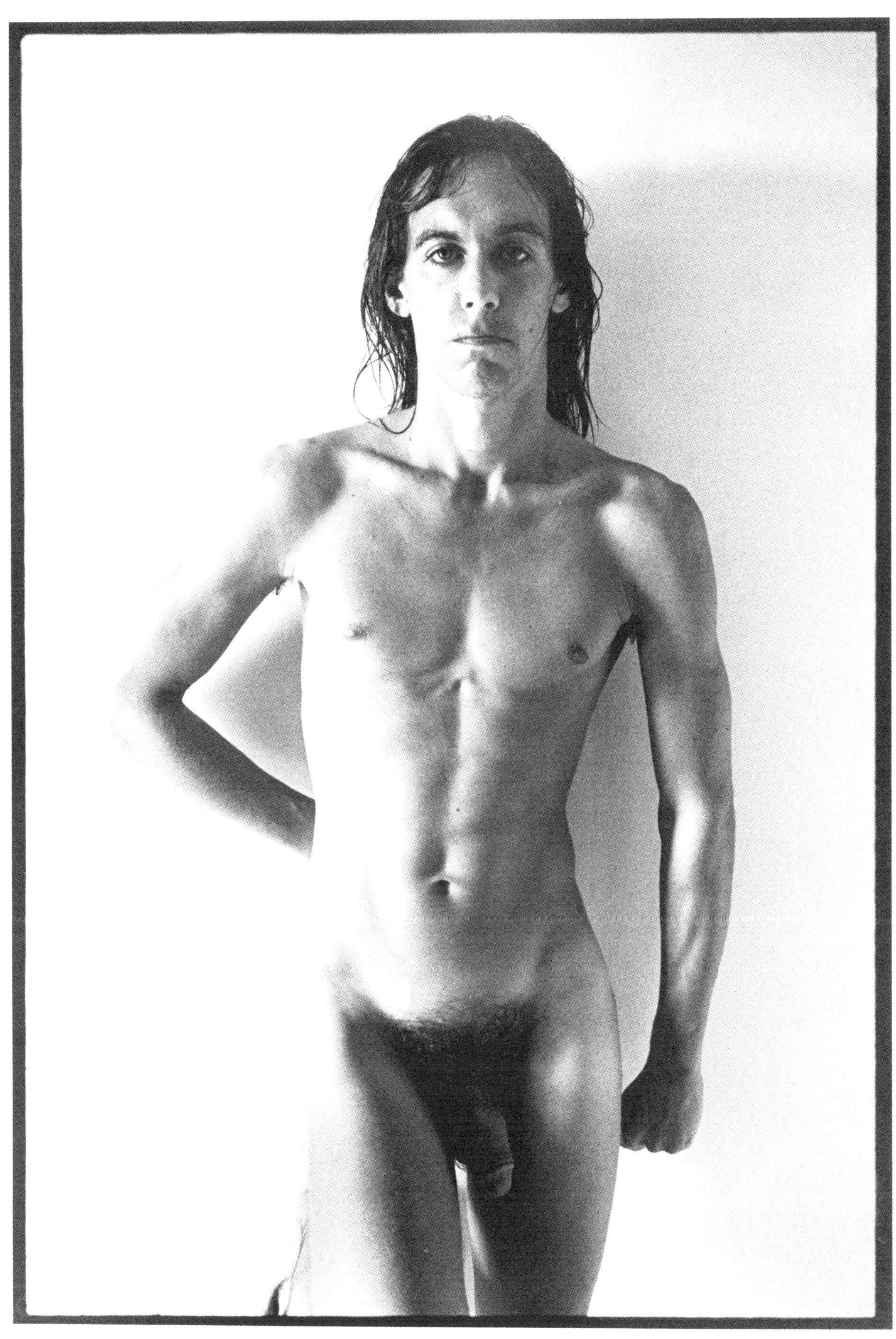

Gerald Malanga, *Iggy Pop*, 1971

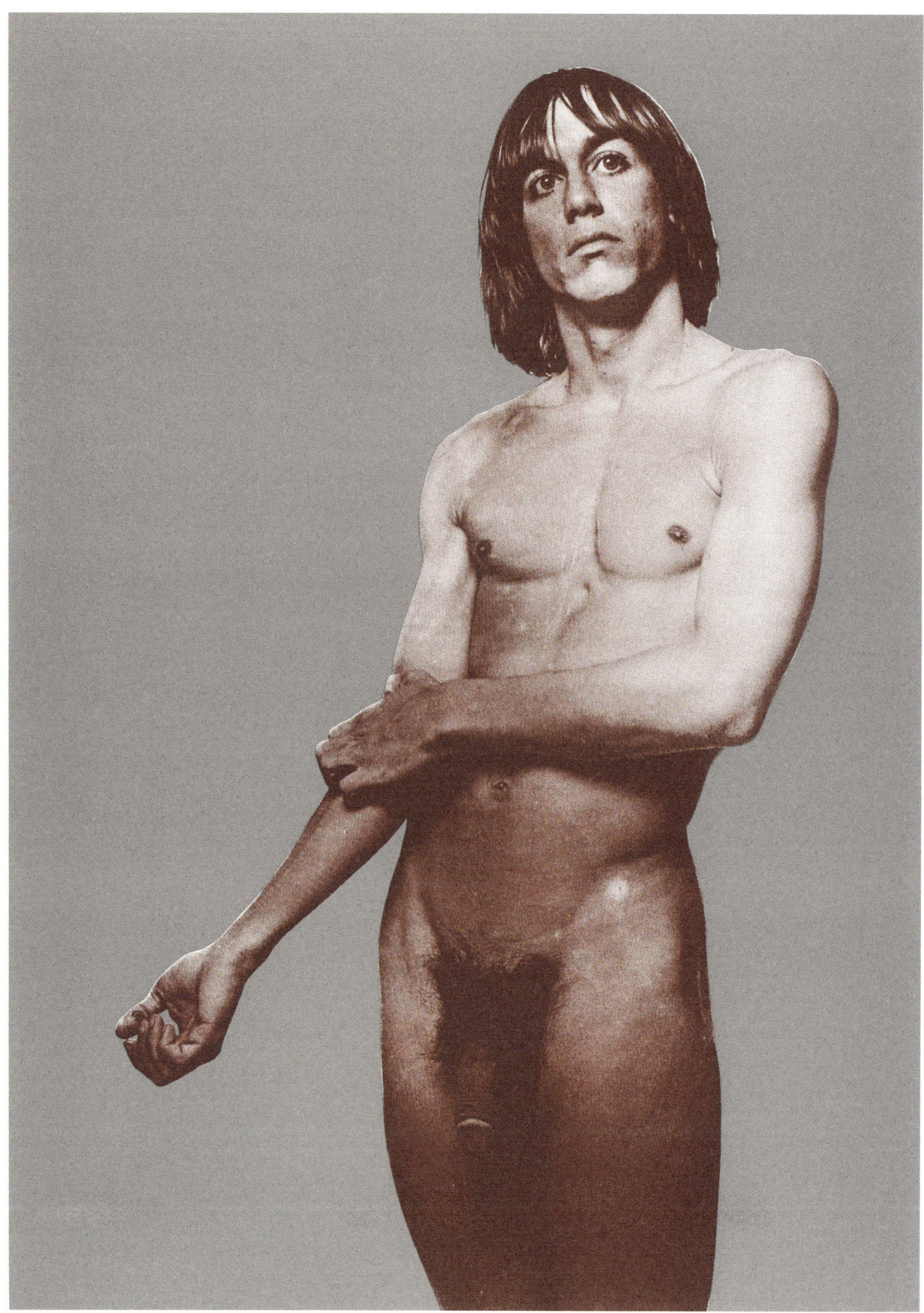

Richard Bernstein, *Iggy Pop*, 1972

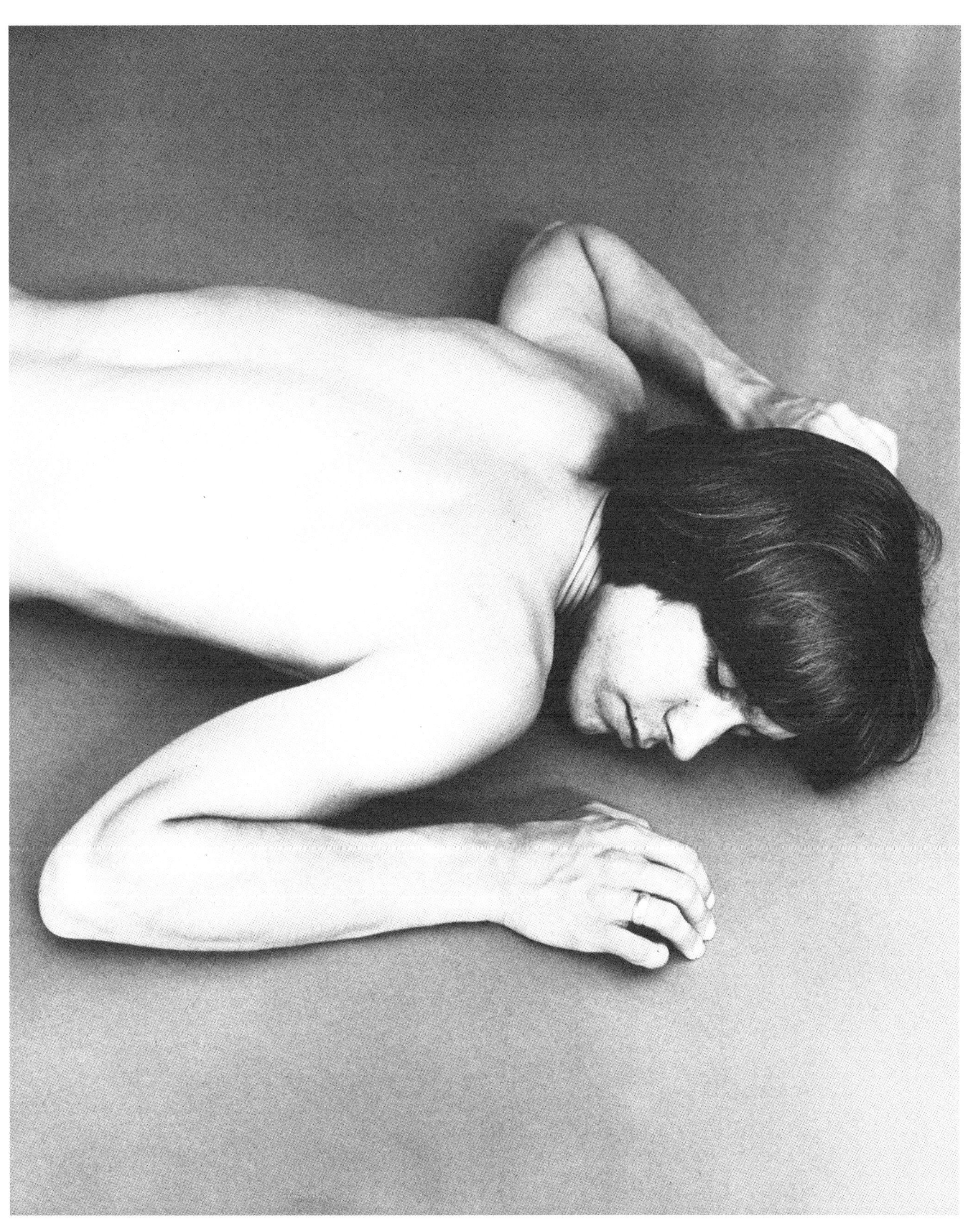

Peter Hujar, *Iggy Pop Lying Down*, 1969

It's an interesting piece, and they even got the—there was something I was doing with the arch of my left foot—and they even got that in that particular piece. They got the attitude, really, and I just had an instinct.

The most important thing, I kept saying, "Well, how am I going to meet these people?" And I'd asked you about it, "How am I going to enter?" Because first impressions are really important. And, you know, if you just get some dweeb waltzing in there with a nice butt formation or something, but without the propensity to live, artists get bored. They're still an audience. They're scribes in a way, and then also, you know, they're going to begin percolating and creating. So, it was a great choice.

You asked me early on did I just wanna come and meet them first, before we all got into the room. And that was great. I could walk over with all my clothes on, and they had all their clothes on … and they were just wonderful, happy, American students of all ages. And we were all able to say hi and have a little grin, and everything was cool. And that was done. And what I want to say, let's put it this way: it was the social opposite of a receiving line at Buckingham Palace, you know? It's what Americans, I hope, do well once in a while; there's a certain way of being formally informal that is an icebreaker for American people. And, I felt good about that, and then it was pretty easy. I found myself really relaxed about the taking-clothes-off part.

I was more curious than anything else, but I didn't feel like, "Oh, my God! How do I look?" Or anything like that. And, the toughest part about the standing/sitting still was to remain mentally engaged during it. And that's where I used my songs, basically. That's what I do when I work live, too, you know? I've got this song, and it starts at Point A, and I know it's gonna go to Point B, and it's a thread that carries along through that part of my life. So that was the idea … I mean you're letting them know, "I'm interested, so maybe you'll be interested too?" I guess that would be it.

Jeremy: So you almost had a set list running through your mind when you posed. It was like you were having a concert in your head?

Iggy: Yes, I did. I had a set list. I was just picking out songs. I'd come in and I'd think, Well, let's try "The Passenger." How 'bout "No Fun"? I had "1969" in there. I had "Gardenia," from my new record. And as I told them, I knew, "Well, that one takes four minutes and fifty seconds." So if you go through, then you say add the next one, but there may have been something, some psychic energy, in the fact that I was hearing those songs in my head, you know? That might have transmitted. It's possible.

Jeremy: The students, afterward, I don't know if you're aware, they said to me what a brilliant model you were. They were so impressed by your poise throughout the session.

Iggy: Ah, that's great. I guess they see a bit of that sort of thing, you know?

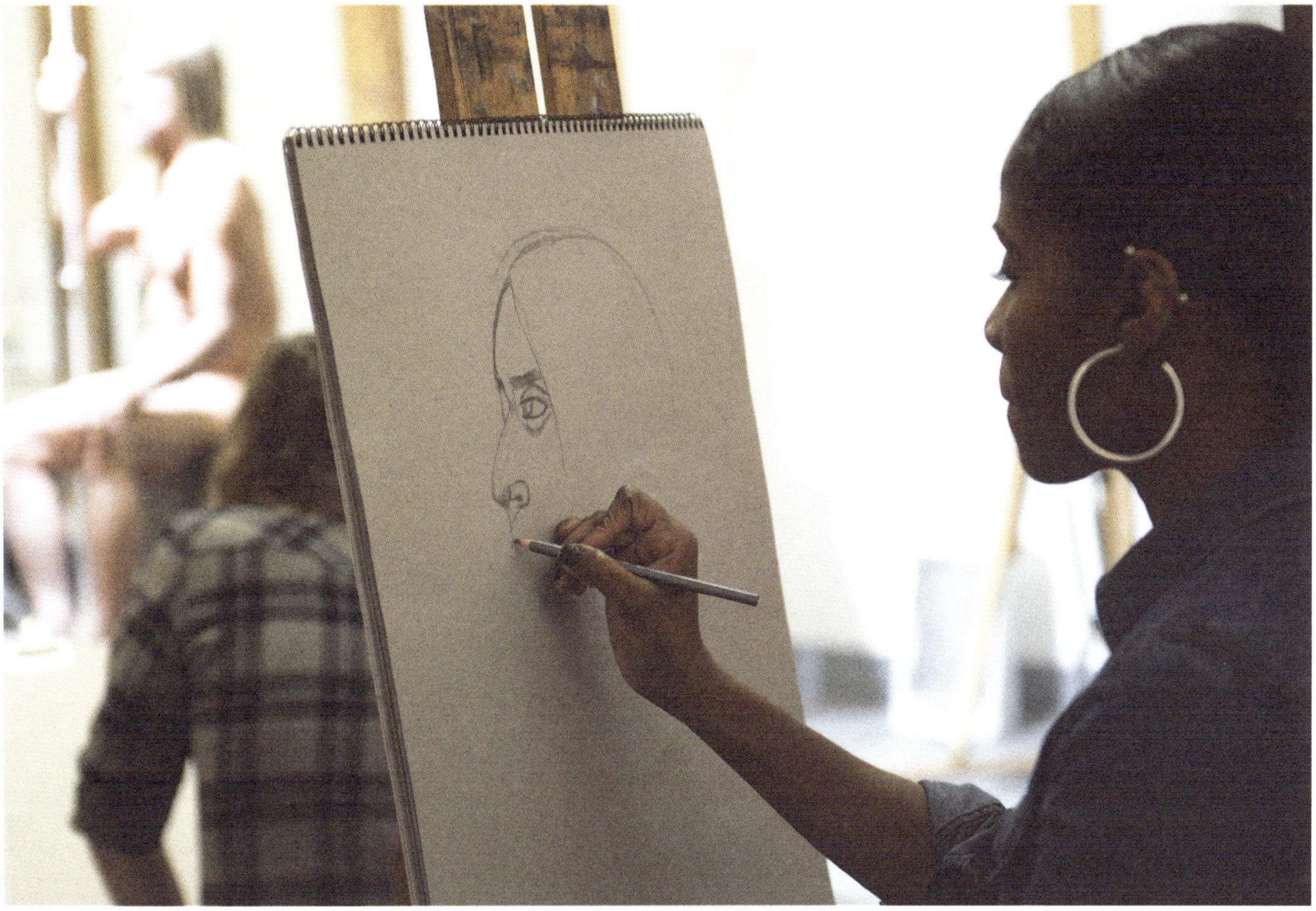

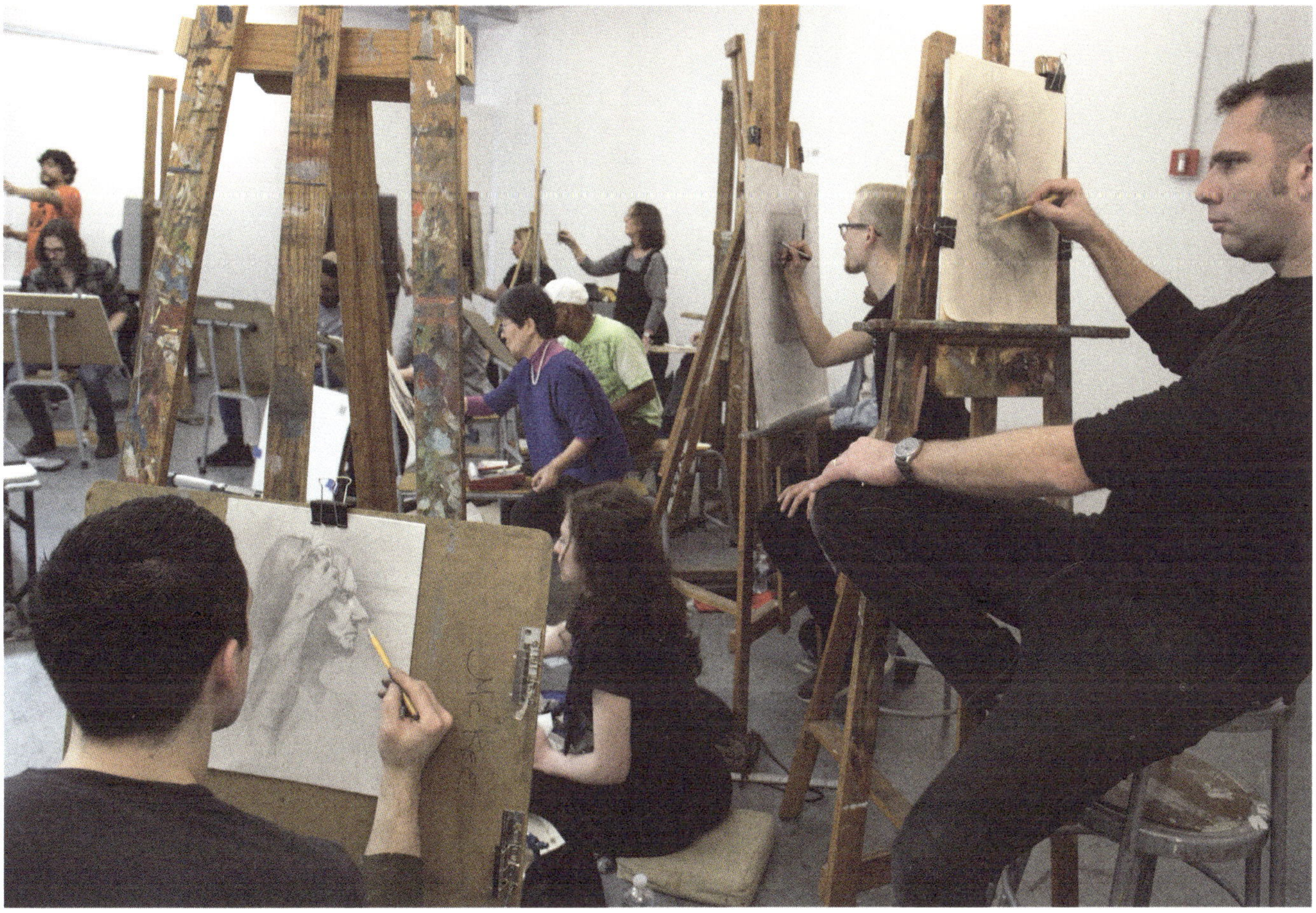

Iggy Pop Life Class in progress, February 21, 2016, New York Academy of Art

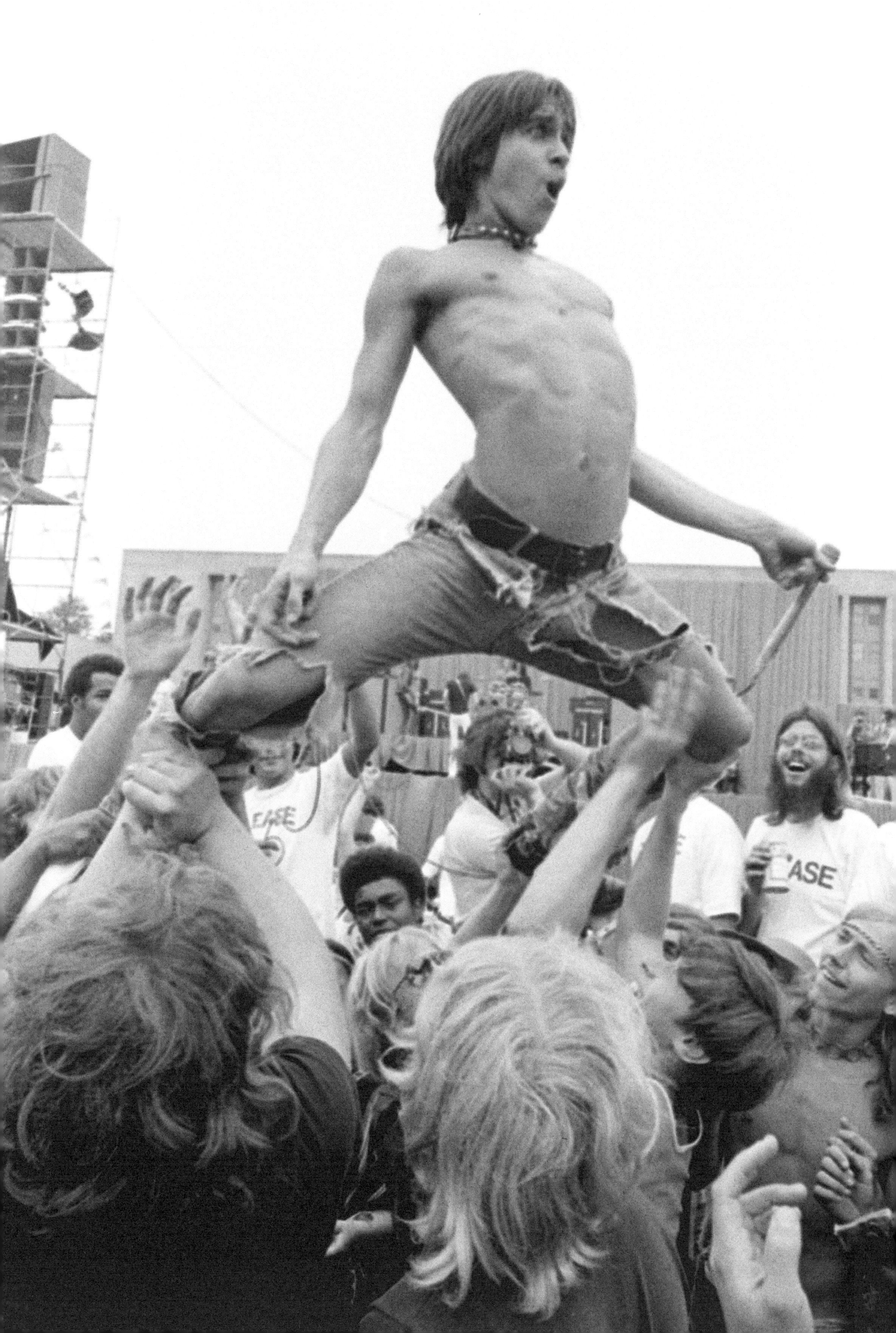

Jeremy: Yes, exactly; they know what a good model is.

I'm interested in the way you've used your body through your career. It's always been such an important part of your persona. Were you always conscious that you were going to do that? You've kept doing it, as well. Is that a statement, to keep showing your body?

Iggy: Well, yes. Part of it is that I played in bands for several years before I started venturing out in front. And I noticed the difference between music that finds its way into the souls of the listeners and music that doesn't. And, it wasn't until later that I noticed you needed kind of a transmitter or transformer sometimes. Someone or something to receive that energy that's being made with the musical tools and the musical instruments, and the motifs, and interpret it or translate it in a way that allows it to engage. I guess that's the best way I could put it.

You see I was always keen on Haitian music and art, which basically comes from the Benin area in West Africa; there are really, really complex rhythms, but they're always surrounding the peristyle temple. In the middle they're dancing around this basically endless beanstalk, if you will, that will get them to heavenly energy. So I just fell into those things as a way of transmitting, and also I maybe got a little possessed, or I do. I just let the music take me over and I try to get in there.

And, then later I'll have a peek, but not too often, and see, "Well, did that look all right?" You know? "Is that cool?" Sometimes it's cool and sometimes it's not. It goes both ways, but that was the idea.

There's definitely a kind of an instrument to express, but I don't know. I didn't sit down and write a dissertation about that or something. It just happened.

I discovered early in life, much to my sadness, that I was one of many people in the highly developed white Western, post–World War II tradition who had sort of been robbed of their ability to do anything except be some sort of damned student in a lecture hall—couldn't dance, get picked up … just couldn't get it, you know? Somehow that seemed to me like entering the category of nebbish-hood, a life not worth living.

So I definitely was exposed through my brief college education to Social Anth 101; I knew there were men in New Guinea who wore a penis sheath; that was pretty cool.

And at the same time I was playing the drums, and it's stupefying in a way. You play enough simple music and you just turn into this head-nodding beast, and I think that's OK.

Jeremy: Absolutely, I mean this is what rock and roll has given the world. It has given us a reason to do this again, or an excuse …

← Douglas R. Gilbert, *Iggy Pop in Soldier's Field, Chicago*, 1970. Photographic print. Premium Archives. (Photo: Douglas R. Gilbert/Premium Archives/Getty Images)

Eadweard Muybridge, *Animal Locomotion*, 1884–87. Brooklyn Museum →

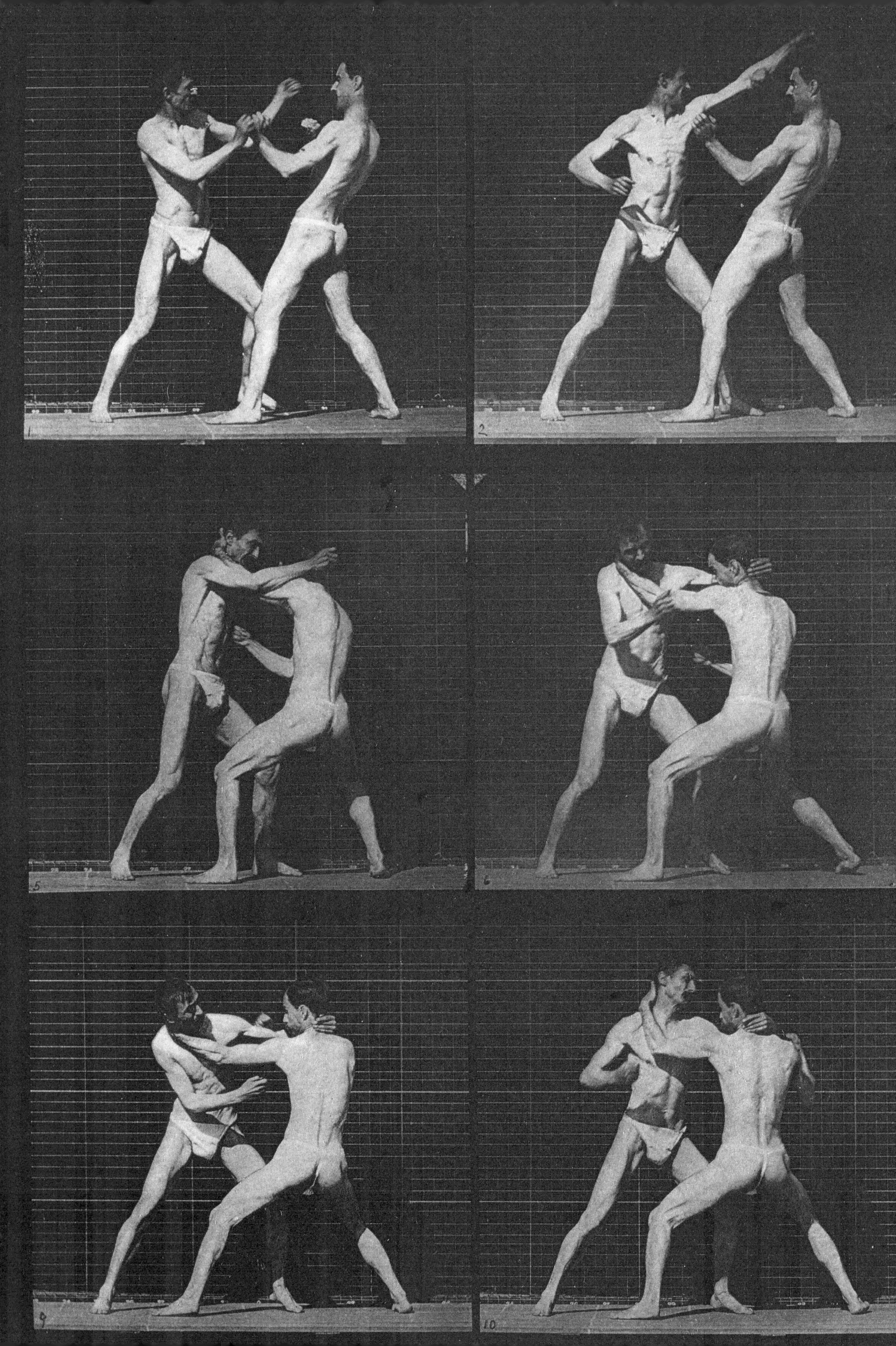

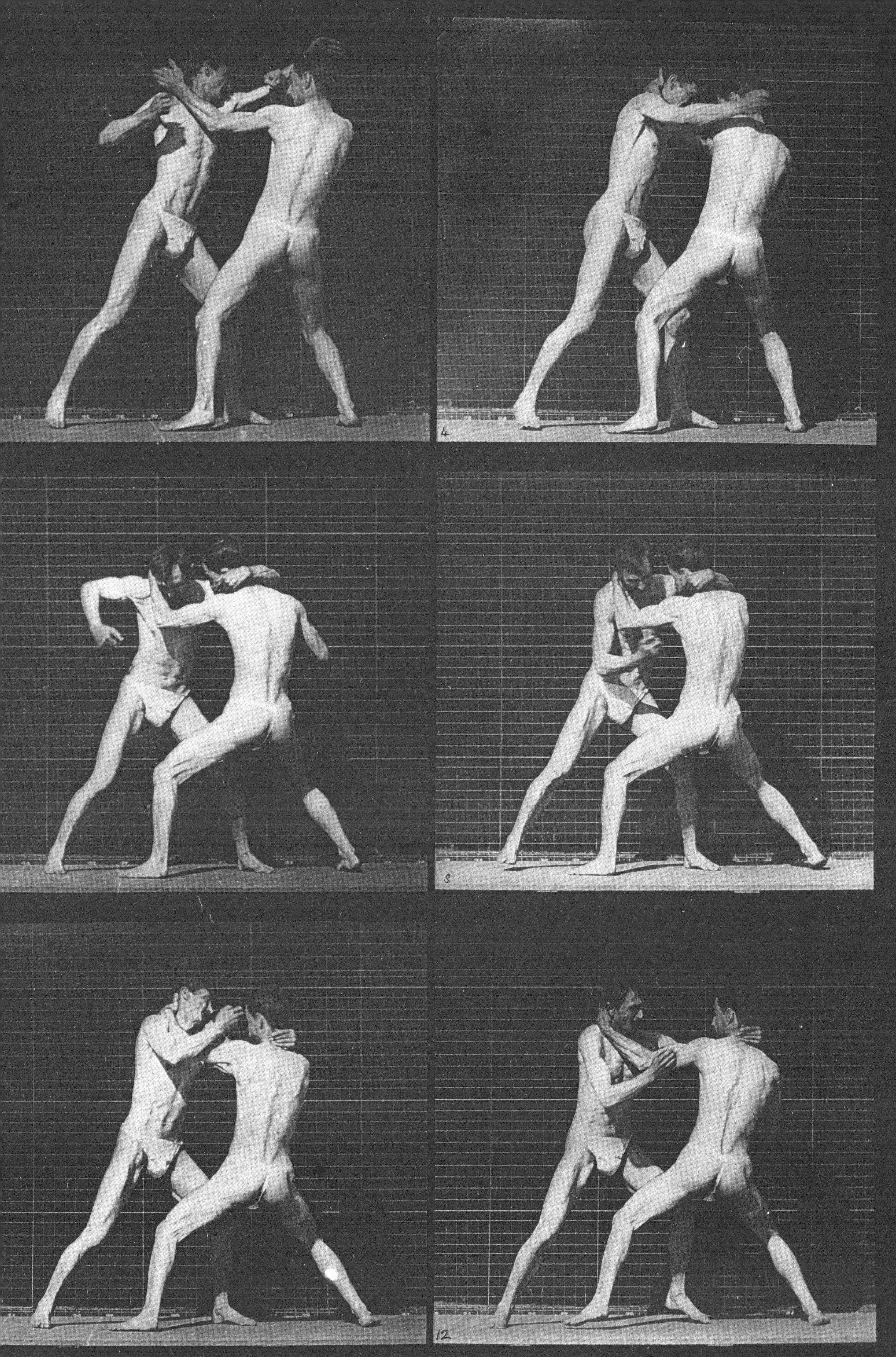

Iggy: Well, I think so, and to kind of make the same movements at the same time.

Jeremy: I totally believe that rock and roll has liberated the male body, more than the female body, almost. It made it OK to behave in a certain way.

Iggy: I think that's a good point, yeah. The guys got to bring out everything from their rebel yell to their female sides through it. And to make a display, as it were.

Jeremy: It's interesting that we're showing a selection of male nudes from the Brooklyn Museum collection along with these drawings of you, and a lot of them are Dionysian in spirit; it's holy, but also it's intoxicated—which is the basis of rock and roll: religion and the profane colliding.

Iggy: Looking at the stuff for the collection installation, it's great. You know I've got the Muybridge (pages 20–21); that's a wonderful thing, then the naughty little satyrs (opposite page) and the torso of Dionysus (page 24); and the Beckmann is beautiful. And then the Heckel (page 25) surprised me.

Sharon Matt Atkins:
I want to understand a little bit too of how you see the life drawings, particularly as they relate to photographs and recordings of you throughout your career—the difference between being captured in a drawing as opposed to a photograph or video.

Iggy: It relates to the way I was photographed pre-1970, for two reasons. One, because back then it was old tech and wasn't so complicated and easy to mess with yet. And two, because at that point I wasn't important enough yet to get on the cover of the kind of magazine where they're going to retouch my belly button or whatever, or do all these sort of horrible reductive things in the service of their inferior thoughts.

So like there are old pictures of me that I love and treasure where some guy just took a snapshot in my house of me completely out of my mind, you know? Or, there's a famous one of just the four Stooges sitting on this filthy couch getting ready to go to our first show, and you know the malcontent of it all rises through.

And there's Leni Sinclair, the wife of John Sinclair, a German woman living in Detroit documenting the sixties who has some very good exhibitions right now in Detroit. She took Super-8 footage of me that felt real (opposite page).

And then little by little what's happened is photography has become such a scam and a sham, and there's so much technology just packed into an iPhone, you know? That now it's lost all impact.

But in the life class you have emotional impact, and I mean I really was knocked out. I had no idea. I think one of the things that happened in that studio was they were, like, I'm just gonna lay it right out here. These people are pretty much unknown to the public; they are not Annie Leibovitz, you know what

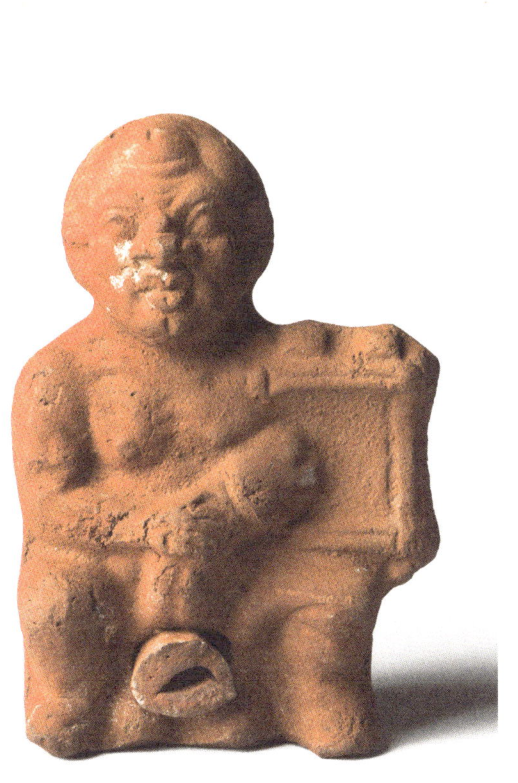

Ithyphallic Man with a Harp, 3rd–4th century C.E. Egypt.
Brooklyn Museum

Satyr Holding a Jar, circa 30 B.C.E.–395 C.E. Egypt.
Brooklyn Museum

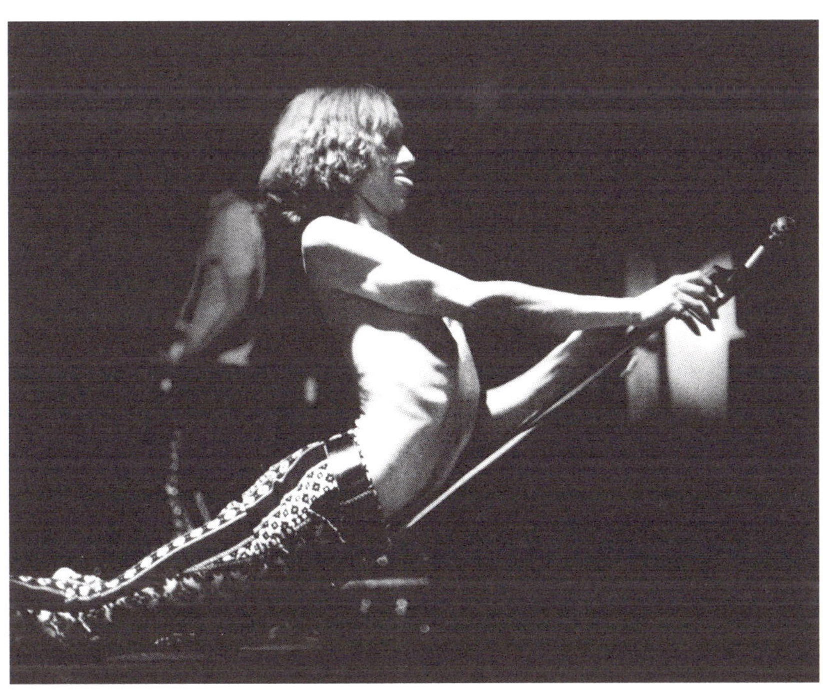

Leni Sinclair, *Iggy Pop*, 1968

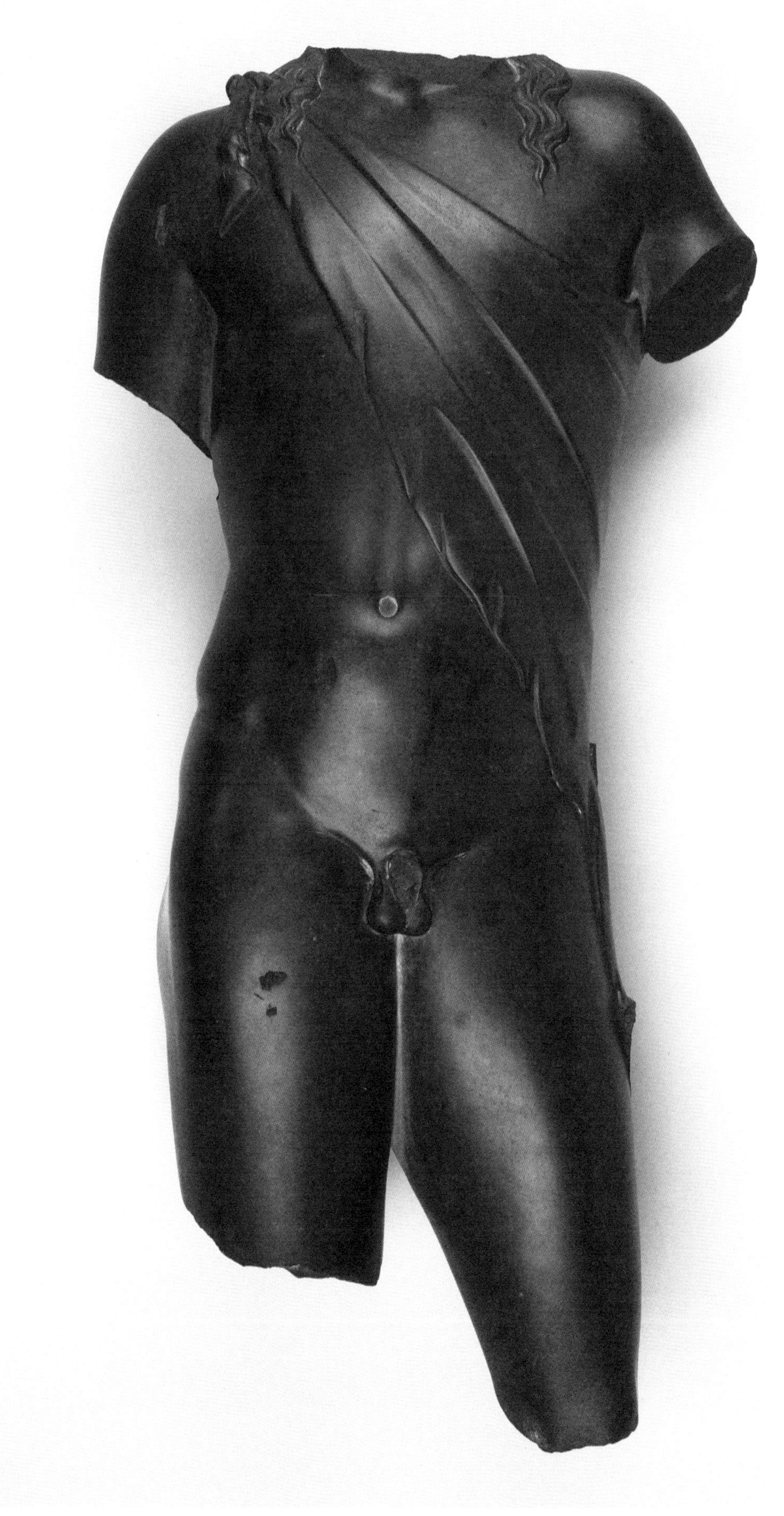

Torso of Dionysus, 2nd–3rd century C.E. Roman copy of a Hellenistic statue. Brooklyn Museum

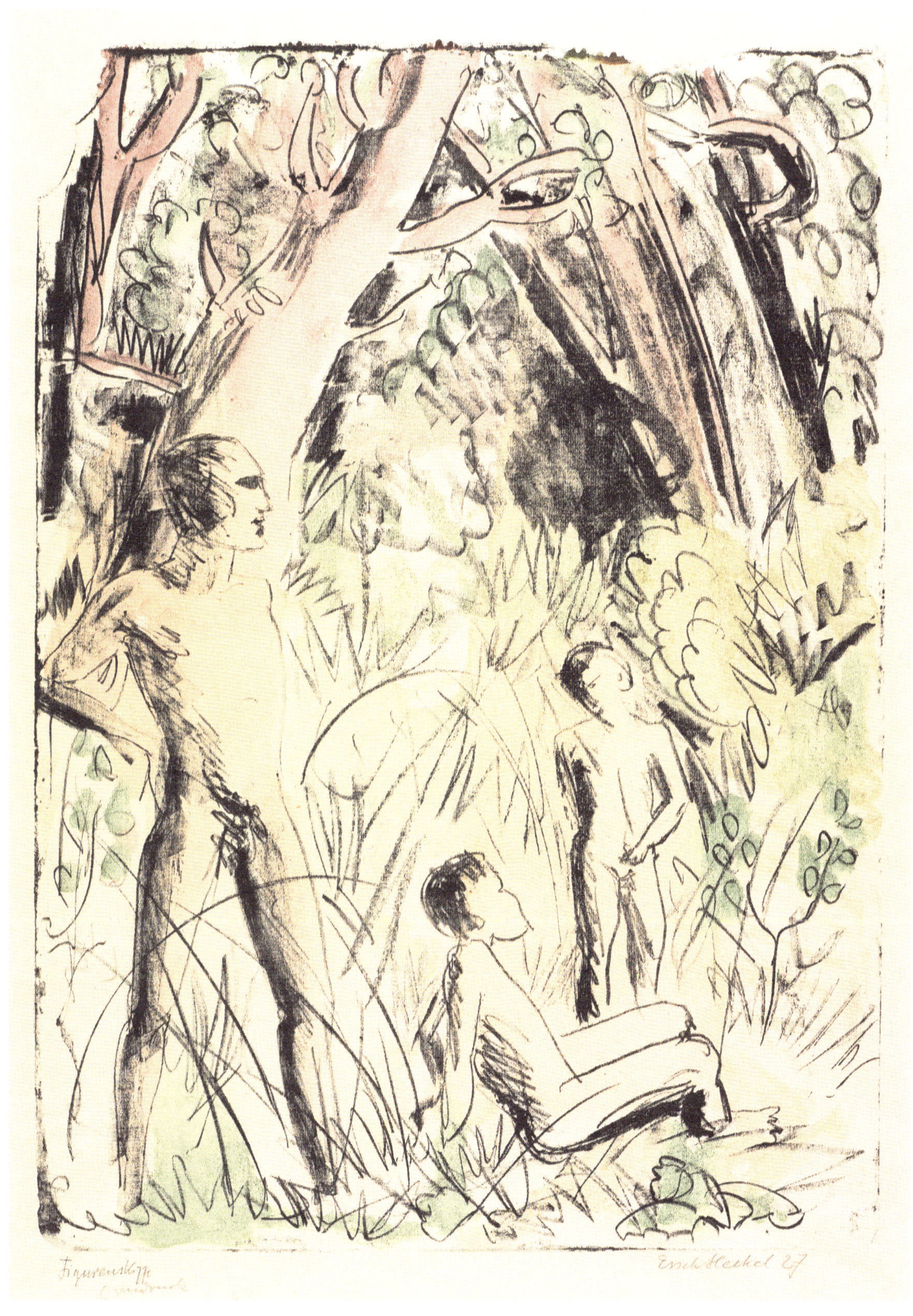

Erich Heckel, *Figure Sketch*, 1927. Brooklyn Museum

I'm sayin'? No. They are just normal people, and in that context, I crossed over to their side. I walked in there Iggy Pop, but I walked out of there sort of cleansed of all that, if you see what I mean. I was cleansed of my billing, and my image, and all that crap, and there I was, as a naked guy, and it was important to me. But you know, those drawings would look odd if they said Iggy Pop on them, you know what I'm saying?

Jeremy: I was a little nervous seeing you naked, if I can say that. I just didn't know how to react! But within about a minute, it was normal, and it was average, and they were drawing you. And it just seemed like a natural thing to happen.

Iggy: That's what I thought, and you know, I think it's good we'll have that beautiful little fragment of Dionysus in the exhibition, or that naughty little Bacchus. Or, you know, even the Egon Schiele nude (opposite page). One thing you understand without really analyzing it: you look at the Schiele nude and you think, "Well, I bet he got up to a lot of other stuff." He didn't just walk in able to do that. He'd been around …

Sharon: One of the interesting things about the class is that we only shared your identity as the model the day before, and the bulk of the class members knew immediately who you were, and responded accordingly. But some of them knew your name, but didn't really have a sense of …

Iggy: No, I'm not that deeply known, you know?

Sharon: But some interesting things came through then, in the way the artists responded after they learned you would be the model the next day. In one case, a woman recalled listening to your music when she was a teenager; she spent the evening before the class listening to your recordings and drawing from photographs online.

Iggy: Oh, wow.

Sharon: And she just found herself responding. Another artist described having in his head all of the images of you that he's seen in the media, and then needing to separate them from that moment in the class and really focus on you, your flesh in that moment, and how to capture that on paper. Yet another artist, who couldn't call to mind your image, didn't look at anything in advance. It was a range, and perhaps that's part of what you're responding to as well.

Iggy: Well, when you get your photo taken, as they say, it's a true cliché that what's going to come out is really, mostly all about how you feel about that person with the camera.

And in the photo situation, you are confronted by that person, and you have to stand up to that moment, and vice versa; they're confronted by you and all

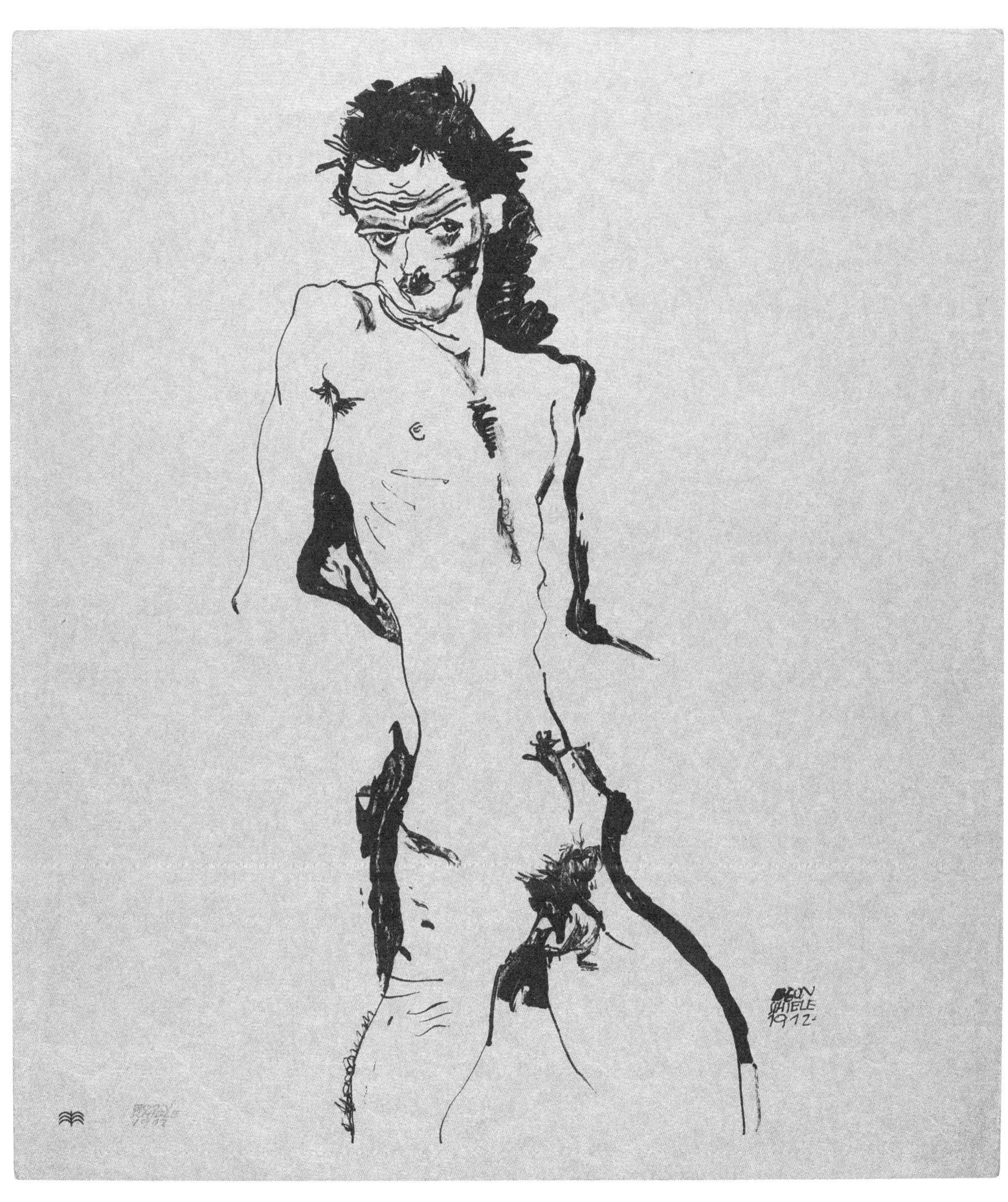

Egon Schiele, *Male Nude (Self-Portrait)*, 1912. Brooklyn Museum

sorts of personal things come into that—things that are wonderfully avoided, I noticed, in the sketches. I didn't feel like any of these people were in my face, and I wasn't in theirs. I remember we talked about where do I look?, 'cause that was important to me, and Jeremy made a mark on the wall, and I just concentrated on that. And so these people were able to do what they wanted with me, without feeling a burden of a confrontation, and it worked that way for me too.

Jeremy: Yes, because I imagine every photographer who takes your picture wants eye contact.

Iggy: Yeah. They all have a different approach: some of them try to be mean, some of them are heavy, some of them try to be nice—but you know, it all comes down to that eye contact.

Jeremy: Yes, they want that look. Do you ever get tired of looking at yourself? Just seeing images, film, and so on, is it ...

Iggy: I'm desperately tired. I'm nearing the end of that line, believe me.

Jeremy: ... I'm just thinking because nowadays, it must be very tough to be someone like you: everyone now has a camera with them, and everyone wants their picture taken with you. You have to negotiate that with the public all the time, I imagine, wanting to have their picture taken.

Iggy: Yeah, I do selfies with people constantly ...

Jeremy: That to me is probably one of the toughest things about being recognizable, if not the toughest—having that attention and trying to be nice to people, and trying to negotiate it.

Iggy: It is, yeah. There are some people, probably smarter than I am, who go out of their way to be pricks about it. I'll usually do a selfie. But one of the weirdest situations is when you've been doing some sort of work that relates to who I am publicly, and maybe there's seven or eight people in the room, and then before I can leave I have to do a selfie with everyone. And I can't help but start suspecting, this little voice is going, "This is because they think I'm a relic, and they think I'm probably going to expire very soon." I'm sorry, but there is that, you know?

Jeremy: I think it's people wanting to be close to someone who's made such an impact on the culture.

Iggy: I see. Well, maybe so. I meet some really, really, really ... I mean I get a lot of good input, too, you know? And just some nice, pleasant, wonderful, good input. All the time. I really do.

Sharon: In breaks during the class, you took the opportunity to chat with some of the artists. What was that exchange like, particularly when you were going back and forth between breaks and posing?

Iggy: Well, I was just curious about them. I'm a human being, and I've just always been kinda curious about other people. And I would have a quick little peek at what they were drawing, and get a quick impression.

Like there was one lady. She was positioned behind me, and she made a drawing of my ass and that thing I sat on. And I just got a big kick out of that, to tell you the truth. And just different people, and how they express themselves. But also I was just wondering who they were. That's all. Who they were, what were they like, what was the vibe … I was just curious, you know, like that.

Jeremy: To be honest, it's only the second time I've been in a life class. And I found the atmosphere interesting. It's intense, very quiet, like a library.

Iggy: It wasn't that different than maybe a good band rehearsal or a good dance performance, where you've got a bunch of other people and you're all working together on the same thing. And you kinda want everybody to be freed, I would say.

Sharon: Yes, although it was different from a typical life class, where they may have two or three more sessions to draw from a particular model, the model even returning to the same pose. We put a considerable amount of pressure on these artists, because they knew that they had only this one morning and early afternoon to capture you, and then they wouldn't be able to continue working on the drawings.

Iggy: You know, that's a very good point. I can't tell you how, again and again, when making a record, a sound recording, it also goes better when people don't feel like they've got all bloody year to deal with it.

Jeremy: Yes, it was like a live performance, in a sense, in that way. But totally quiet and with no movement, so almost like the antithesis of rock and roll, weirdly.

You might not be able to answer this, but who is the person they drew there? Is it your public persona, or is it the other part of you that's the private person? Or, is it a mixture of both when you look at those drawings?

Iggy: I would say it's the public me, but showing things that have been hitherto kept more private. And that's partly me, the expressions on the face particularly; but these artists really caught a couple of things. It was definitely public: there was one, a sketch, mainly the head, and it reminds me a little bit of George Washington. There's sort of a sense of this very stubborn person, who sort of somehow managed to win something, in his own mind if nothing else.

Jeremy: It's like Mount Rushmore. That's what I felt.

Iggy: And, also in the one that's a full nude, seated with the pole. It's a certain look, you know. And then some of the others that are more figure studies, and that's nice too, but they're more honest; there was no stagecraft done, really. I just got up there where you told me to and you know, got it on.

Sharon: To go back to the beginning of our conversation, and your comment about the importance of these works' being part of the Museum's collection, and the idea that they would stay together as a group, but also to be seen within the context of an encyclopedic museum. Why was that important for you?

Iggy: Well, it was. It was important. I enjoy going to see what the Chapman Brothers are up to, all right? But I would rather be in with the Chamba standing male figure (opposite page), from Nigeria. So let's put it that way: I'd feel that's a better place for me. And, it sort of has to do with the general collection and also the fact that, to me, the Brooklyn Museum has proletarian roots.

I think that's fair to say, and yet it's in Brooklyn, where sparks are flying now. And what have you got at the Met? You've got basically fashion, fashion, fashion, fashion. Or, you know, art that's getting more and more conceptual. But I just thought it was important to be there in this place.

I felt Brooklyn had a good combination right now. There's size. There's gravity. There's certain kinds of roots, and at the same time, there's something cultural happening in Brooklyn that's very, very important, because everybody that I would've hung out with when I lived in New York wouldn't be able to live in my old neighborhood anymore. They'd all be in Brooklyn.

So, there were certain considerations, and I enjoyed it when I lived in New York. I was still there when Mayor Giuliani got stuck on Chris Ofili's *Holy Virgin Mary*, with the dung breast, that was shown at the Brooklyn Museum. And I thought that was wonderful. Somebody needed to give that asshole a poke, you know?

That's how I felt, though I'm not really strictly left-wing. When I lived in Manhattan, I was spending a lot of time up at Sotheby's and Christie's, because I found that back then I could walk right in there on a Thursday afternoon, and I could be face to face with a Rubens. And nobody bothered me. They're very accessible, and they organized the art sensibly as to commerce. It was very interesting. I saw a lot of great stuff that way. So, I just wanted to be somewhere solid. That's how I felt. Put it that way.

Sharon: Do you collect art?

Iggy: I collect in a way that every once in a while I'll have a little burst and buy a few things. A lot of what I've got is Haitian or Haitian American. I have one Hector Hyppolite that's beautiful. I've got four or five of Edouard Duval-Carriés. And I've got some beautiful sculptures by Georges Liautaud. And I live with these things. They're like my friends, my companions, my lovers, my entertainment. They're great. They hang … I hang around with them. I also collect nice old antiques, but not feverishly and not replacing them all the time. So I have some Norman things and some Art Deco things and some early American things.

They're basically good companions who make me comfortable, and I don't feel empty, and they don't talk back.

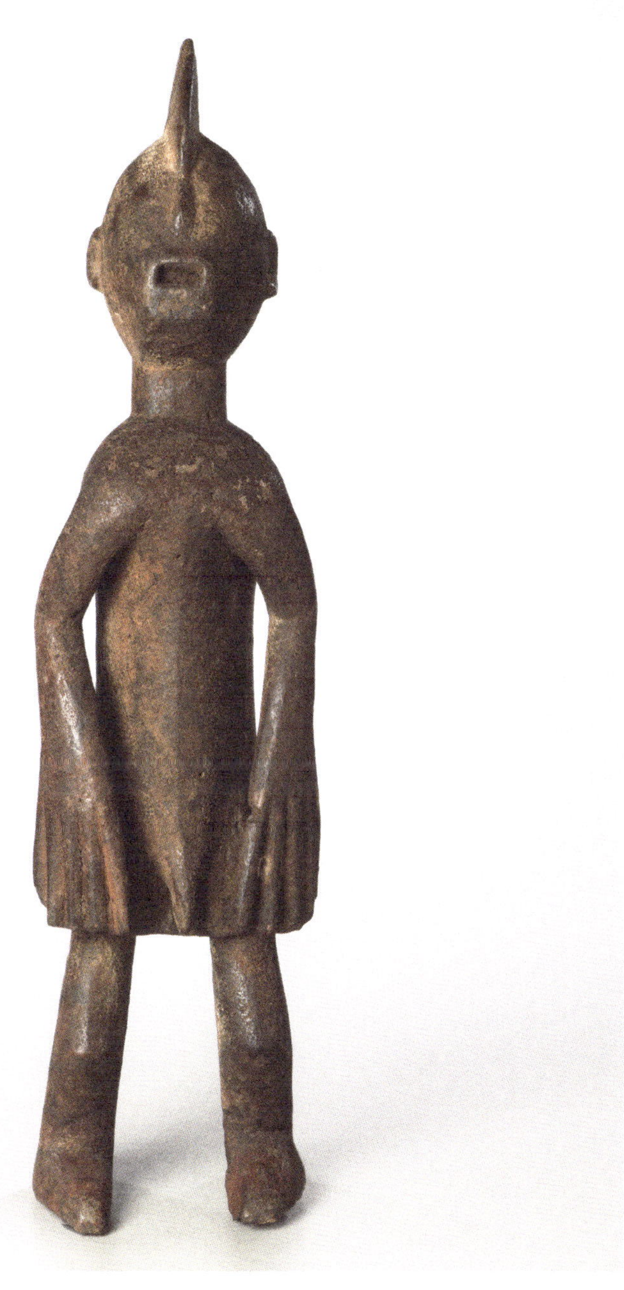

Standing Male Figure, early 20th century. Chamba. Adamawa State, Nigeria. Brooklyn Museum

Participants

Jeremy Day
Jeanette Farrow
Margaret Fisher
Seiji Gailey
Michael Grimaldi
Robert Hagan
Tobias Hall
Deirdra Hazeley
Patricia Hill
Okim Woo Kim
Maureen McAllister
Kallyiah Merilus
Guno Park
Kinley Pleteau
Angel Ramirez
Robert Reid
Mauricio Rodriguez
Danielle Rubin
Taylor Schultek
Charlotte Segall
Andrew Shears
Levan Songulashvili

Life Class Drawings

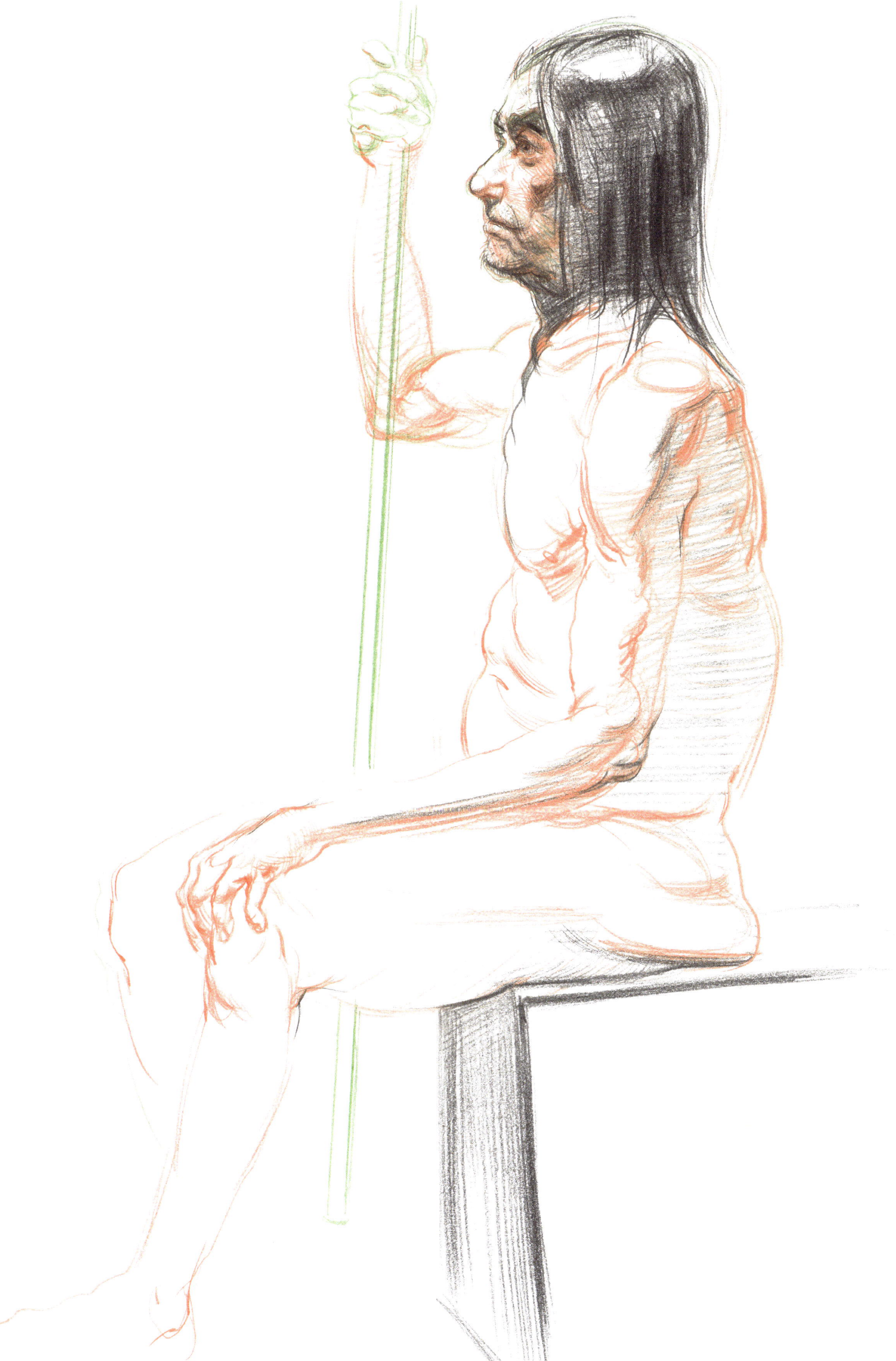

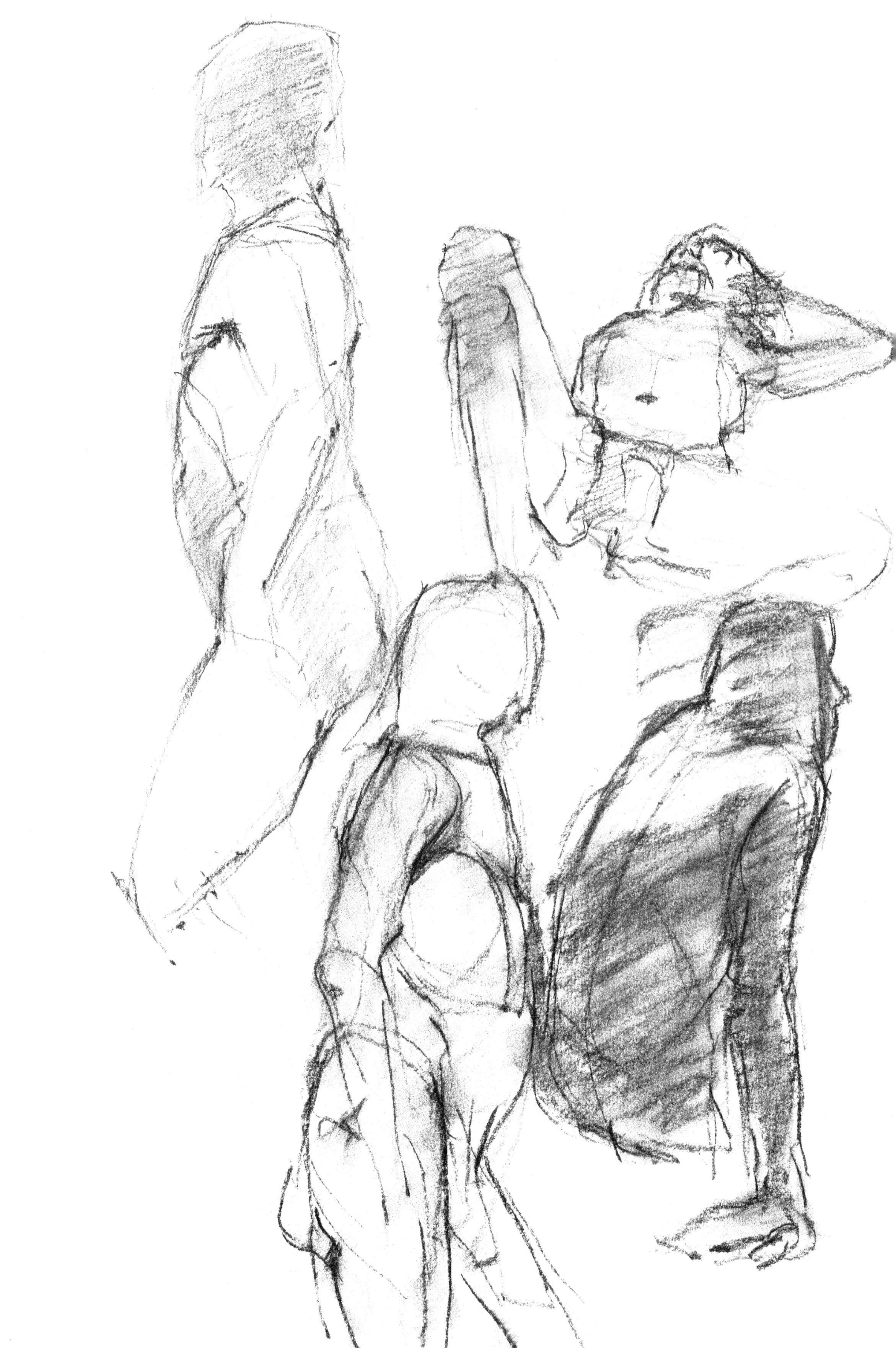

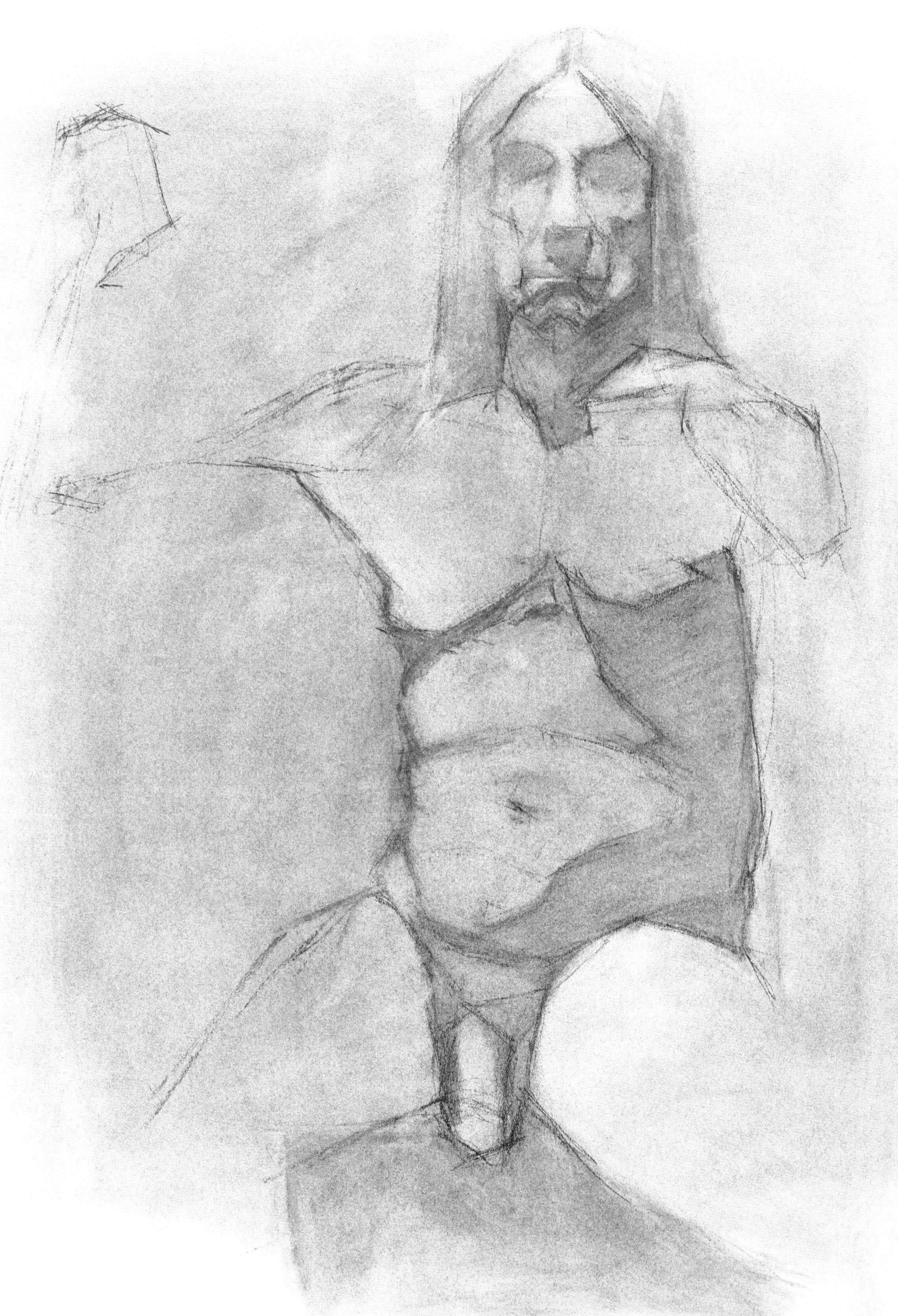

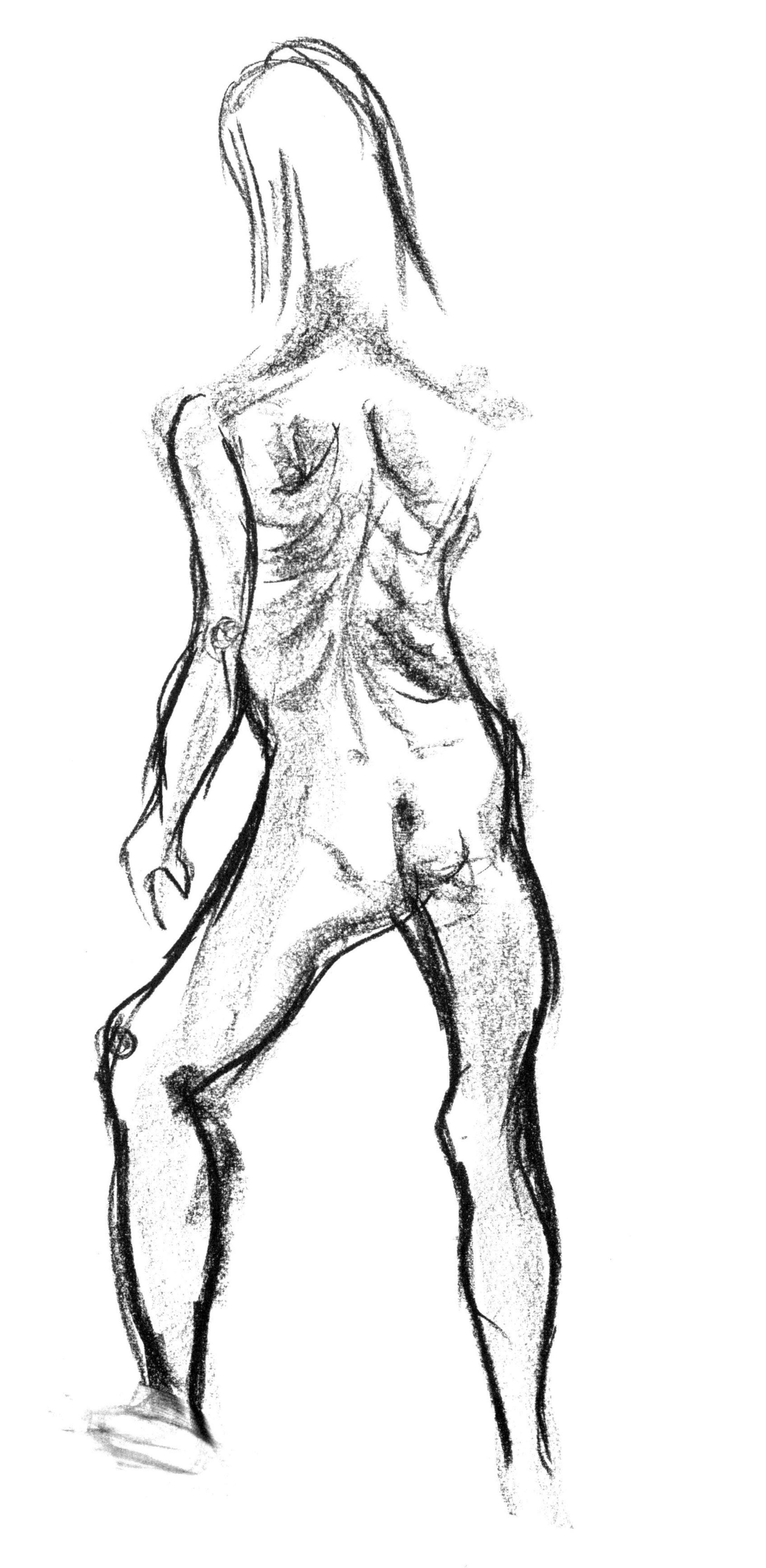

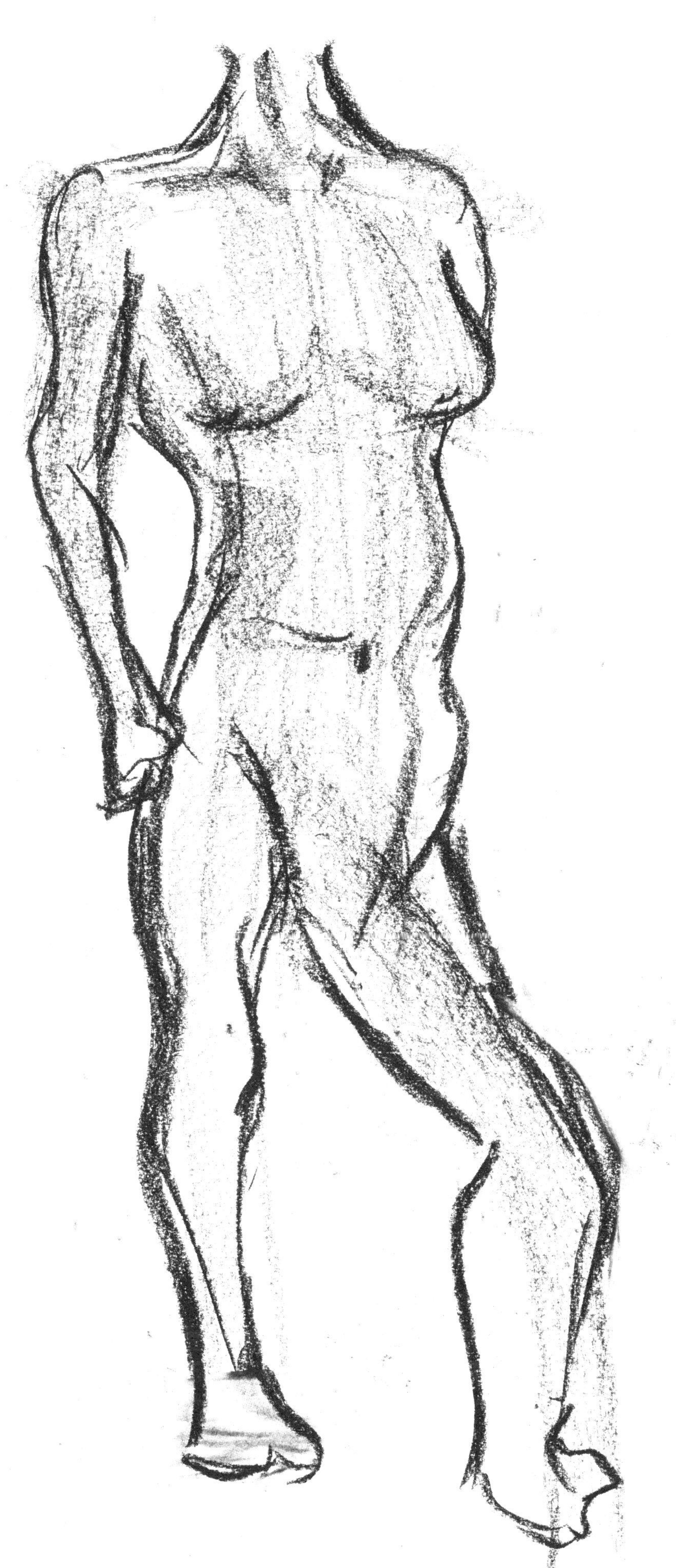

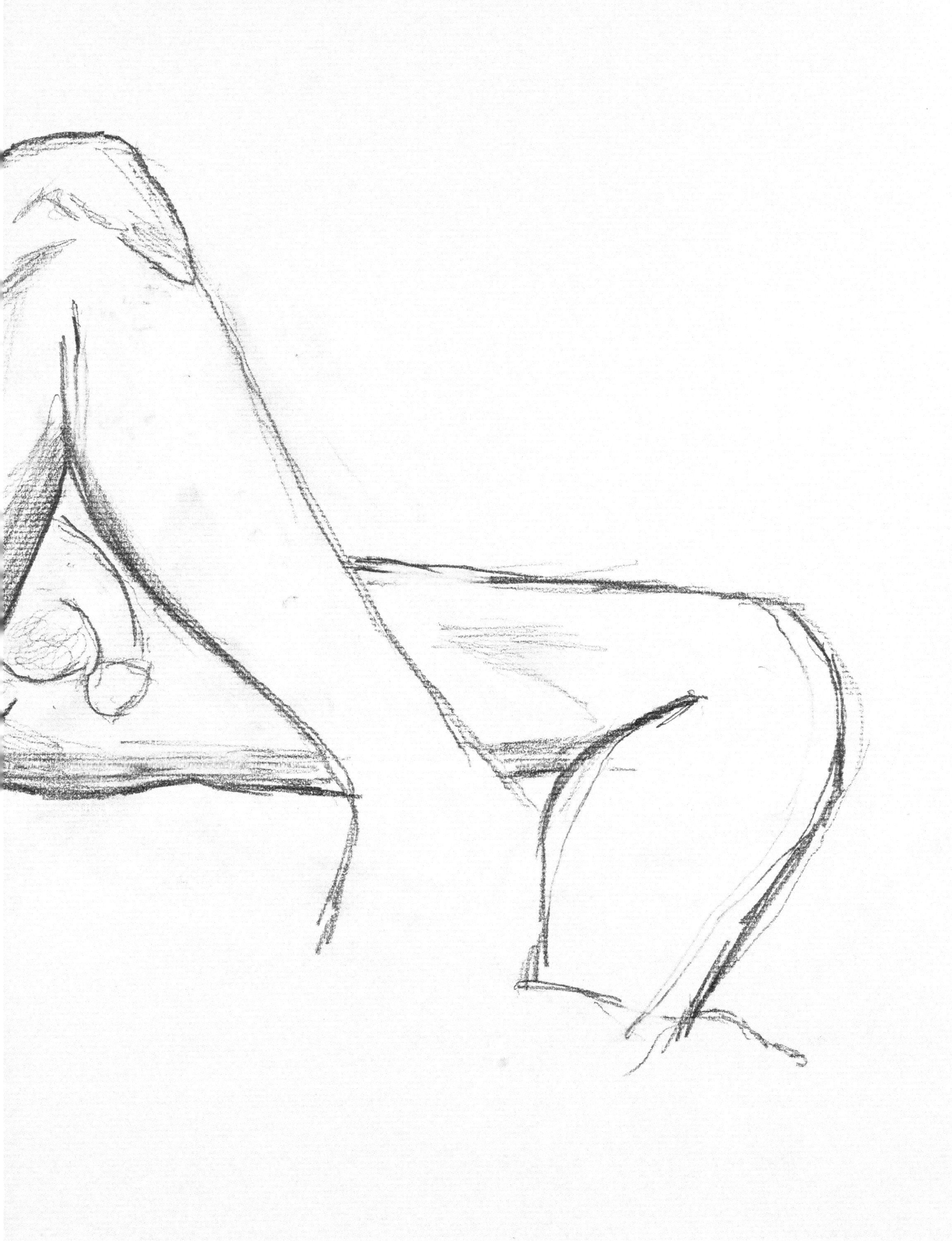

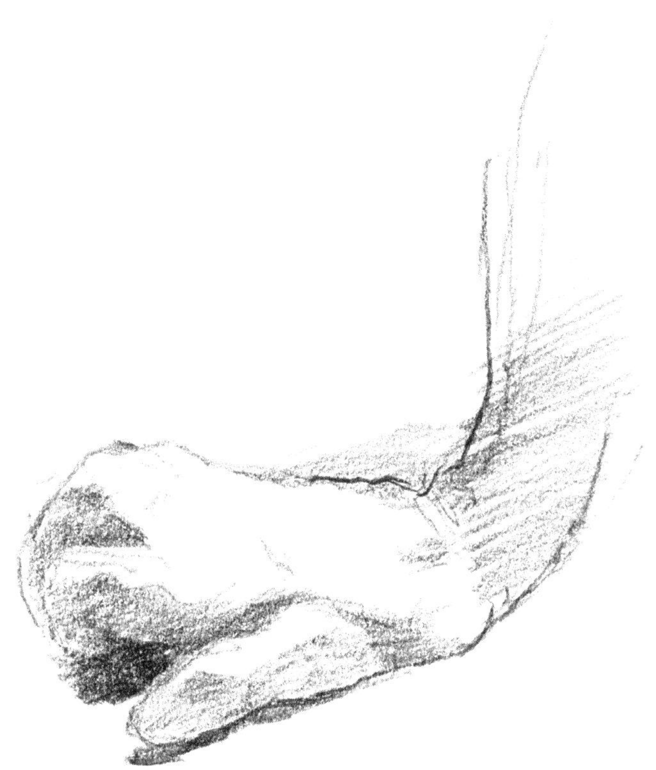

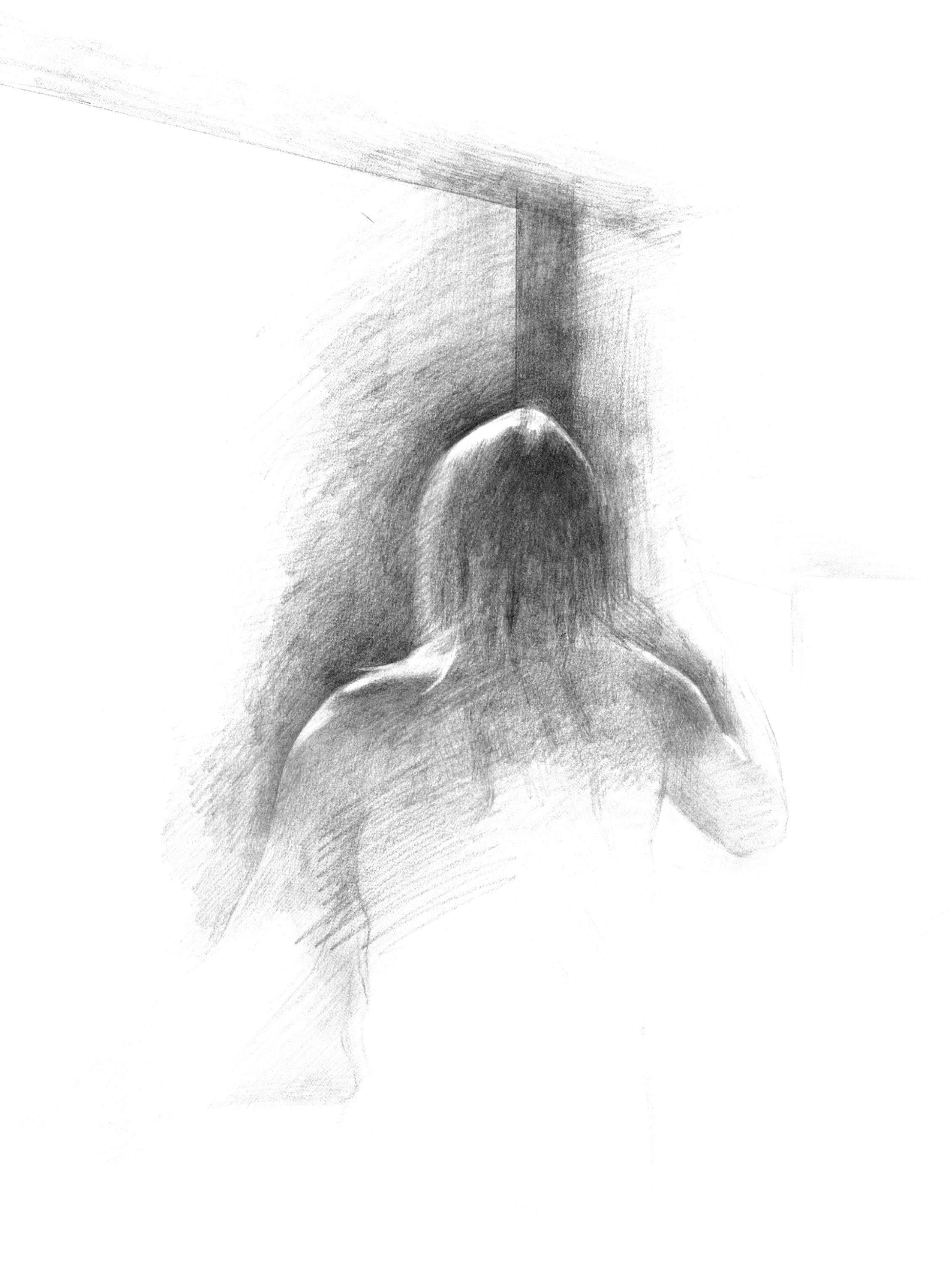

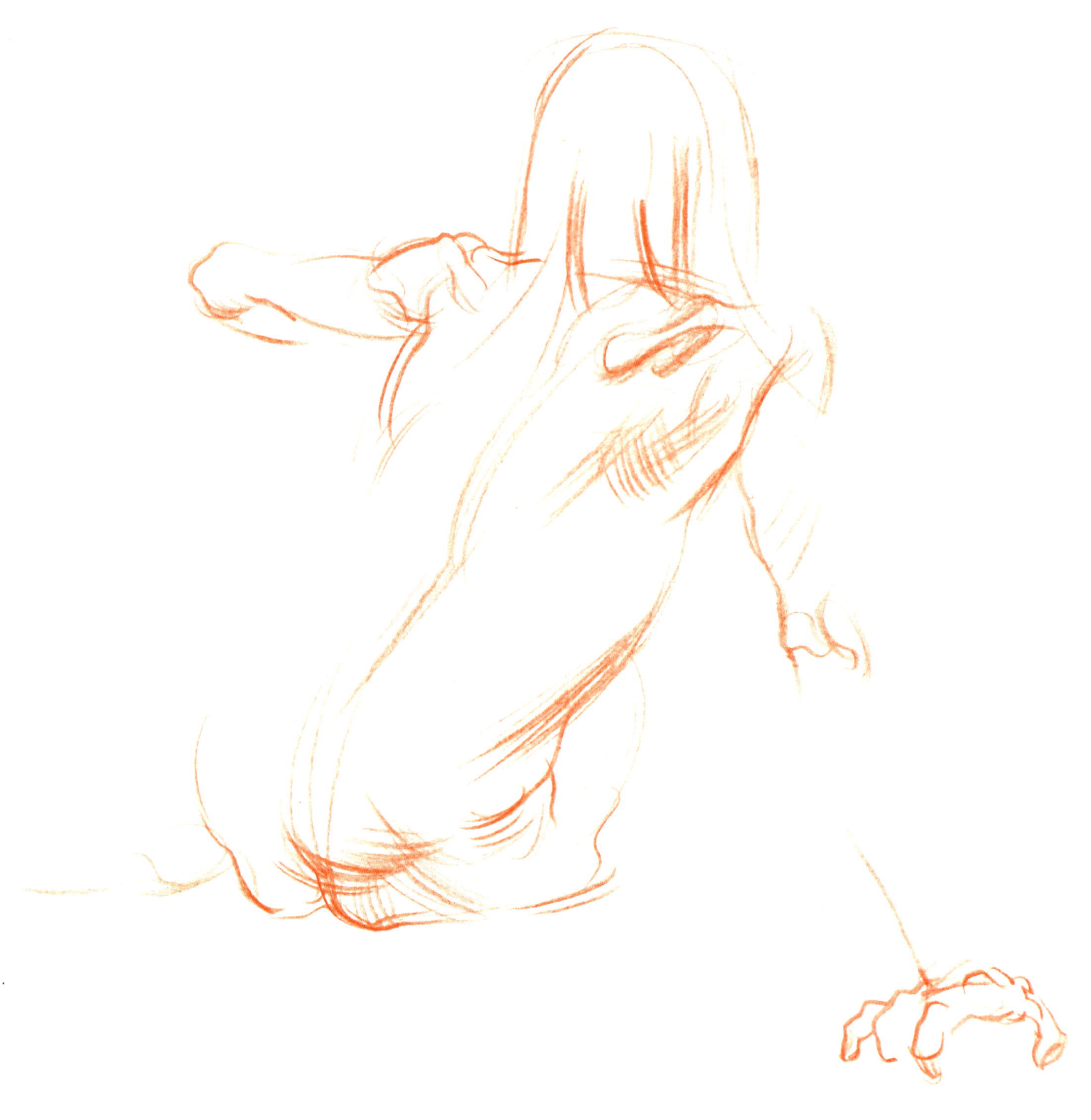

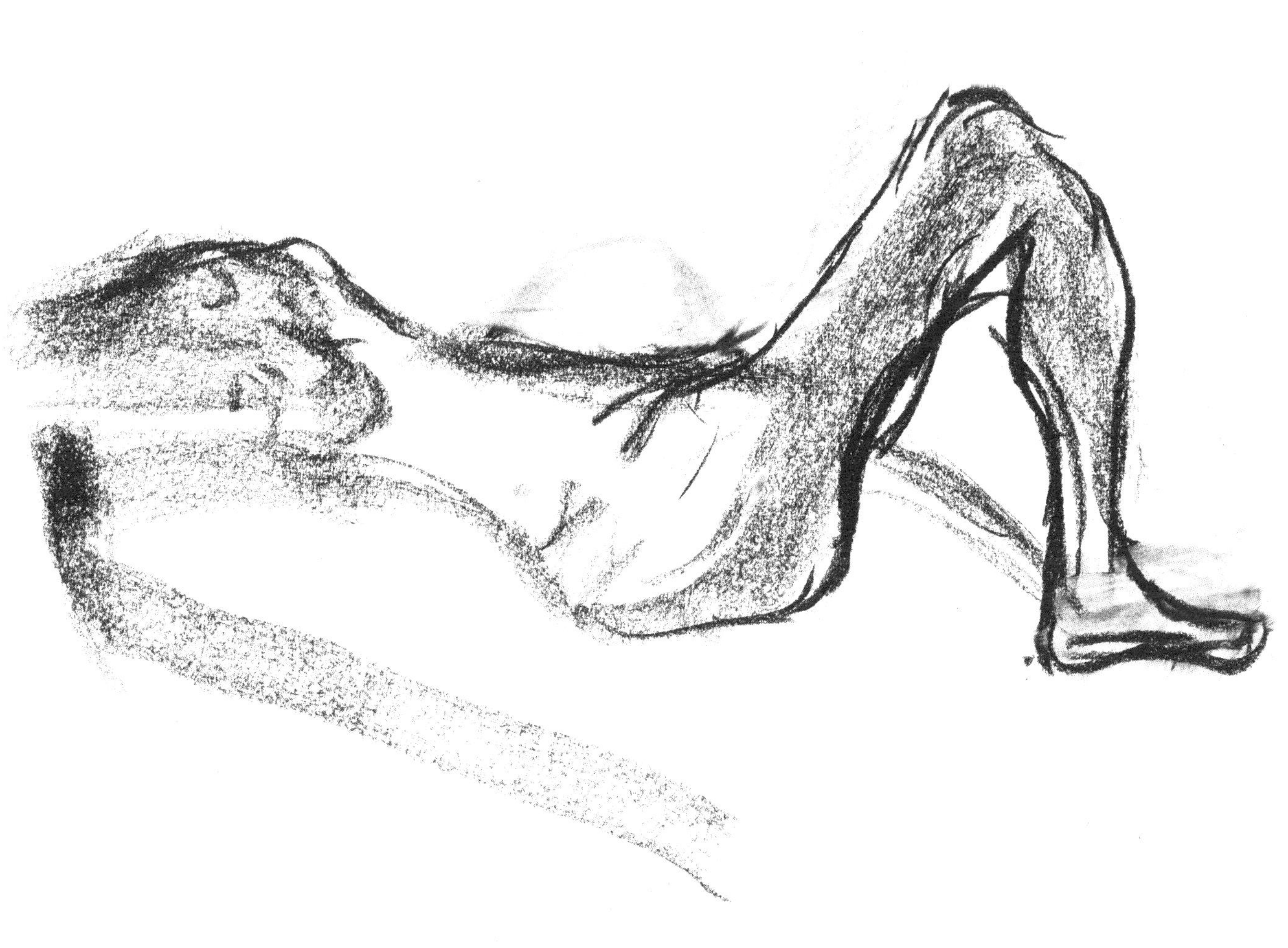

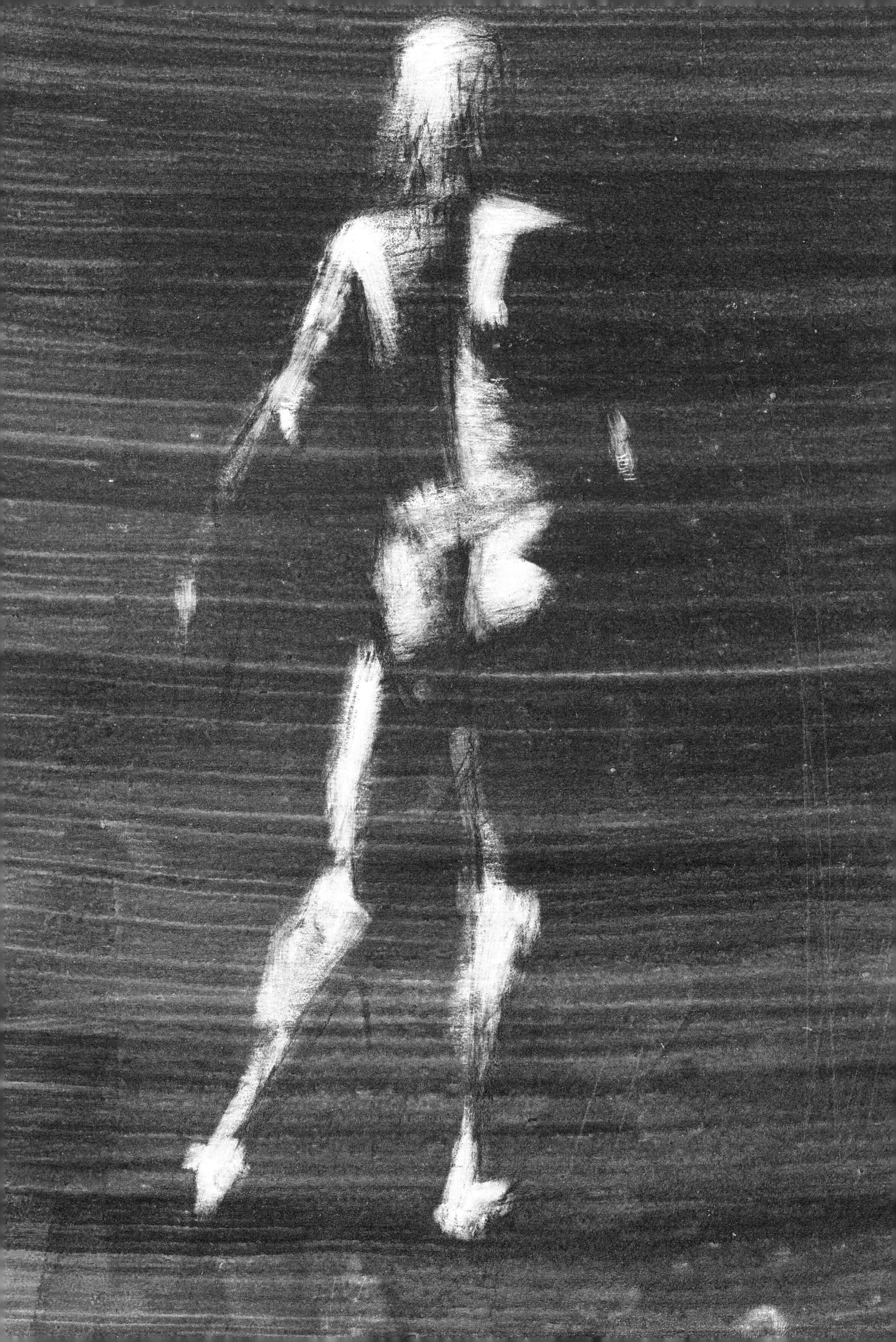

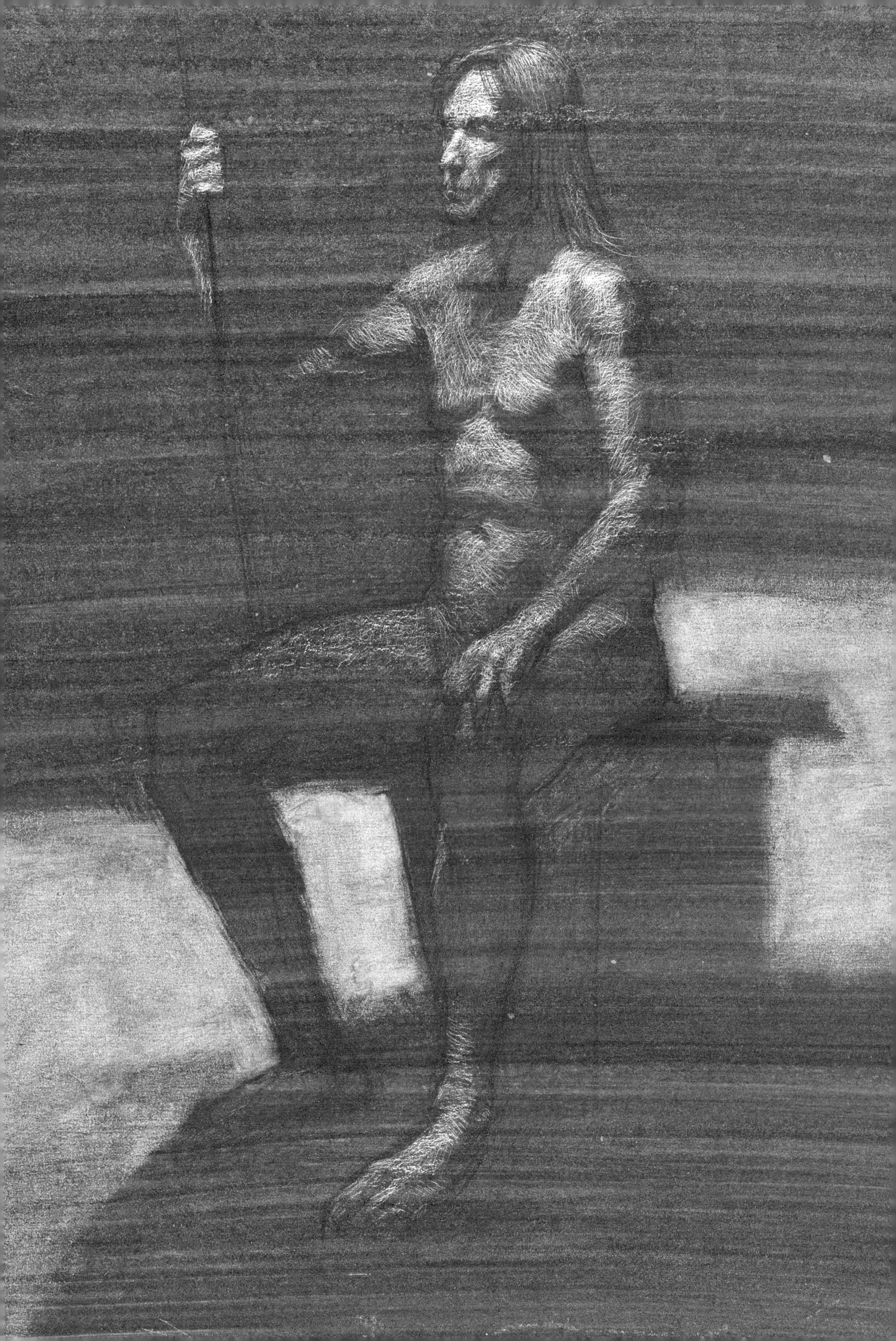

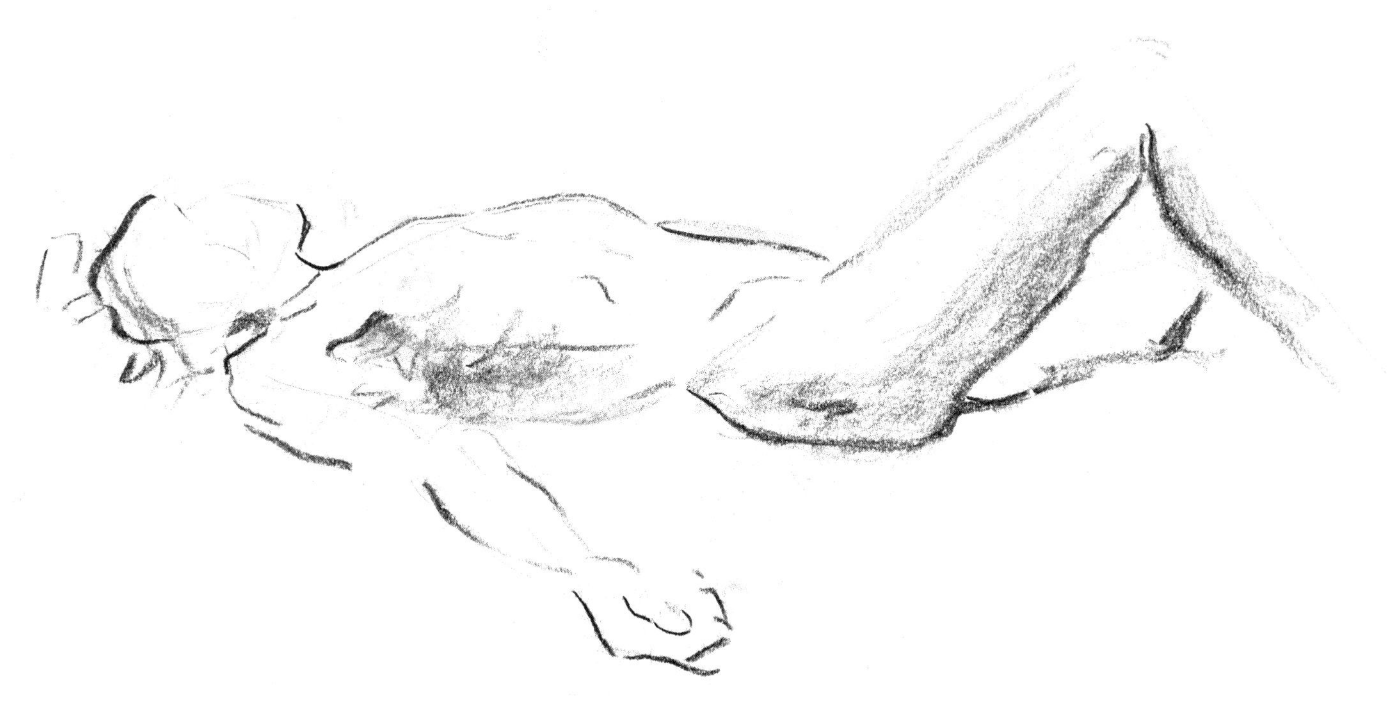

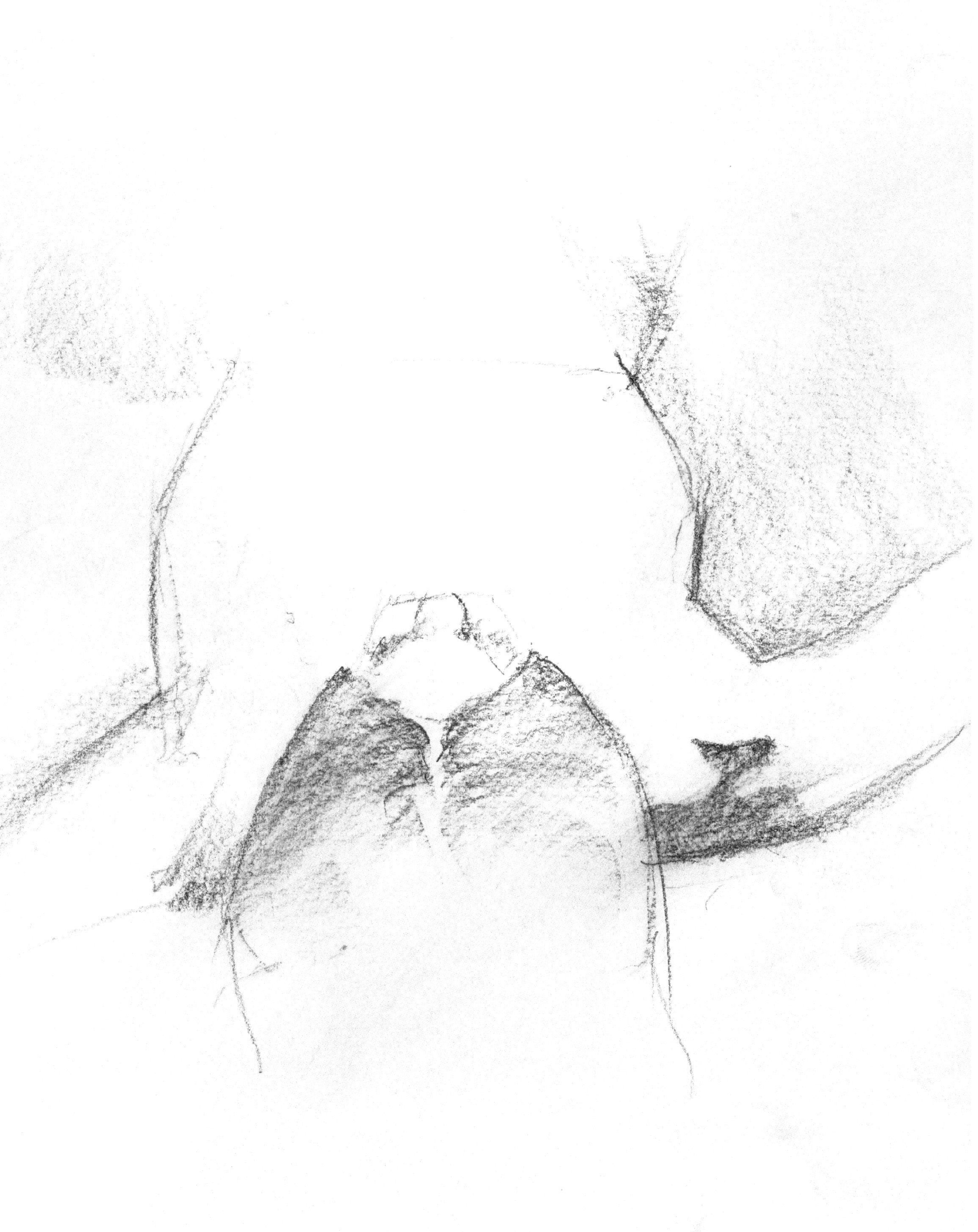

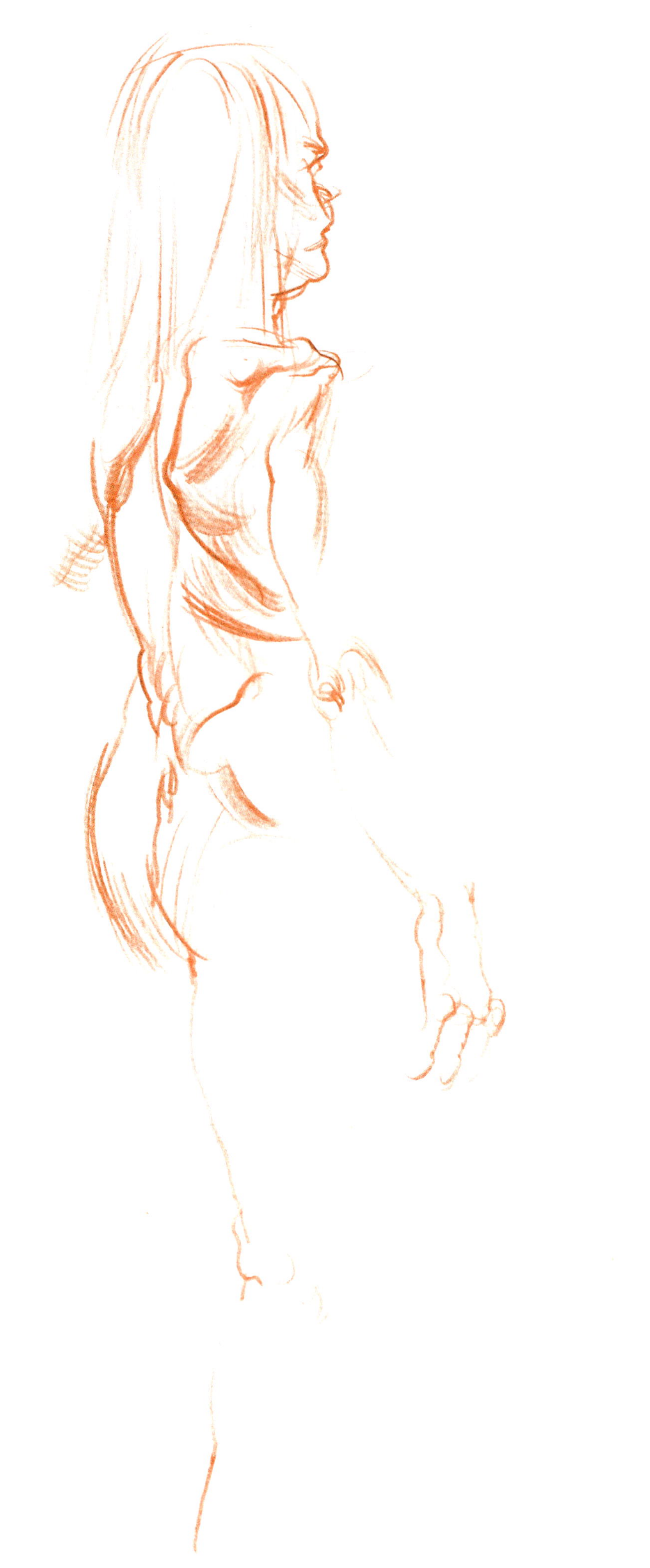

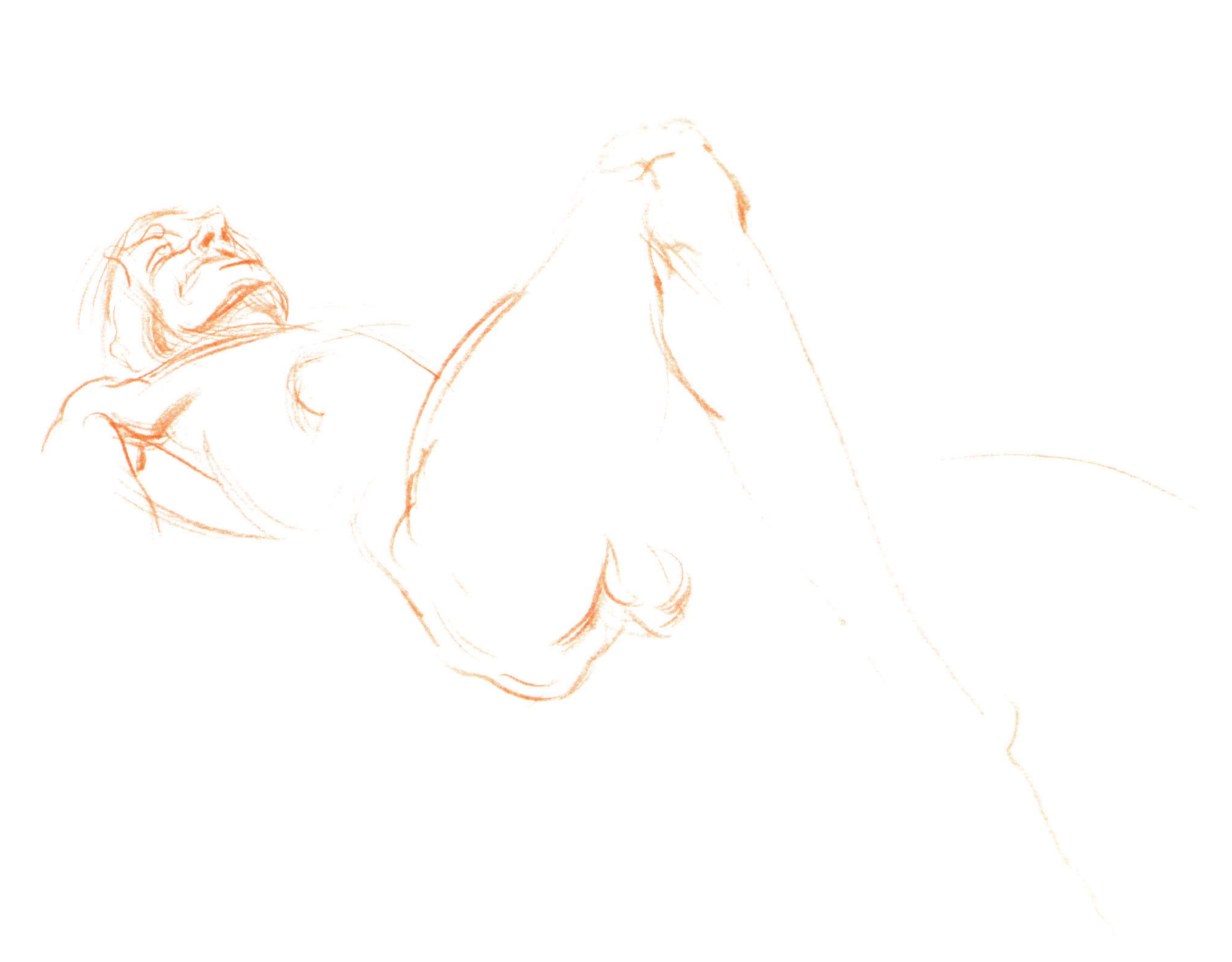

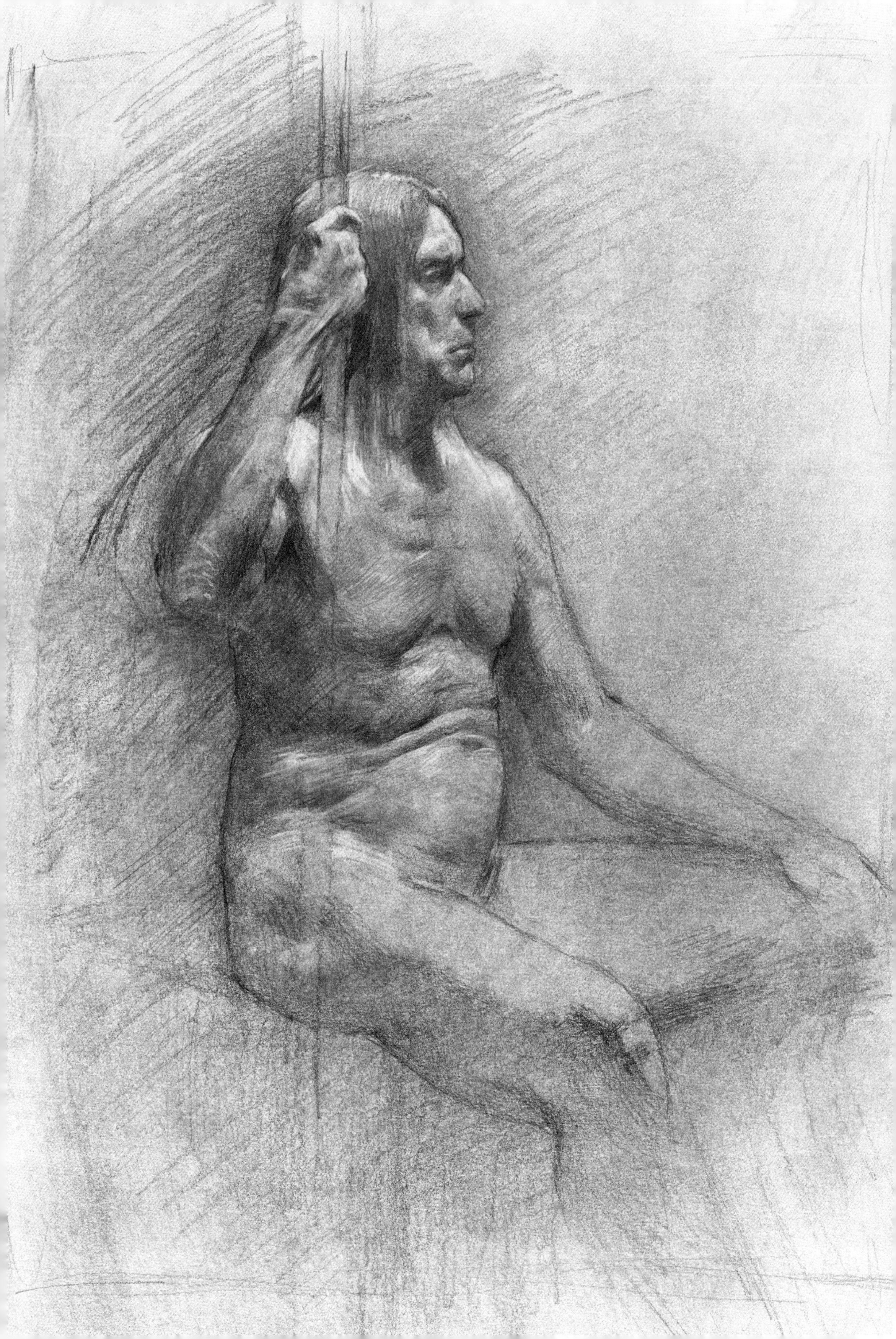

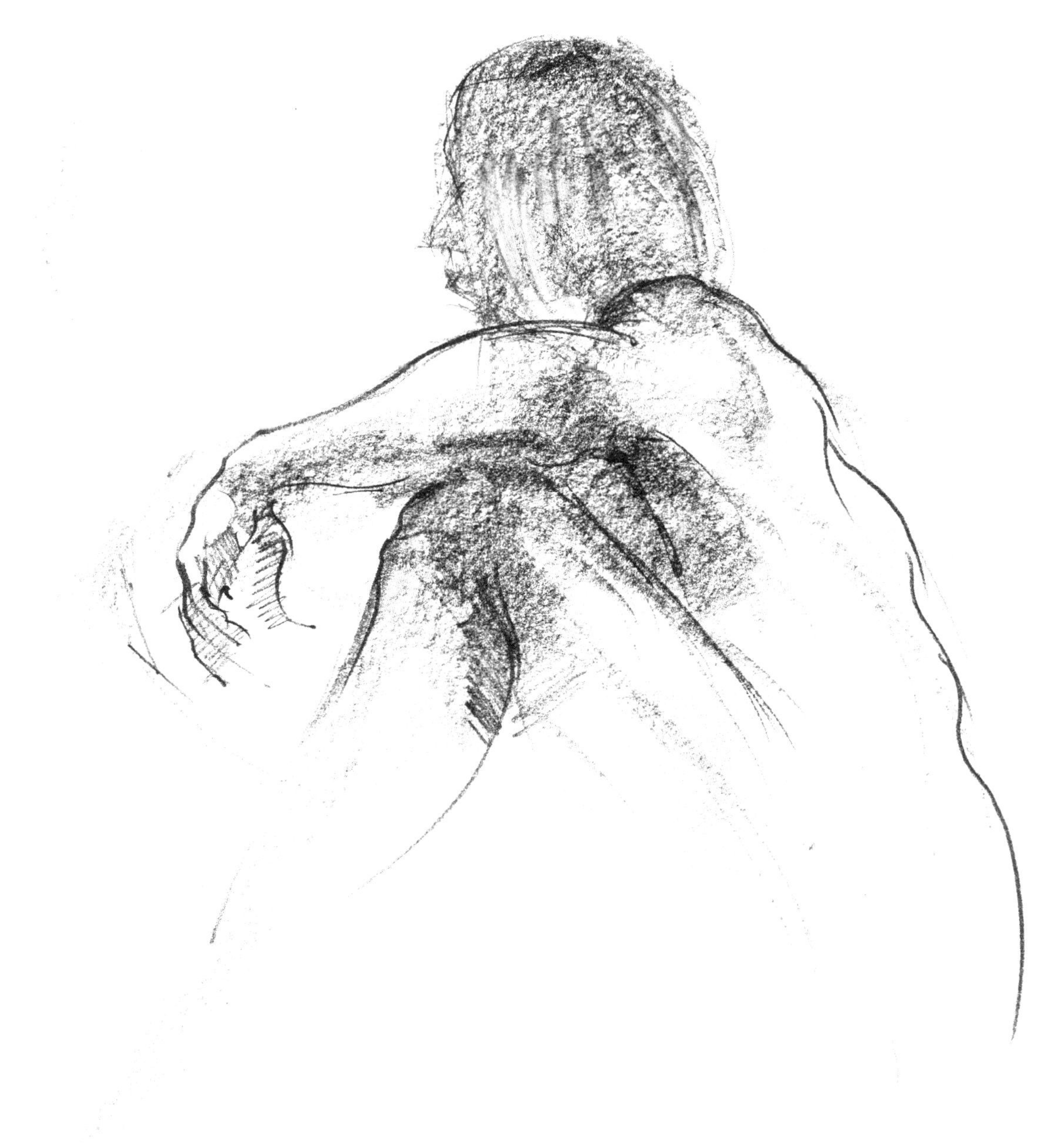

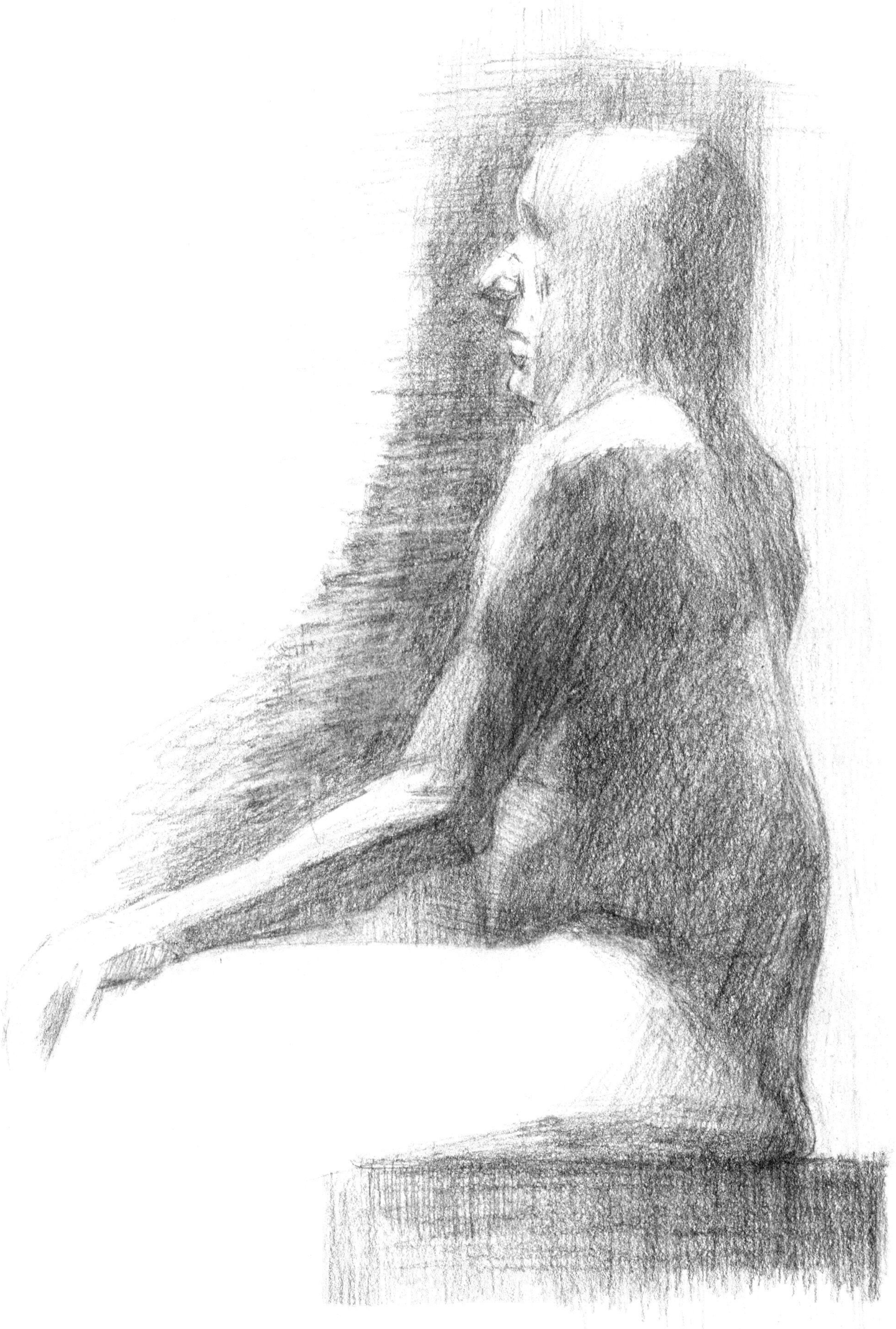

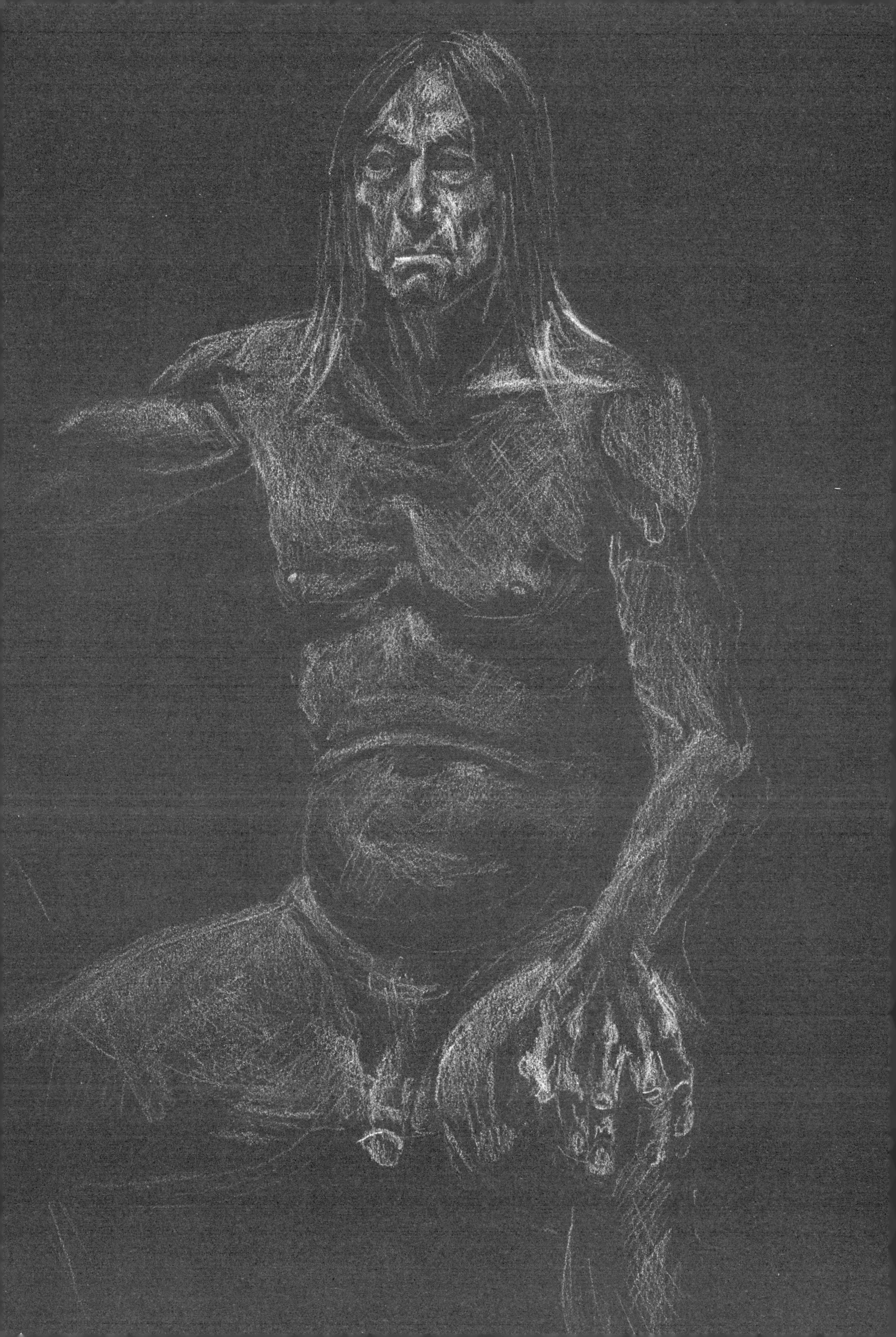

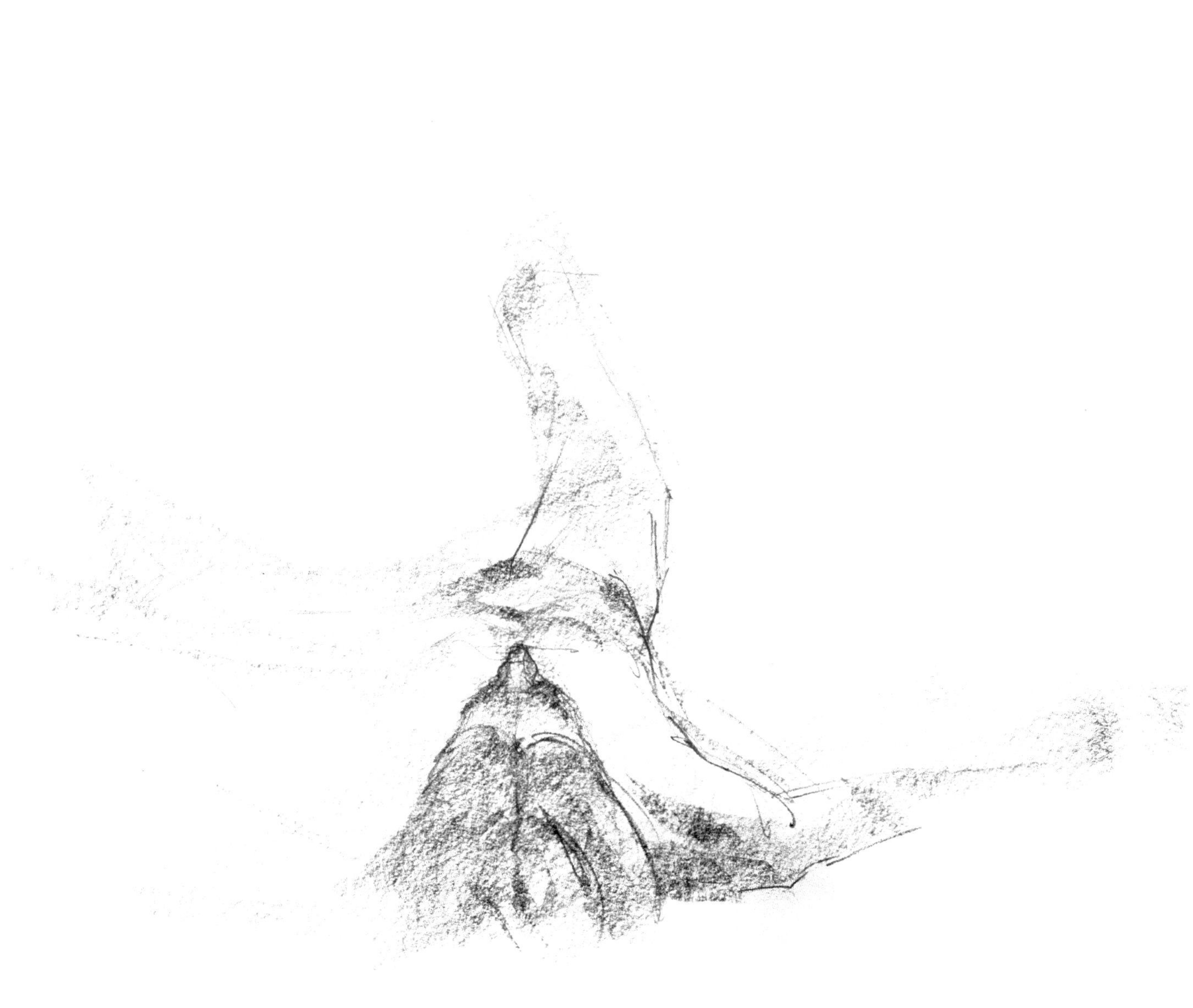

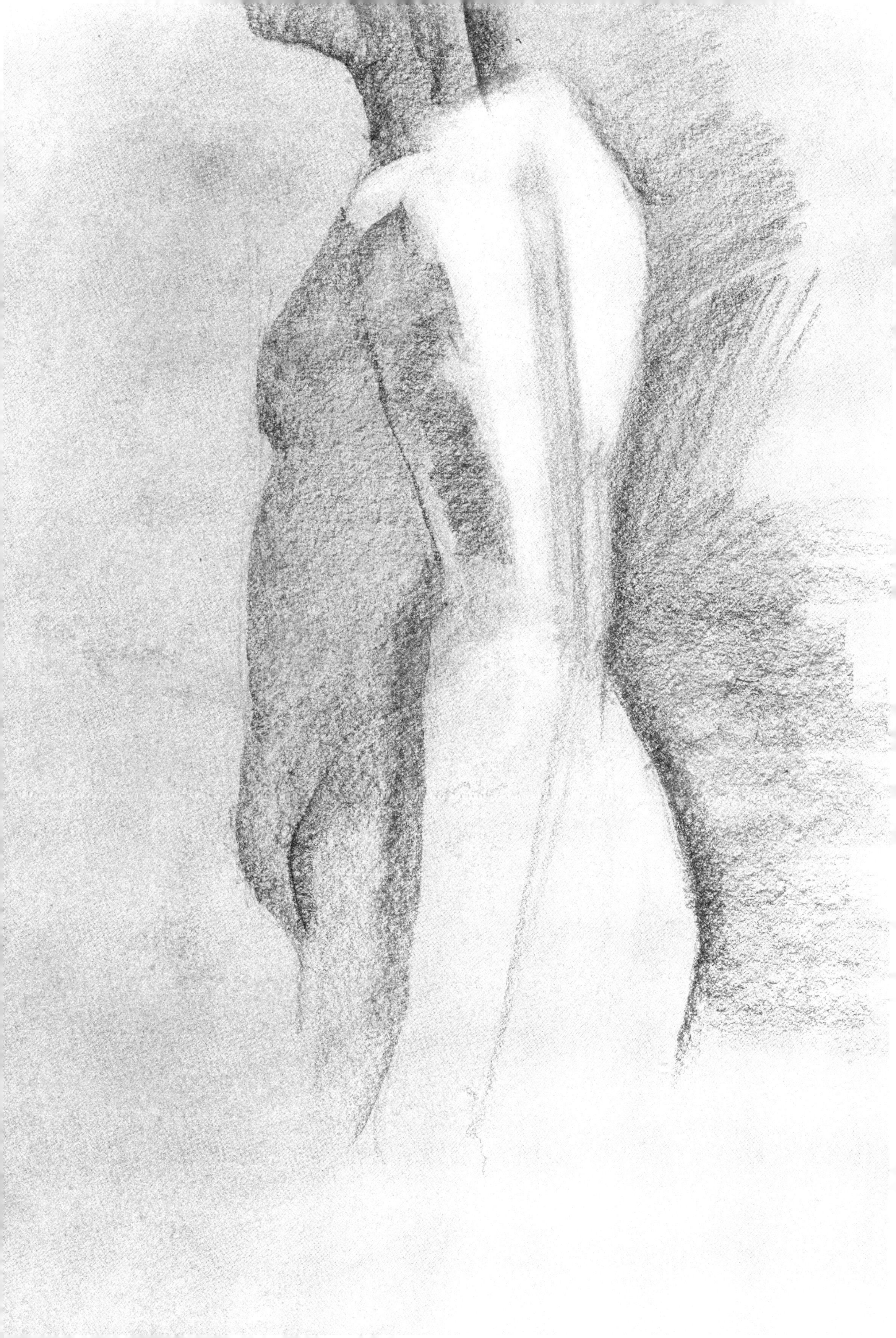

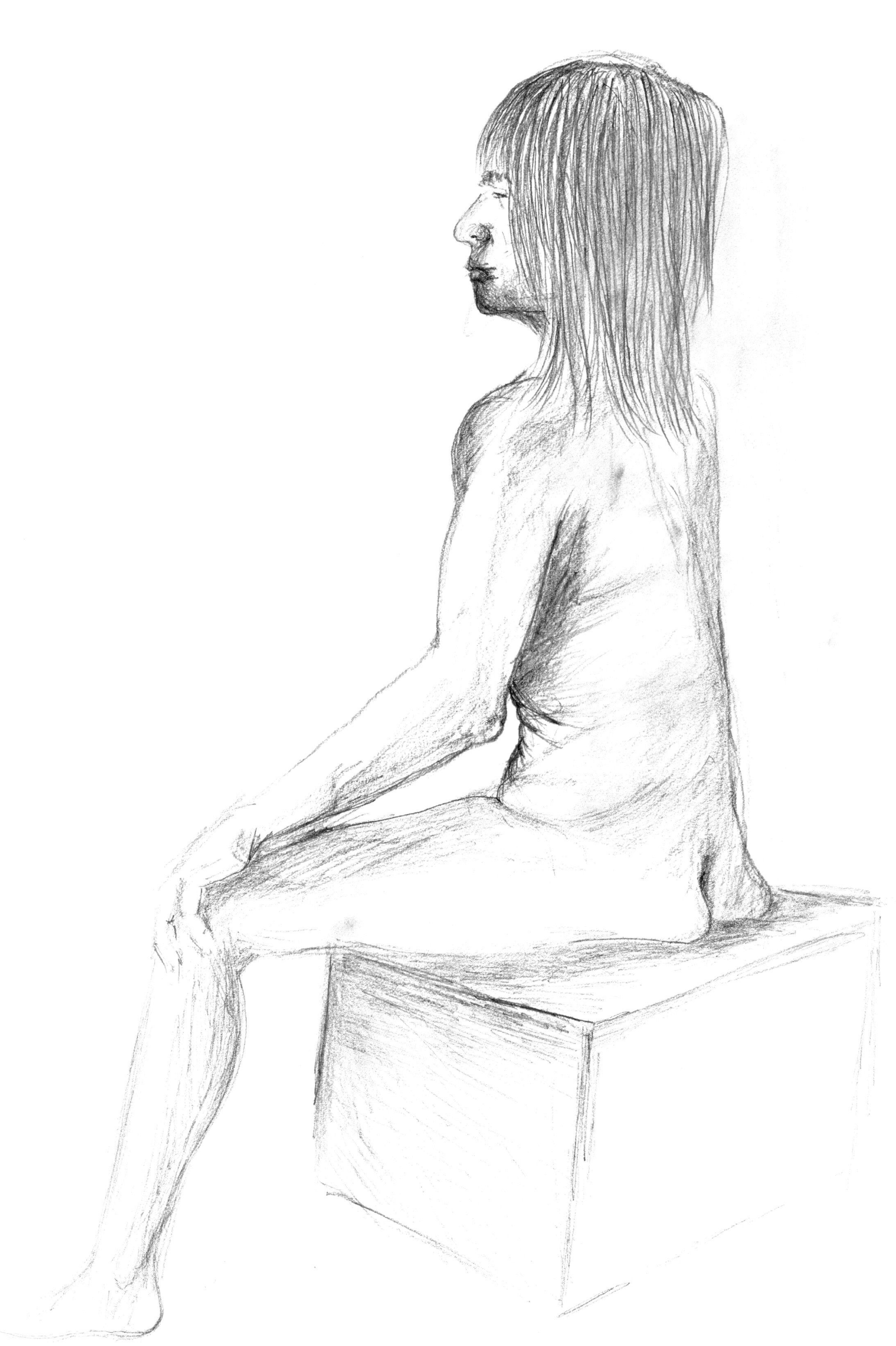

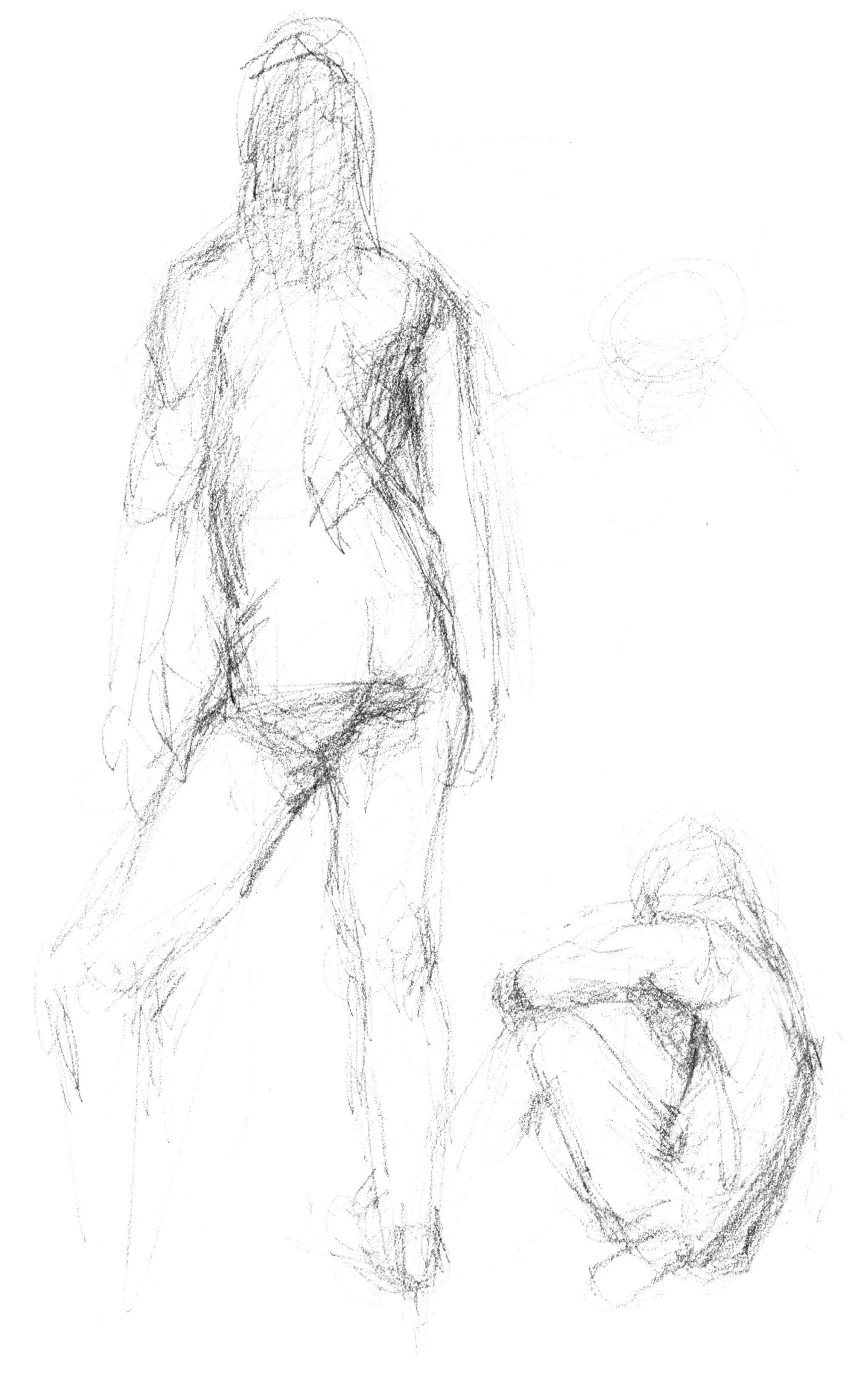

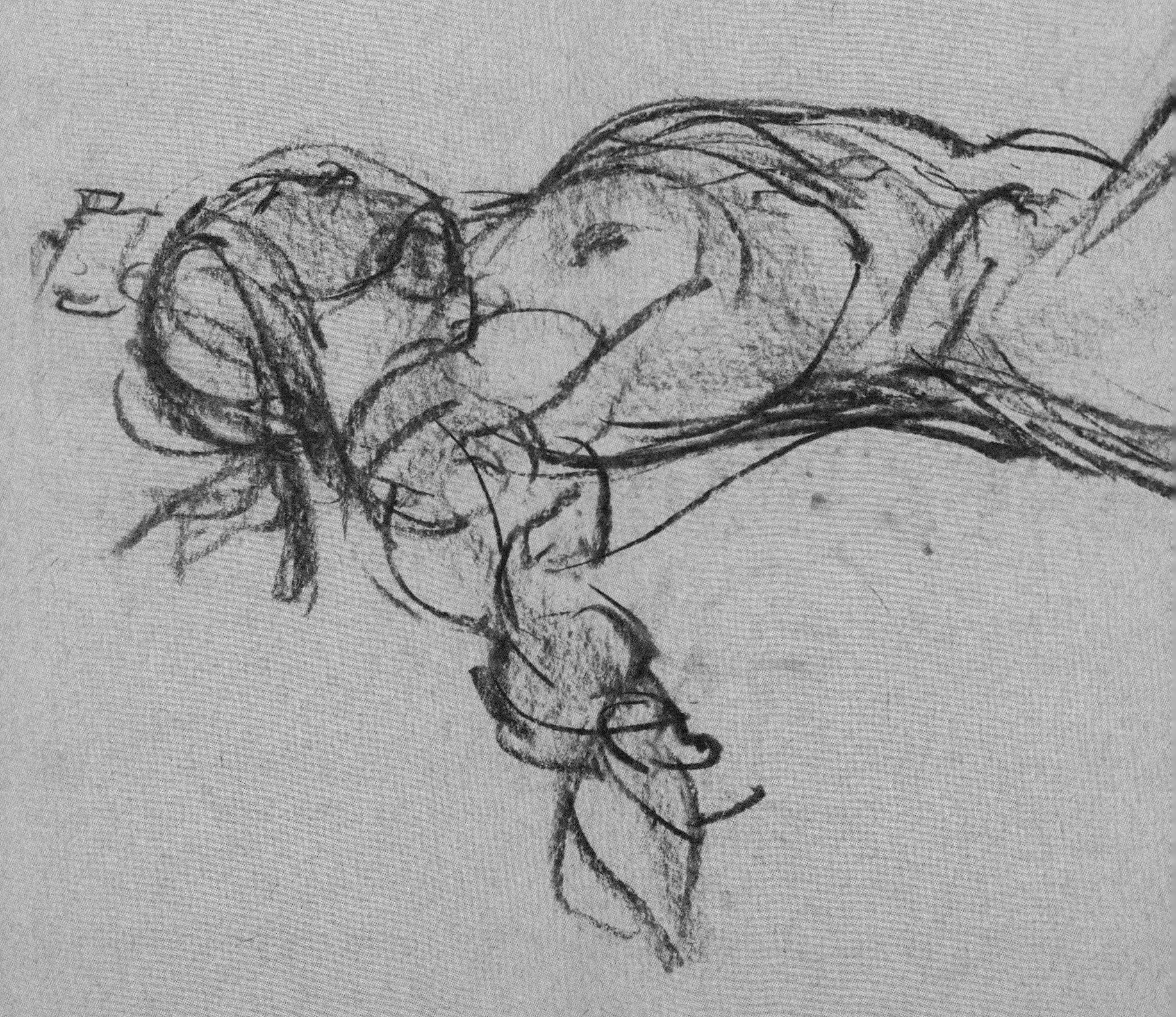

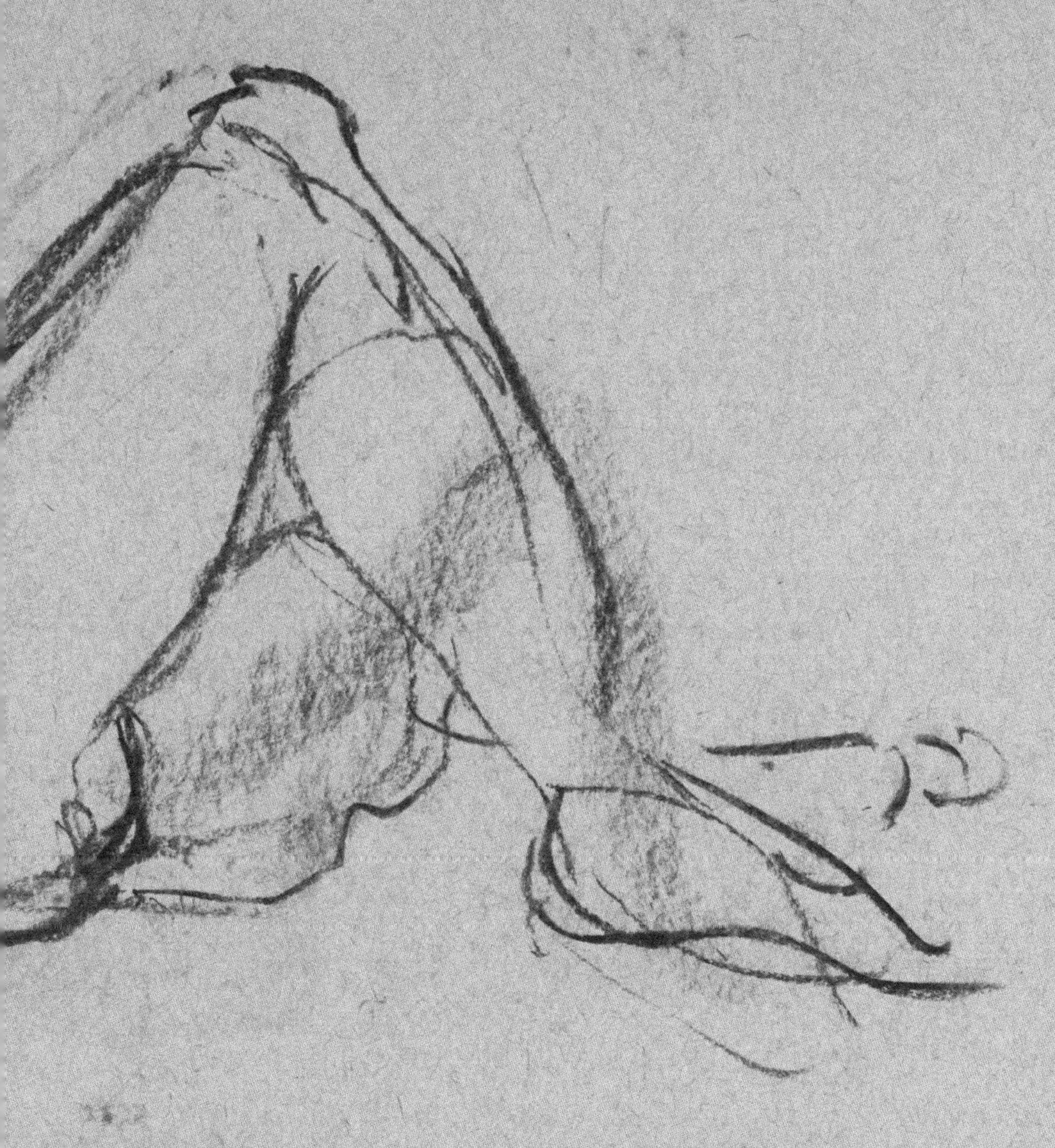

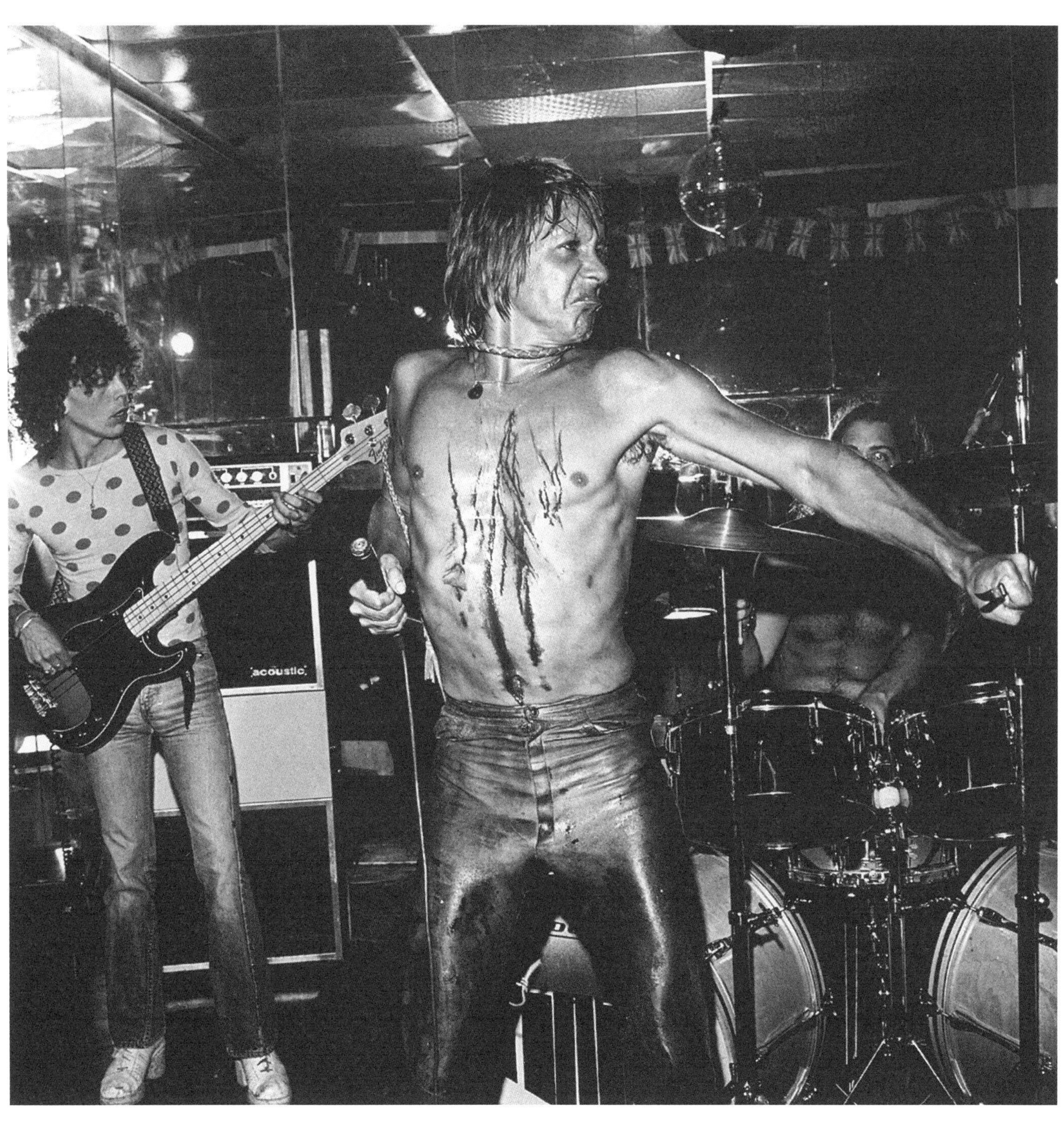

James Fortune, *Iggy Pop at the Whisky à Go-Go*, 1974

"And a flesh machine": Iggy Pop, the Body, and Performance

Mark Beasley

When the Stooges arrived, Iggy was dressed in a ridiculous jazz-dancer's outfit, a kind of leotard with spangled skirt. His eyes were sloppily ringed with eyeliner, and a cigarette drooped from his lips. His whole demeanor said, "Fuck you." I could feel the current of hatred spread through the bikers. Iggy was the total front man; the rest of the band barely moved. They stood stiff and erect like store window dummies, their faces blank. They were the perfect foil; all eyes were focused on Iggy, a master of body gesture. Every move was charged, and his moronic, contorted dancing seemed inspired, like an acrobat possessed by the spirit of an epileptic Jerry Lewis.... It was the best piece of theater I have ever seen.

Mike Kelley (1991)[1]

Did I ever throw up onstage or bleed onstage? Yes! The first time I did, it was out of frustration. I just felt very bad at the time, and music's an expressive medium that can sometimes get out of hand, and suddenly you're playing and you want to express a truth and the truth of that moment was I ought to be cut ... so I cut myself!

Iggy Pop to Tom Snyder (1981)[2]

It's 1981 and a post-Stooges, post-performance Iggy Pop sits slumped and grinning, legs dangling over the arm of his TV-studio seat. He's lost a tooth, having split his lip mid-performance, and blood's trickling from his mouth. The *Tomorrow Show* host Tom Snyder, in an attempt to regain control of a potentially wayward situation, resorts to mimicry, copying his interviewee's slouch. Pop's body never conforms even when seated. The studio audience giggles nervously. Snyder begins his line of questioning: "Is it true you once threw up on your audience ... that you cut yourself onstage ... that you roll around in glass ... why do you do that?" Given that Pop has just karate-kicked and contorted his way through an explosive three-minute performance-to-camera, he's on point and deals adroitly with his interlocutor, steering the conversation from the sensational matter of vomit and blood toward higher

1. Mike Kelly, "Some Aesthetic High Points" (1991), in Kelley, *Minor Histories: Statements, Conversations, Proposals*, edited by John C. Welchman (Cambridge, Mass.: MIT Press, 2004), p. 42.

2. "Tom Snyder *Tomorrow* Show 2-12-81 Iggy Pop," *YouTube* video of TV broadcast, accessed Sept. 16, 2015; https://www.youtube.com/watch?v=Bh97e3gjkA8.

thinking, as he describes the Dionysian versus Apollonian nature of his art. Snyder looks nonplussed, clearly troubled by the pretensions of a rock and roller who doesn't know his place. This is the interviewer as riled everyman, affronted by a seemingly unrepentant, disheveled, and noncompliant upstart. His barely concealed contempt and inability to match, or want to, the erudite and truth-seeking Pop are apparent. Here sits a pariah to be called to account for his perceived iniquity: the sin of free expression without remorse.

*

Pop (born James Newell Osterberg, 1947) has been prowling the stage and surfing the crowd (pages 72–73)—he's credited with inventing the form—for close to fifty years. For Osterberg, raised in a trailer park just outside Detroit, music presented the opportunity to "escape the life that was planned,"[3] and with the help of his assumed stage name and the spirit-possessed persona of Iggy, he and the Stooges all but single-handedly defined the soon to be punk-rock pose and attitude. Often termed the godfather of punk—a title and a crown that gets passed variously from Lou Reed to Richard Hell to Joey Ramone to John Lydon—Pop and the Stooges have serious claim to the throne. Their early albums (*The Stooges*, 1969; *Funhouse*, 1970; and *Raw Power*, 1973) set the scene for a driving, antagonistic rock and roll and created a proto-punk template for those angry youth to come, from the Ramones to Nirvana. The Ramones were early fans and name-checked Stooges gigs as their prompt to action; the Sex Pistols covered their songs; and Kurt Cobain—a musician whose every named musical influence immediately achieves iconic status—called *Raw Power* his number-one record in his posthumously published *Journals* (2003).

Pop's introduction to rock and roll arrived courtesy of the trailer park and the teenage guitar-owning son of a Tennessee family who repeatedly played the guitar riff from the pre-surf instrumental "Bulldog."[4] The social politic of the trailer park, its music, and its fluctuating community cemented his understanding of "rock and roll as a working-peoples' folk music."[5] The rhythm and the groove stuck. And as Pop learned the drums and worked in various high-school bands (notably The Iguanas, from which the name Iggy derives), playing Chicago blues clubs, and with the realization that other people played—or, in the case of the British Invasion, copied—the blues "better," he sought his own groove: enter the Stooges and their white suburban delinquent music.

But what of Iggy, the shape-shifting, bleached-blonde-trickster-stripper, jerking his way across the stage? Pop's body, his writhing, cavorting frame, is fixed in the mind of anyone who's seen him perform, watched footage or picked up one of his many (twenty-three and counting) albums. From the cover of the Stooges' 1970 *Funhouse* (opposite page), Pop's long-gloved arms held aloft as his

3. "Iggy Pop," *The South Bank Show* (TV arts magazine), produced by ITV, Season 28, Episode 9, Dec. 5, 2004.
4. The Fireballs, "Bulldog" (song), released by Top Rank Records, 1959.
5. "Iggy Pop," *The South Bank Show*.

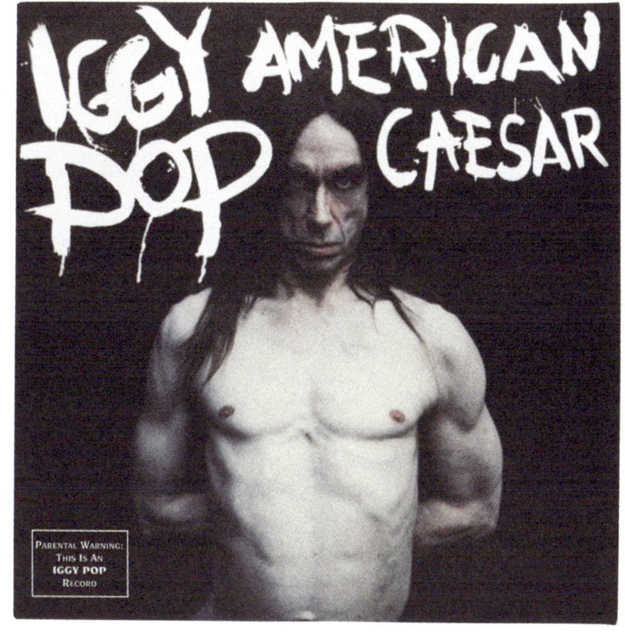

Iggy Pop: American Caesar, 1993. Virgin Records

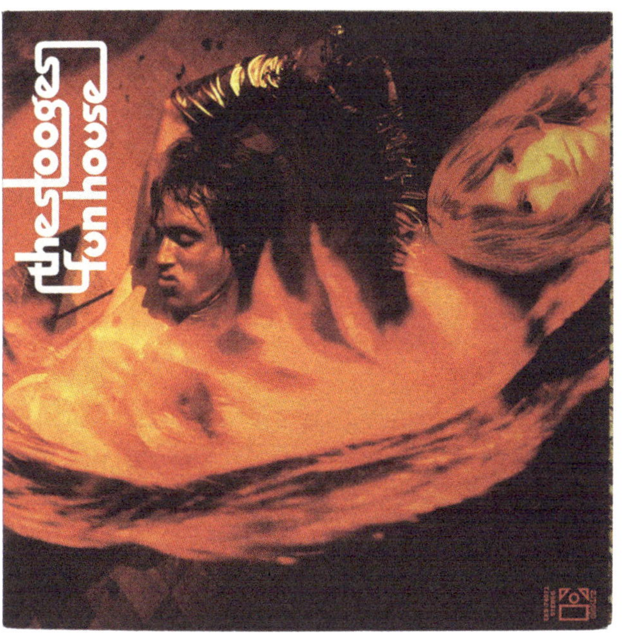

The Stooges: Funhouse, 1970. Elektra Records

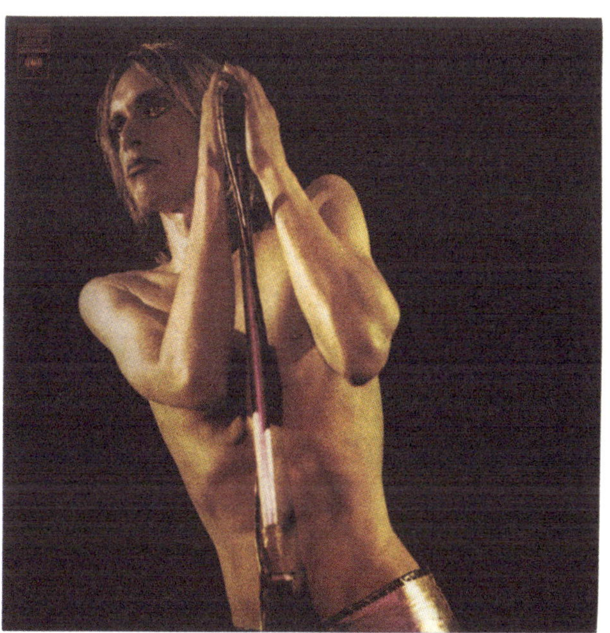

Iggy and the Stooges: Raw Power, 1973. Columbia Records

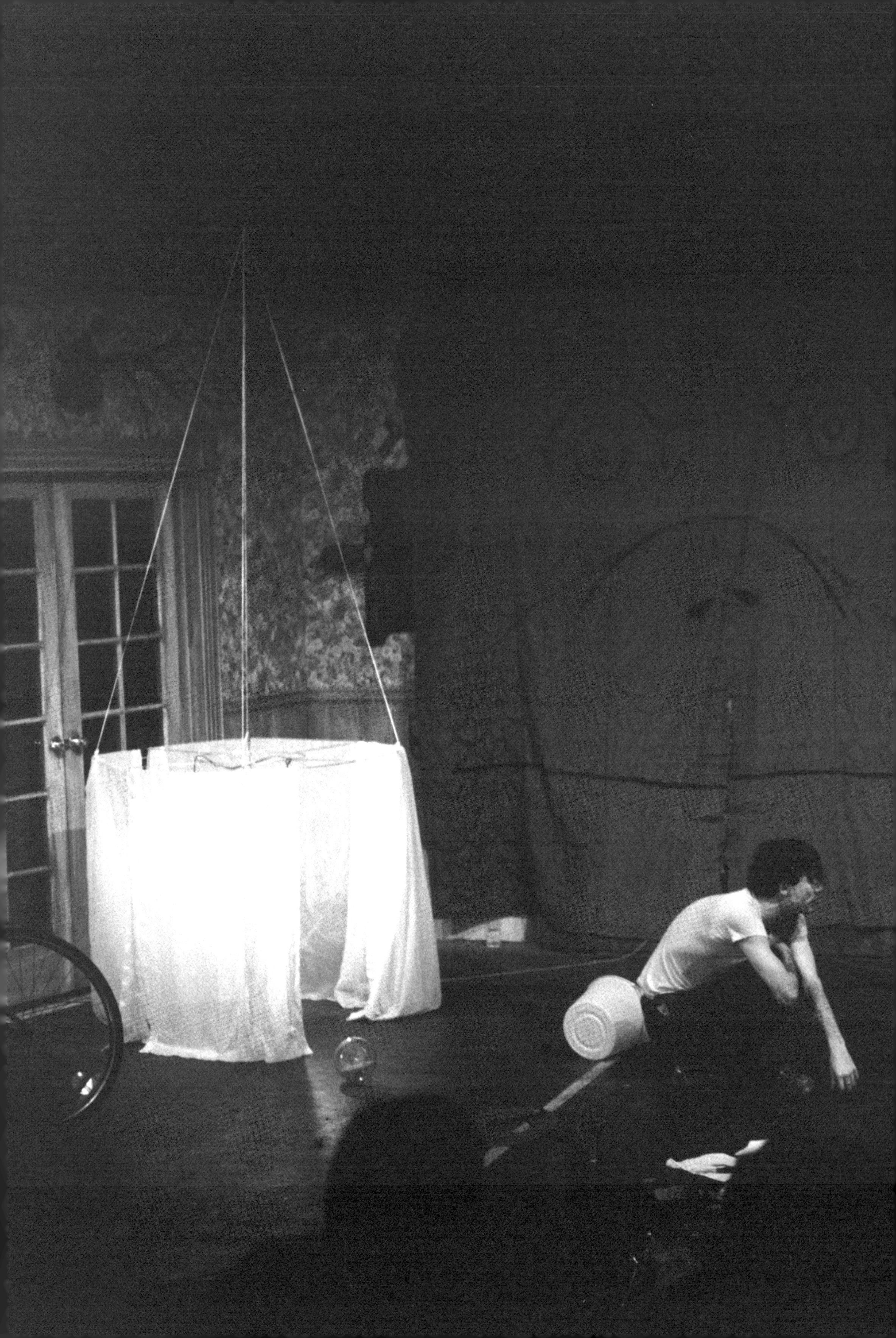

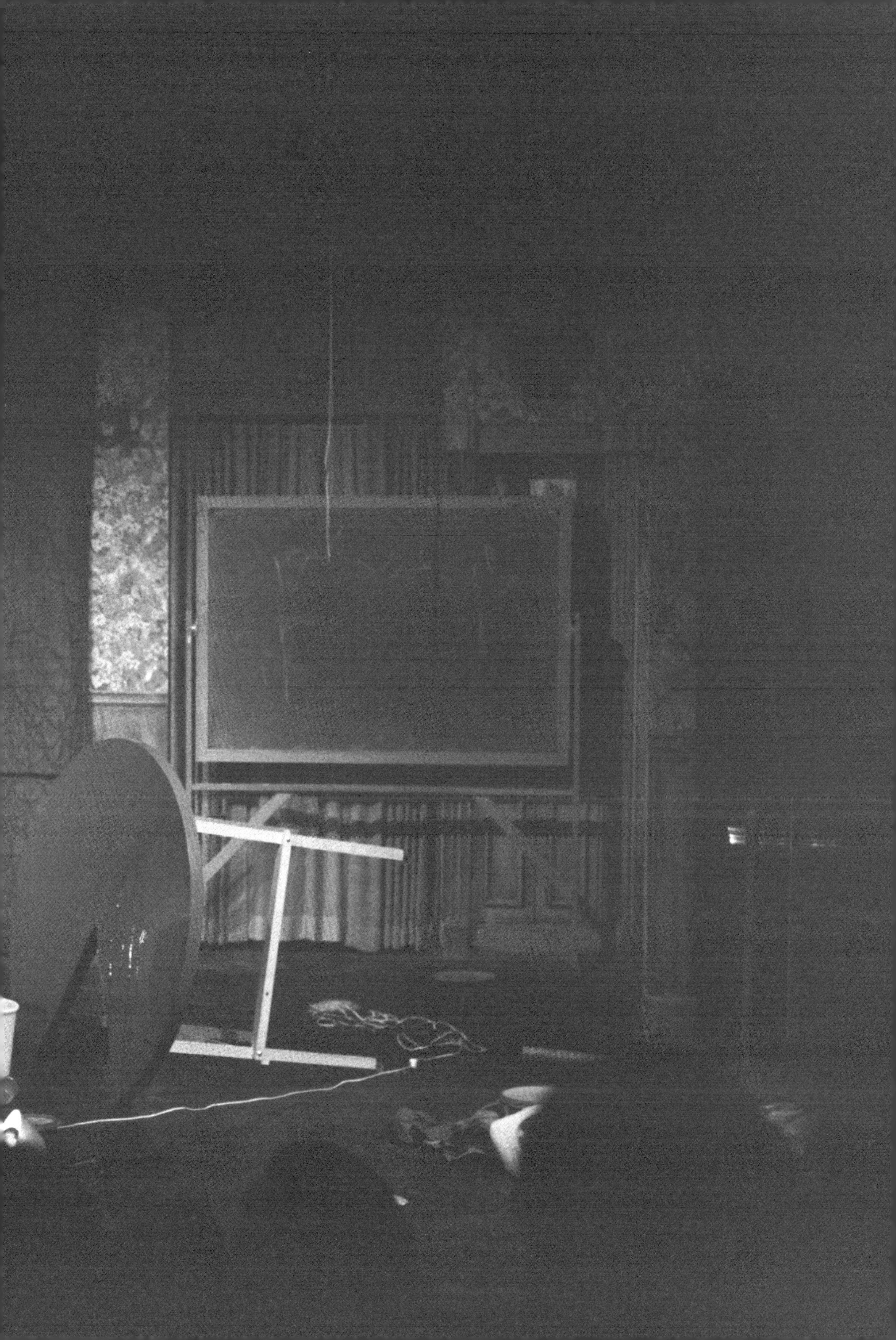

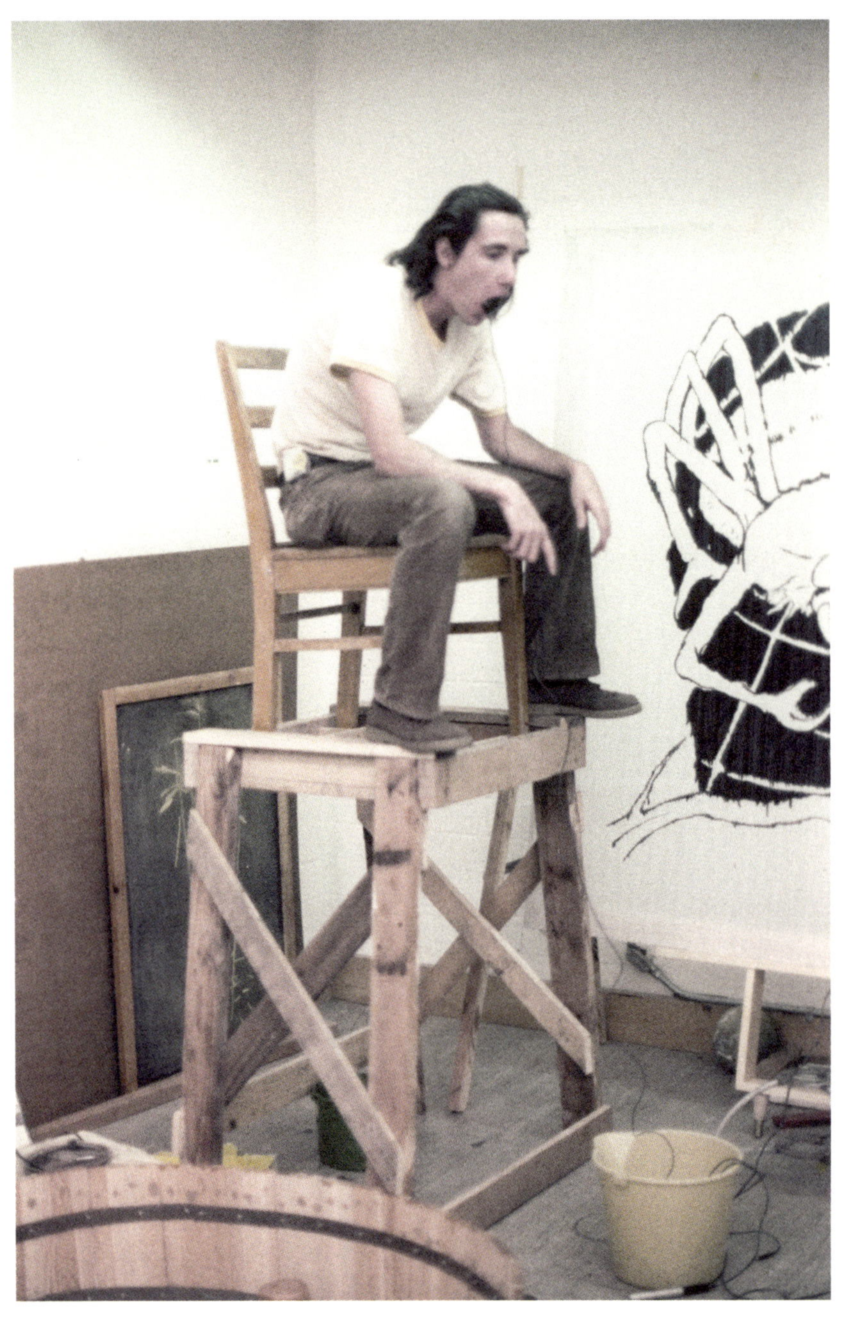

Mike Kelley, *The Oracle at Delphi*, 1978. Performance at CalArts

← Mike Kelley, *Confusion: A Play in Seven Sets, Each Set More Spectacular and Elaborate than the Last*, 1983

wiry torso explodes in a psychedelic burst of solar flared red and orange; to the follow-up *Iggy and the Stooges: Raw Power* (1973; page 67), and his sinewy male torso reminiscent of the arrow-pierced, bound, and martyred Saint Sebastian; to his later solo LPs and the cadaver-pale torso of *American Caesar* (1993; page 67) or the slumped impish "fuck you" stare of *Naughty Little Doggie* (1996), his body has been foregrounded. Throughout the various shared flats of my youth, the apartments, and now family home, there has always been Iggy staring out from one corner or another, from the record sleeve or poster, his body as well as his music keeping time and marking the passing of years: impish, knowing, and forever rock and roll.

If you've never seen him onstage and in the flesh (pages 72–73), there's much to be gained by perusing YouTube clips of Iggy in full flow. When interviewed on the BBC's *South Bank Show*, Pop described his response to sound: "A certain kind of music suggests the way a song should be performed and if it gets physical, it gets physical. As Elvis said … I just can't help myself!" Driven by the raw power of brothers Ron Asheton on guitar and Dave Asheton on drums, Pop's torso writhes and twists as he romps onstage. The Stooges came of age at a time of amplification. It's hard to imagine now, but in the mid-sixties it was rare to see anyone standing in front of a microphone, as only a few performers (Sinatra, Bennett, Presley) had mics. In regular unamplified clubs, a singer would have to strain to be heard, fighting over instruments, the clink of glasses, and the orders at the bar, which in turn gave the blues its particular singing style: Howlin' Wolf howled for many reasons. The Stooges were the sound of a new and *plugged-in* generation, and for the first time instruments and vocals could both be played at volume. Guitarist Asheton describes the sound of their early gigs at the University of Michigan as assaulting and hallucinatory. As the Marshall amp stacks rang out, the room literally vibrated and the band and audience were swallowed up in sound.[6]

The call of the amp and the guitar is still evident in Pop's recent Post Pop Depression Tour (2016). As the opening power chords of "Lust for Life" (1977) ring out, Pop comes haring from the back of the stage to greet the crowd, the crowned jester of the court of rock and roll he helped invent. "Here comes Johnny Yen again / With the liquor and the drugs / And a flesh machine / He's gonna do another strip tease.… I got a lust for life!"[7] As sound waves crash on the stage, they're met by Iggy, who translates sound into movement—our interpreter, the flesh machine.

Written in lieu of a biographical statement for a monograph, Mike Kelley's "Some Aesthetic High Points" (1991) describes two key influences and performances. One was Sun Ra at the Ann Arbor Blues and Jazz Festival; the other was Iggy Pop and the Stooges at a small biker bar in Wayne, Michigan (both 1973). Paraphrasing Kelley's account, as Pop continually baited the crowd, hurling insults, mocking their complicity in the "freak show" spectacle of rock and roll, he and the band repeatedly played "Louie Louie" (Richard Berry, 1955),

6. *Lust for Life* (documentary, 40 minutes), directed by Bram van Splunteren, VRPO TV, Nov. 1986.
7. Iggy Pop and David Bowie, *Lust for Life* (album), RCA, 1977.

Thomas Copi, *Iggy Pop*, 1970. Photographic print. Michael Ochs Archives. (Photo: Tom Copi/Michael Ochs Archive/Getty Images) →

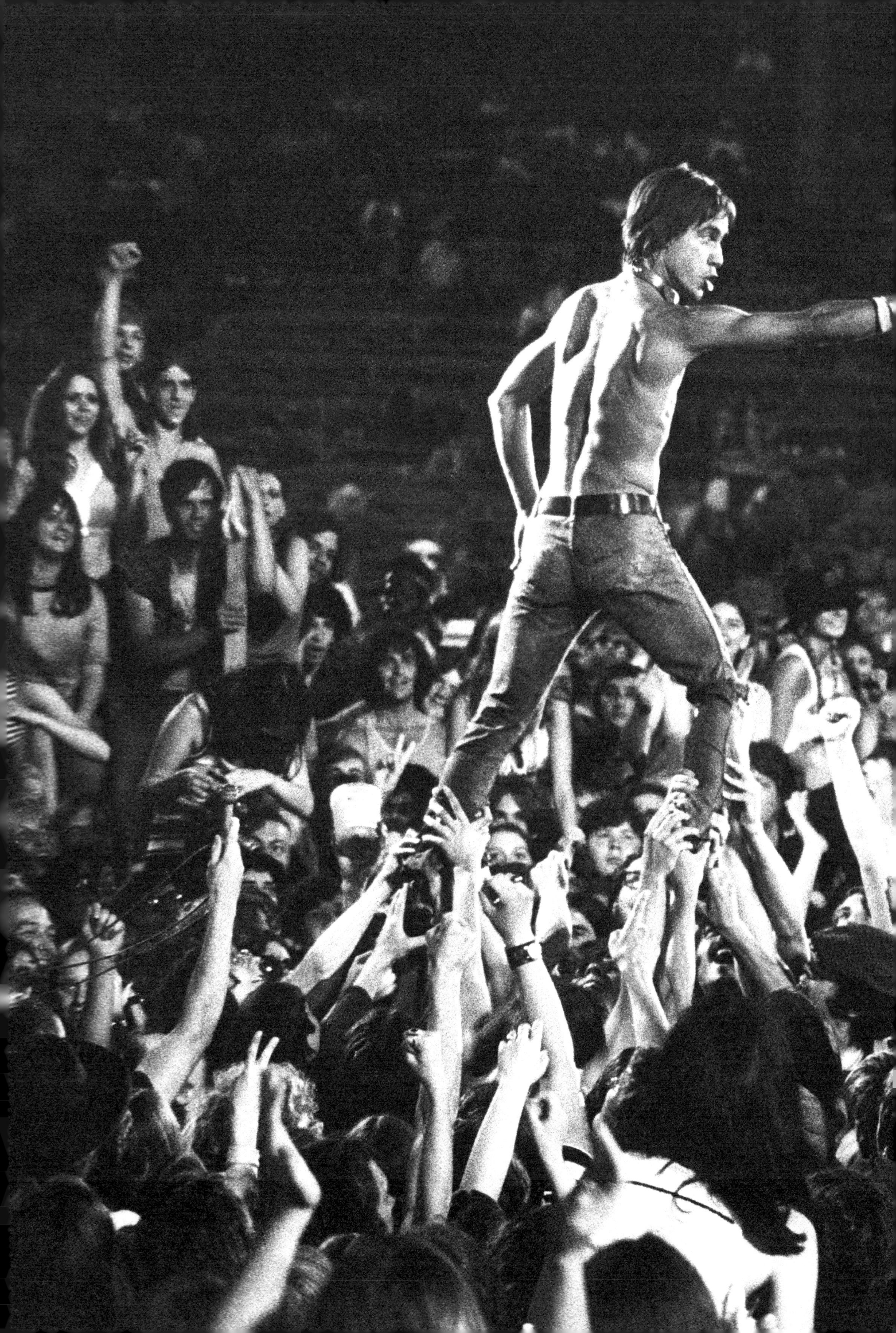

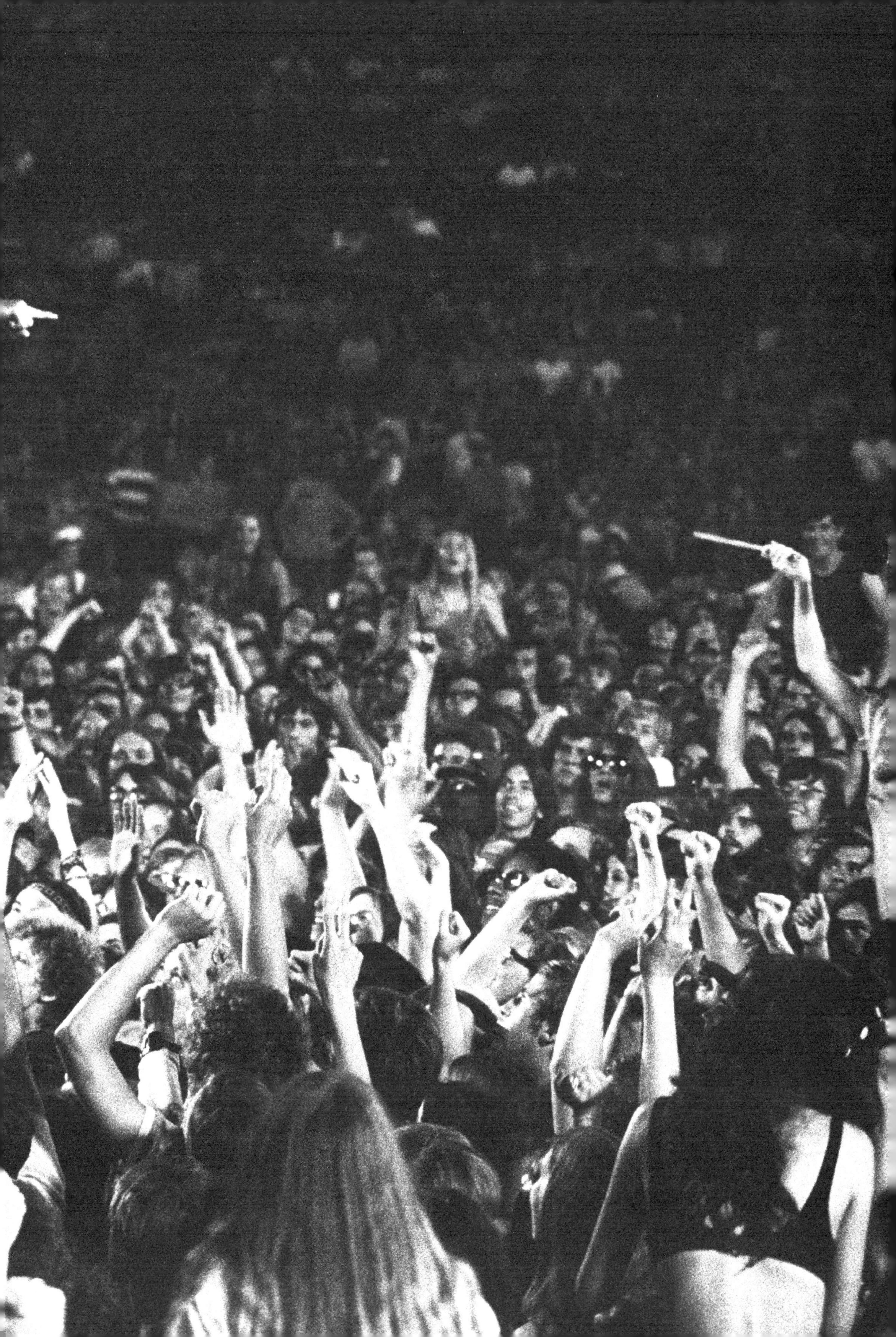

much to the audience's increasing ire and bellowed demands for other Stooges tracks. Pop's mixing of gender norms, dressed in stripper-drag and smeared in make-up, further confused the biker crowd who, growing more restless, found solace in the inevitable bar brawl. One can only imagine Pop's smirk and the glow of a job well done! For Kelley, Pop is the trickster-in-chief, possessed of the Brechtian spirit of living theater: nurtured by the sounds of Detroit's auto factories, the Detroit Twelfth Street riots of 1967, the psych-rock music of the MC5, and the far-left gospel of John Sinclair's White Panther Party. Kelley, fellow Detroit native and musician, with his band Destroy All Monsters (Ron Asheton would later join a more overtly rock-and-roll version of DAM), finished his bio with the line, "Everything of major importance that I know about performing, I learned from these concerts."

Kelley's performances (pages 68–70) employed both music and dance, moving fluently between low and high cultural form (his critical championing of American low-vernacular pop culture is chief among his many achievements). His work with bands such as Sonic Youth (on the performance piece called *Plato's Cave, Rothko's Chapel, Lincoln's Profile*, 1985, as well as the broadcast *The Peristaltic Airwaves*, 1986) and on collaborations with choreographer Anita Pace that fused contemporary dance with metal music's slam-dancing (*Pansy Metal/Clovered Hoof*, 1989) make Kelley's understanding of the dynamics of rock-and-roll performance clear. In his final performance, *Extracurricular Activity Projective Reconstruction #33, Plus* (2009), at New York's Judson Church, he appeared in a flowery bonnet and skipped and flounced his way around the room, welcoming the audience with mock-solemnity and satiric glee. New York had long been a documented source of frustration for Kelley, its critics too Eurocentric and its artists (specific disdain was reserved for Jeff Koons) too quick to employ pop culture as surface skin without depth. As curator of *EAPR #33,* I'd watched Mike rehearse and direct other performers, dancers, and musicians for weeks, resulting in an exactingly detailed and choreographed—both in dance and in music—performance. Yet, I'd rarely seen him perform in rehearsals; this flower-bonneted host appeared from nowhere, fully formed and fluent in movement, chaotically in control and, as with Iggy, out to trip expectations from gender norms to the presumed *politesse* required to receive New York's great and good.

Pop's impact as popular performer, his flailing body and legendary "leap into the void" to the waiting arms of the crowd, rewired audience and performer relations. No longer is the performer—that Holy of Holies—at one remove from the audience, but is now thoroughly implicated. In one online TV clip, a confused presenter immediately cuts to a commercial break as a midair Iggy launches himself into the crowd, his status as a performer presumably entirely undone by leaving the stage. Now an MTV awards show trope among punk-derived bands, for Pop, its inventor, it suggested and suggests togetherness, a willful breaking of the rules of the stage. But it's perhaps his sadomasochistic leanings ("Now I wanna be your dog") that have the greatest push on, or parallel to, visual arts performance. It's a relationship best exemplified by an early work of Chris Burden. In *Through the Night Softly* (1973; opposite page), Burden worms

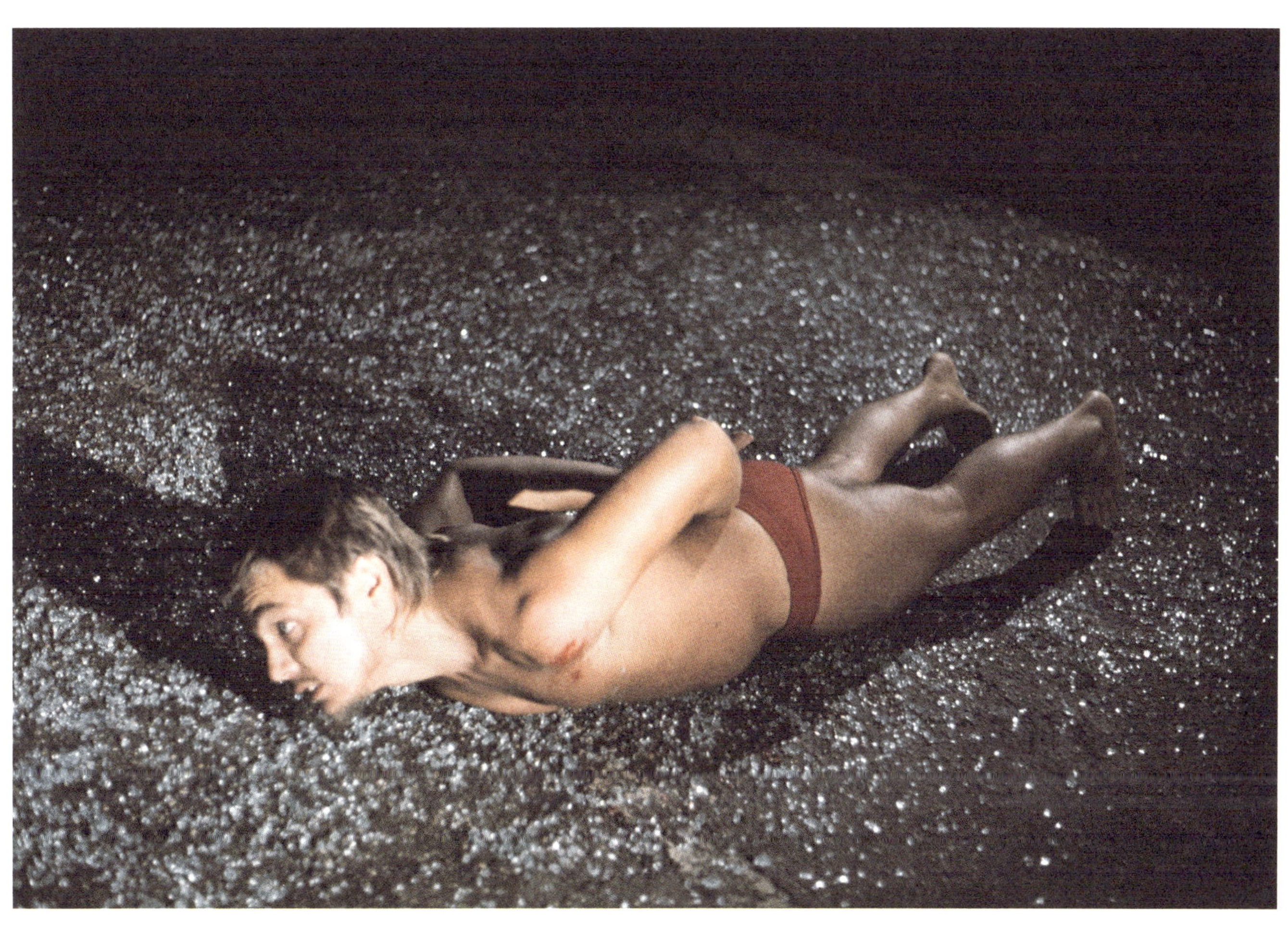

Chris Burden, production still from the film *Through the Night Softly*, 1973

his way naked through fifty feet of broken glass. In the video, placed as a ten-second TV ad on a local station—all the airtime that Burden could afford to buy—the glass shines like stars in the night as Burden bleeds. That same year, the Stooges were monthly residents at New York's Max's Kansas City nightclub, and as Iggy walked from the stage across the tables, glasses were smashed and the stem of a wineglass became a weapon for self-mutilation. "I just couldn't stand myself anymore, so I went behind the amps with this piece of broken glass, having decided to cut my jugular vein. I just didn't have the guts, though.... I was aiming for the vein, but just couldn't make it. I cut up my chest instead."[8] It makes for difficult reading. Far from heroic pose, the male body as presented by Pop and Burden is a wretched, crawling, and scarred presence. As Vito Acconci's *Seedbed* (1972) or Burden's earlier performance work *Shoot* (1971) questioned presumed relations between the gallery audience and performer (viewer and perpetrator), Pop's chosen forum, the gig, is continually tripped up, made curious and strange, through acts of abjection and revolt.

As Pop coquettishly raises his arms above his head and turns his back to the crowd, we are reminded that the musician's body (as with guitar, drum, and voice) is also an instrument: it too can change its tune, from aggression to seduction. The body is a poeticized text, of sorts; we read the way it moves. It's part of the tale. In addition, as music theorist Simon Frith states, it is through "learning how to dance to music that we learn how best to listen to it."[9] Anyone who has (and forgive the cliché) been lost in music, in dance, and in movement can attest to the body's instinctive reaction to sound. Iggy as performer allows us access to the music (and specifically new music, as it was back then), a flirtatious spirit-guide moving to the call of rock and roll's endlessly potent beats.

Performance is essentially a social form, and to be understood it relies upon a shared understanding between audience and performer. For it to be anything else would result in endless drift and being lost in unreadable gesture. (As we've seen, even bikers recognize codes and when they're being "put on.") To this extent, even the most radical "in the moment" and unscripted performances rely upon some form of rhetorical gesture that, if not altogether socialized, can be read. In turn such radical posturing calls for an equally radical empathy as we look for ourselves in the actions of another. As fans, we don't, as is commonly suggested, consume pop stars—what they wear, where they holiday, what they eat; that's simply the by-product. Instead what we consume is their performance, as they're fitted into our own private understanding of the world. We read *us* into the movements and actions of performers.

If David Bowie continually shed his skin, Jim Osterberg, in the guise of Iggy Pop, kept his, and over the years we've watched it dance, writhe, age, and wreak havoc onstage. Reading Iggy, as he climbs the walls and leaps from the stage

8. Martin Patrick, "Chris Burden, Iggy Pop and the Aesthetics of Early 70s Performance Art," *Art Monthly*, 276 (May 2004); accessed on the *Art Monthly* website.

9. Simon Frith, *Performing Rites: On the Value of Popular Music* (Cambridge, Mass.: Harvard University Press, 1996), p. 203.

or skitters like a herky-jerky scarecrow, is to understand something of an embodied resistance—to the postindustrial life of the Midwest, to the Vietnam draft, and ultimately to the boredom of straitjacket America, straitjacket anywhere. Pop's acting out, his delirious giving over to the music, is an escape from alienation and from the hidden injuries of America's social and class system. In every small town there's an Iggy Pop; this one happened to think, dance, and howl his way out. Pop is the boundary-crosser; his belief in music as a liberating form has taken him from the trailer park to the concert hall and finally to the museum.

Many of Pop's concerts end with an invitation to the audience to join him onstage to riot in the glare of the concert spotlight, and in recent concerts he has taken to pointing out members of the crowd and exclaiming, "I am you, I am you." Clearly we can't all be Iggy, but within the moment of encounter, at the gig, we are momentarily lost in the collective identifying ego. If Kelley's, Burden's, and Acconci's actions made the gallery productively curious and strange, then Iggy Pop took it to the masses, infecting a working-class people's music and the macho seed of rock and roll with forthright lyrics and outré moves. The battle scars of an American subcultural landscape are written in the possessed, seductive, brutalized yet ultimately triumphant body of Pop. We are all implicated, all lost in the dance.

Studio venue for the Iggy Pop Life Class, February 21, 2016, New York Academy of Art →

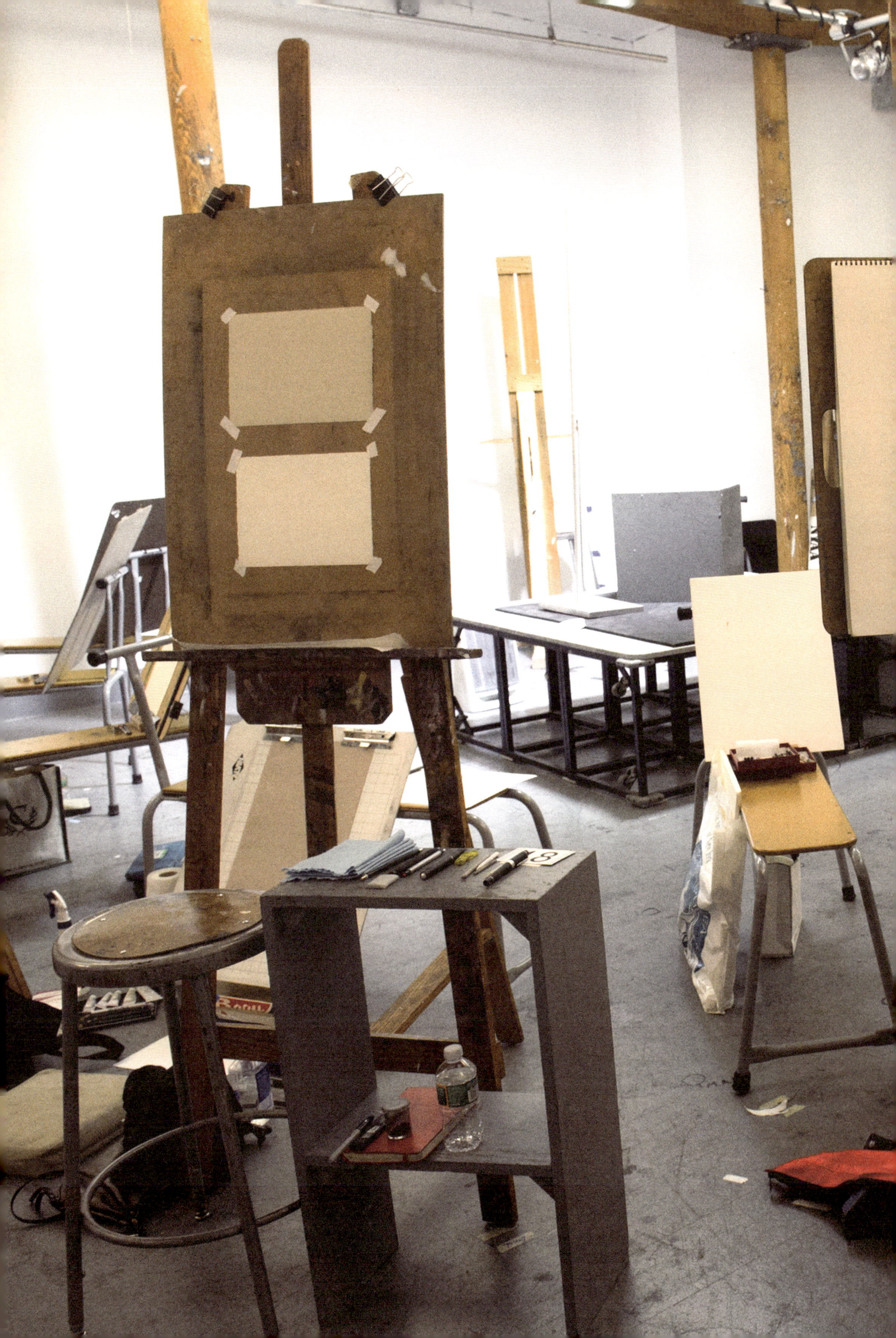

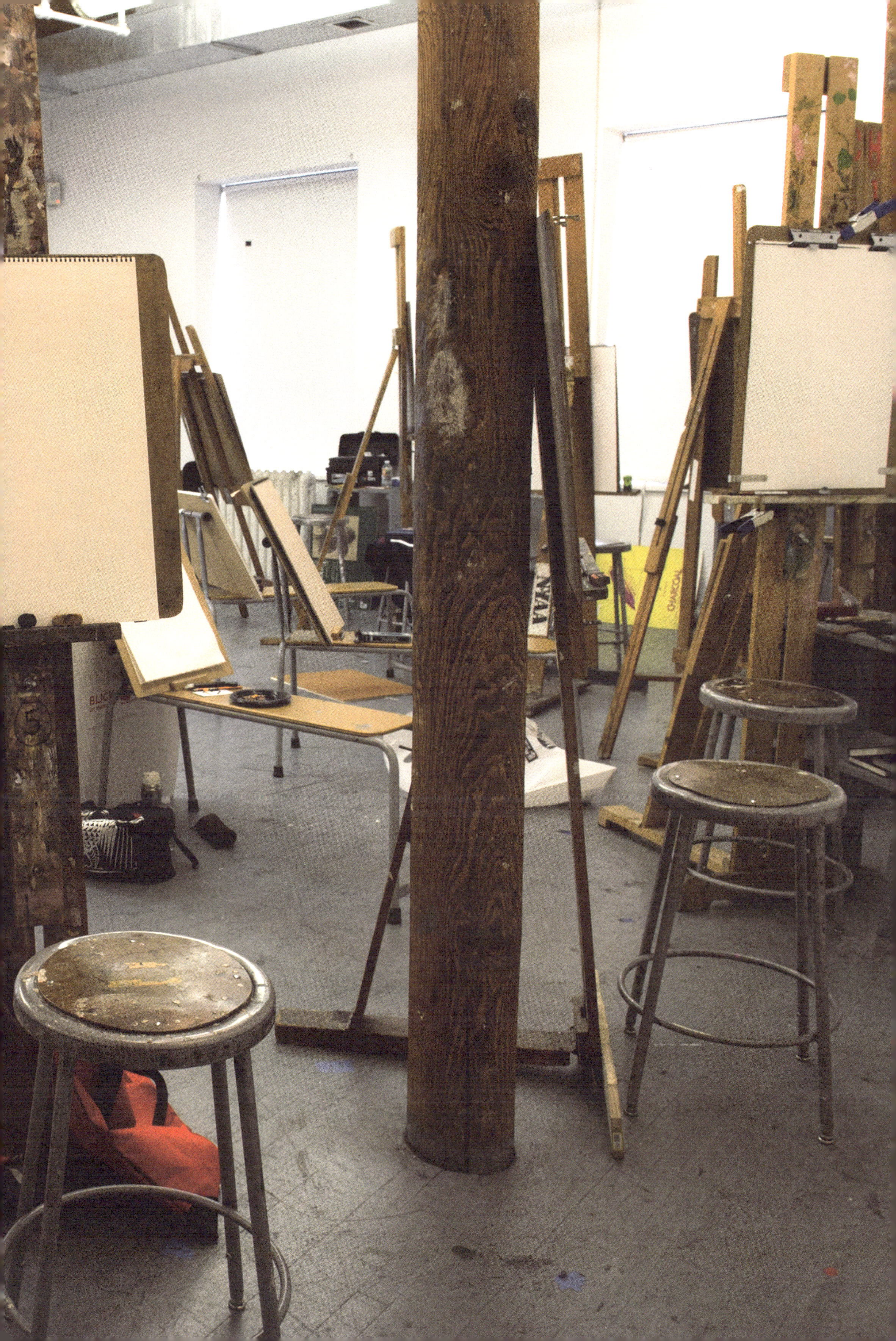
NYAA
CHARCOAL

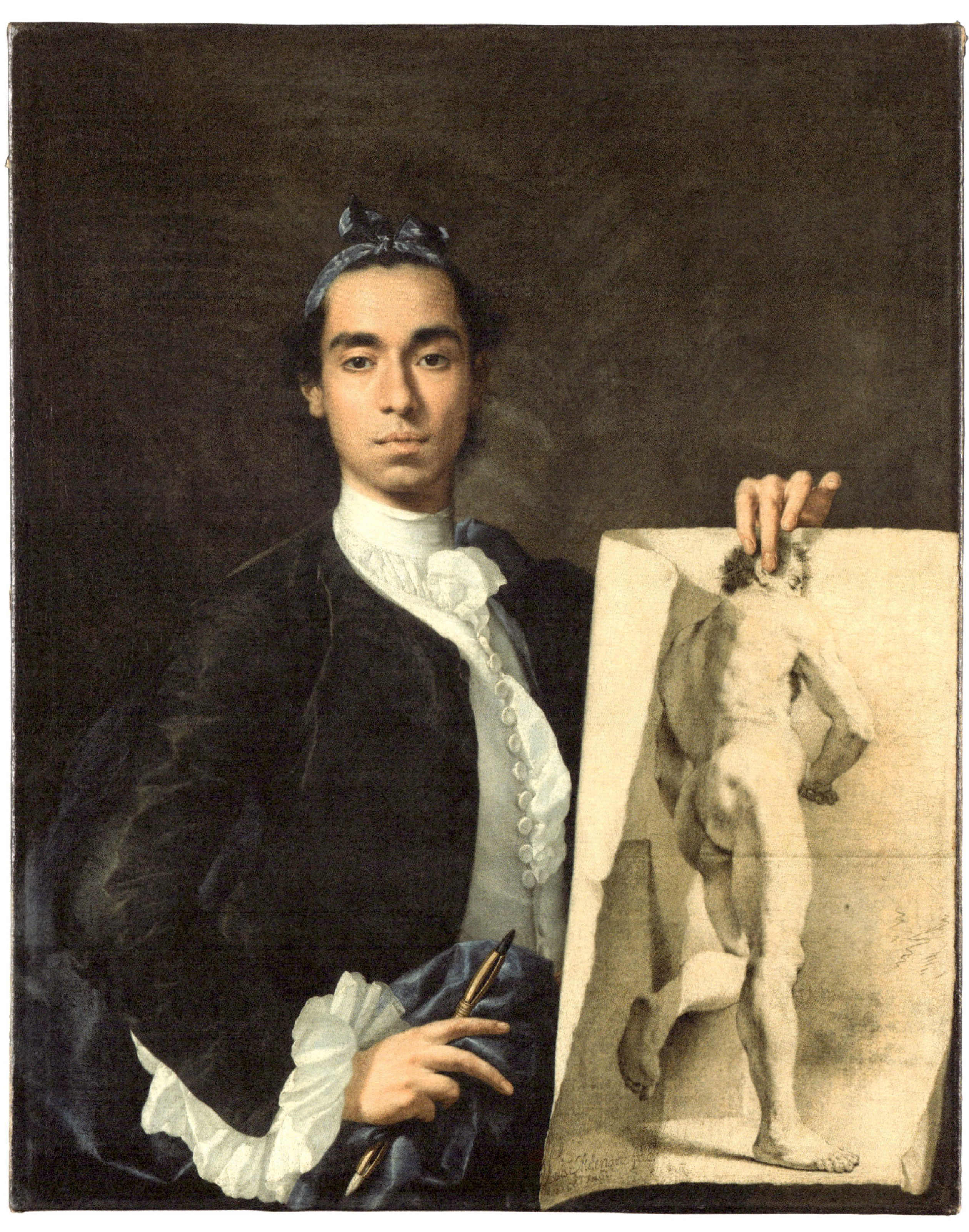

Luis Meléndez, *Self-Portrait Holding an Academic Study*, 1746. Musée du Louvre, Paris

Life Drawing and the Male Model

Frances Borzello

We have an image of a life class in our heads: a naked human holding a pose in front of a group of clothed students silently transposing what they see into pencil, paint, or charcoal.

Jeremy Deller calls the life class the foundation of art and art history. "The life class is a special place in which to scrutinize the human form. As the bedrock of art education and art history, it is still the best way to understand the body."[1]

But what does bedrock actually mean? To most people, mastery of the nude proves the artist's ability to draw properly, "properly" meaning in a realistic manner. And that is certainly part of it. But the life class has a bigger history, one held as intimately in the history of post-Renaissance Western art as is the pencil in the hand.

Authority for the life class can be traced back to Leon Battista Alberti's *On Painting*, an Italian treatise of 1435 devoted to promoting the new, realistic, and scientifically based way of painting, as a fine art involving intellect, as opposed to the old-fashioned medieval way of treating painting as a skill-based craft.

This new, modern art from Florence was inspired by a growing awareness of the high standard of classical art, a standard that became a goal for the fifteenth-century artists of the Renaissance. It was underpinned by Filippo Brunelleschi's invention of the perspective system two decades earlier and the conviction that a good artist should be able to draw from life: that is, could paint trees that looked natural as opposed to the stylized broccoli stems of medieval art. The aim was to see a painting as a window in the wall, a standard that remained in place until the end of the nineteenth century. As part of his argument, Alberti claimed a hierarchy of subject matter that had at its summit paintings of classical history, a category soon expanded to include episodes from history and the Bible. These moral and uplifting subjects demanded the ability to portray convincing figures to play their part on the painted stage.

Within a hundred years of Alberti's treatise, artists were gathering to draw the nude, particularly in Rome and Florence, where the Medici sponsored the visual and literary arts in the sixteenth century, and then wider afield in the seventeenth century. In Paris in 1648, art as a respected profession received a royal seal of approval with the opening of the Académie Royale de Peinture et de Sculpture, a move that was followed in most European countries by the end of the eighteenth century and in America with the founding of the Academia de San Carlos, in Mexico City, in 1781, and the Pennsylvania Academy of the

1. "Brooklyn Museum Announces *Iggy Pop Life Class*, Conceived by Artist Jeremy Deller, to be the Focus of an Exhibition in Fall 2016," Brooklyn Museum press release, Feb. 2016.

Fine Arts, in 1805. The journey is visible at first in prints and drawings showing informal groups around a model, and later in ambitious paintings of life classes in the prestigious national academies, their intriguing new subject matter guaranteed to attract attention.

Unlike the smaller schools and informal groups, which typically met by lamplight to draw the nude, the national academies prided themselves on their rigorous standards, and by the start of the nineteenth century a formalized course of training had emerged that, with minor variations, was common to them all. Whereas all aspects of art were taught, from portraiture to the achievement of landscape perspective through color, it was the mastery of drawing the naked body that was the aim of the most ambitious students, the ones wishing to produce works that dealt with the serious matters of life and would therefore be taken most seriously. Study of the human figure was privileged because the figure was the basis of history painting—Greek and Roman history, mythology, and biblical subjects.

The national academies introduced students gradually to the human body, teaching them what lay beneath the skin in anatomy classes, then having them copy bodies from admired drawings, paintings, and sculptures, and only then allowing them to work from the living model. The life class was the drawing student's final destination, one that had to be earned through completion of all the other exercises. The prior anatomical information and knowledge of past masterpieces was not only to familiarize the student with the body, but also to help him (and until the end of the nineteenth century, it always was a him) improve on the less than perfect life class models by subtly bringing their flawed reality closer to the most glorious painted and sculpted nudes already in existence. Proof that a student had mastered the ability to draw the nude was evidence that he had successfully completed his training. In a self-portrait of 1746, the young Spanish painter Luis Meléndez proudly displays his *académie*, the French name for the finished life drawing that was the gateway to his profession (page 80).

Choosing models for the life class was a serious matter. As far as academic teaching was concerned, it was the male body, with its clear delineation of muscles, that was the most fit for this purpose. Alberti's statement of 1435 still held: "Before dressing a man, we first draw him nude, then we enfold him in draperies. So in painting the nude we place first his bones and muscles, which we then cover with flesh so that it is not difficult to understand where each muscle is beneath."[2] We can assume that the four male models whose pay marked the first expenditure of the newly formed British Royal Academy in 1768 were the finest specimens available. Diaries and letters offer evidence of what this meant. "I frequently see an old beggar without legs in Holborn," wrote the artist C. R. Leslie in 1812, "who was one of the rioters at the time Newgate was burnt, and had both his legs shot off by a chain-shot in that very street … I am told his body is remarkably fine, and that he has frequently sat to artists—very often to Mr West"[3]; Benjamin West, that is, the history painter who had left Pennsylvania

2. Leon Battista Alberti, *On Painting* (New Haven, Conn.: Yale University Press, 1971), Book 2, p. 73.

3. Tom Taylor, ed., *Autobiographical Recollections by the Late Charles Robert Leslie, R.A.*, 2 vols. (London: John Murray, 1860), vol. 2, pp. 12–13.

to study in Europe and became president of the Royal Academy in 1792. Models whose bodies approximated the most admired painted and sculpted predecessors were particularly valued and became known as the Rubensian or the Michelangelesque model. The Royal Academy council minutes of 1815 record turning down an applicant after inspection because "his figure is not sufficiently good for that of a model." In 1822, the Academy decided to pay a professor of gymnastics to instruct a model called Thomas Bromhead in "various exercises for the purpose of developing his form."[4]

It was not by chance that the first models hired by the Royal Academy were men. The male nude came with an unblemished classical pedigree. When the ancient Greeks worshipped the human form, it was the masculine human form that they revered. Apollo was the most attractive of the gods, Hercules the strongest, and both their bodies were modeled on those of the finest athletes. The classical pedigree of male nude sculptures, together with the muscular bodies of the models who resembled them, made the male nude model far more valued than the female, whose putative fleshiness disqualified her from active poses. Translated into life class practice, the male body became indispensible for teaching young artists the structure of the body.

Women had a different history. From the start, the notion of the female model was circled with an aura of unease. According to ancient Greek and Roman historians, women indeed modeled, but a female model is never once mentioned without a certain underlying sense of innuendo. Unlike the men, who were sculpted in all their naked glory, as befitted the marble representation of the perfect bodies of gods and heroes, the lower halves of female classical statuary were wrapped in marble drapery or had their sex coyly covered by a hand. Their beauty was considered lowlier than that of the men, who stand straight and strong without a stitch, their genitals nestling below the tidy rows of pubic pin curls. This view of the female body as an imperfect version of the male, animal-like and inharmoniously designed, was inherited by the Judeo-Christian tradition, where it was explained anew by Eve's original sin and viewed as a container leaking milk and blood and all things lowly (an intriguing opposite to the "sugar and spice and everything nice" version of females in the nursery rhyme). In Renaissance Italy, Christ was painted with the body of a classical god; not until Sandro Botticelli painted *The Birth of Venus* in the mid-1480s did a female nude appear in art to match its beauty (page 84).

The fact of a naked woman stared at by surrounding men was a problem for authorities concerned with educating the young and raising the status of art. When, within a few months of its opening, the Royal Academy hired two female models, it paid them more than men in an attempt to attract a better class of woman: not a prostitute, in other words. Until the nineteenth century, all academies employed more male than female models, and in some countries, Spain for instance, no females at all. In the eighteenth century, the Royal Academy allowed only married men and those over twenty into the female

4. Council Minutes of the Royal Academy, June 8, 1815; and Nov. 29, 1822.

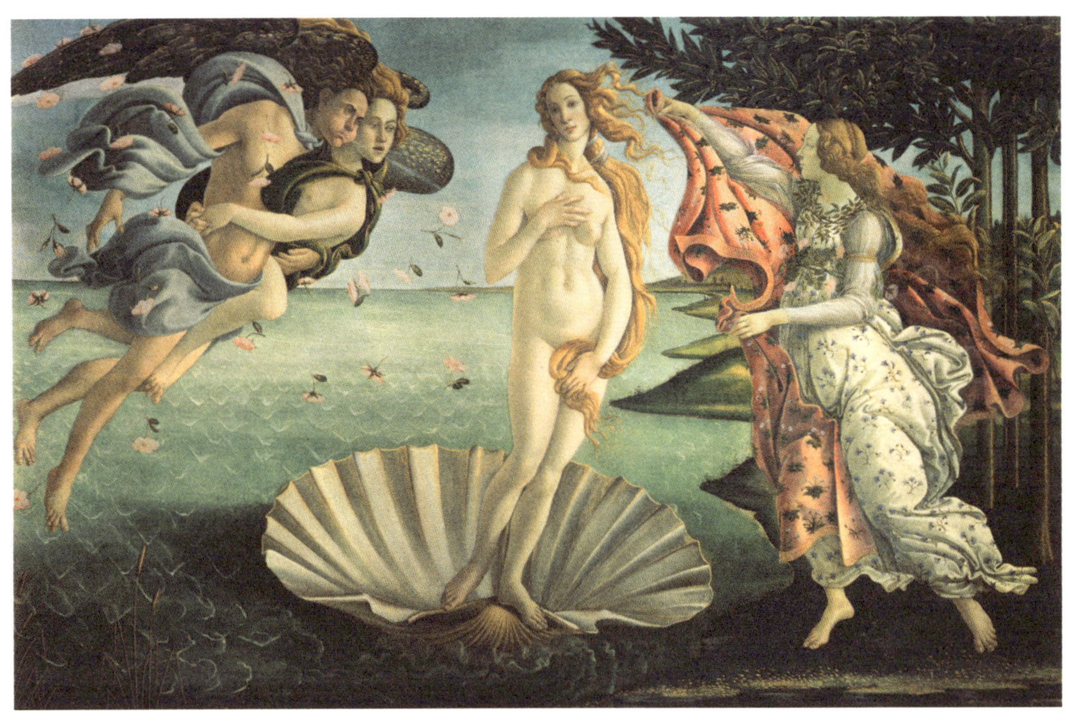

Sandro Botticelli, *The Birth of Venus*, circa 1486. Galleria degli Uffizi, Florence

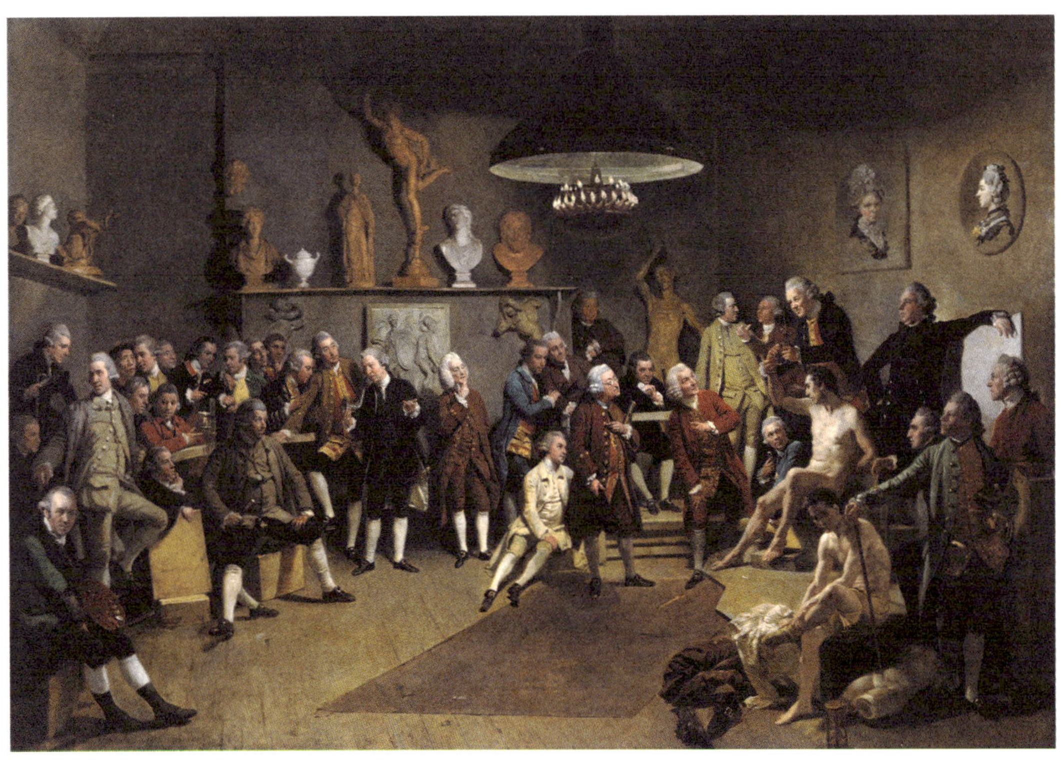

Johann Zoffany, *Life Class of the Royal Academy (The Academicians of the Royal Academy)*, 1771–72. Royal Collection Trust, U.K.

model life class, and the official minutes hint at rowdiness that had to be contained: in 1792, the supply of bread to use as erasers was stopped due to students' habit of throwing it around.[5] When the painter to the British court Johann Zoffany included two of the institution's well-known male models, one in the process of disrobing, in his celebrated painting *Life Class of the Royal Academy* (1771–72), the two female founding members of the Academy, both successful artists, were included as portraits on the studio wall (opposite page). Showing them in the actual presence of naked male models would have ruined their reputations and scandalized the picture's viewers.

A reverse of this situation occurred at the end of the nineteenth century, when women students were finally allowed into the Academies. Nobody stated their fears surrounding the life class in so many words—though such anxieties were satirized in *Punch* (page 86)—but the authorities were clearly terrified about what might develop when a male model posed naked in the midst of a group of women. In 1890s Britain, a nervous Academy Council decreed that the male model in the women's life class should first put on bathing drawers, then wind nine feet of fabric around him, and finally secure the whole outfit with a belt—presumably to guarantee that the costume stayed in place.[6]

With the spread of art academies, a life class routine emerged of regulated posing sessions and rest pauses for the model and rules of silence for the students. Models were expected to be punctual, sober, and able to hold their pose; fraternizing with the students was frowned upon. A raised dais enabled students to see clearly, and an assortment of boxes, poles, and ropes helped models hold the more difficult poses, such as the one seen in Maillais's rendering of an archer (page 87). For reasons of expense, models usually posed singly—though as an end-of-year treat, a master might set two or even three models as a grouping from an admired work of art—the Three Graces, for example, or a group of gladiators, or a contrasting group of light and dark models. Until the twentieth century, for reasons of propriety, male and female models were forbidden to pose together. The stove that kept the heating high for the models meant that students worked in air filled with smoke and the smell of tobacco.

In the nineteenth century, the cult of the ideal body began losing ground to Realism. The classical dream of an ideal nature (looking at five male torsos to construct the perfect torso) was replaced by fidelity to nature's idiosyncrasies. Nineteenth-century narrative painters were unable to put brush to canvas without the perfect model standing before them—even if the perfect model required flea powder, and brown paper to stand on, as the Victorian painter Luke Fildes recalled.[7]

By the second half of the century, the art market greedily gobbled up paintings, particularly narrative paintings. In 1845, Charles Dickens recognized half the models in the model market at the Spanish Steps in Rome from the walls of the Royal Academy's summer exhibition: he lists the "assassin" model, "who leans against a wall with his arms folded"; the "haughty" model,

5. Council Minutes of the Royal Academy, vol. 2, p. 245.
6. Royal Academy Annual Report, 1894, p. 18.
7. See F.L.V. Fildes, *Luke Fildes, R.A.: A Victorian Painter* (London: Michael Joseph, 1968), p. 25.

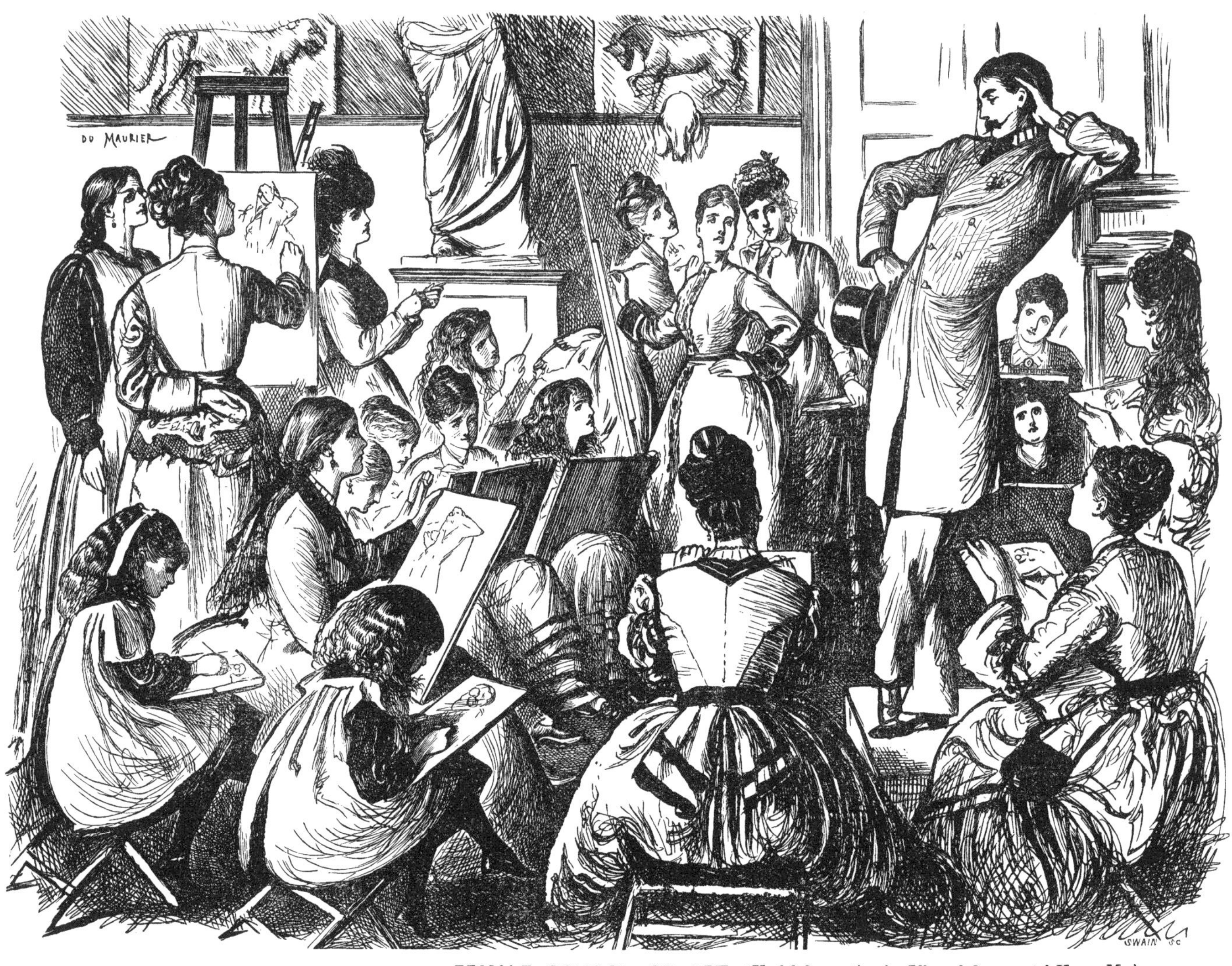

George du Maurier "Female School of Art: Useful Occupation for Idle and Ornamental Young Men." *Punch*, May 30, 1874

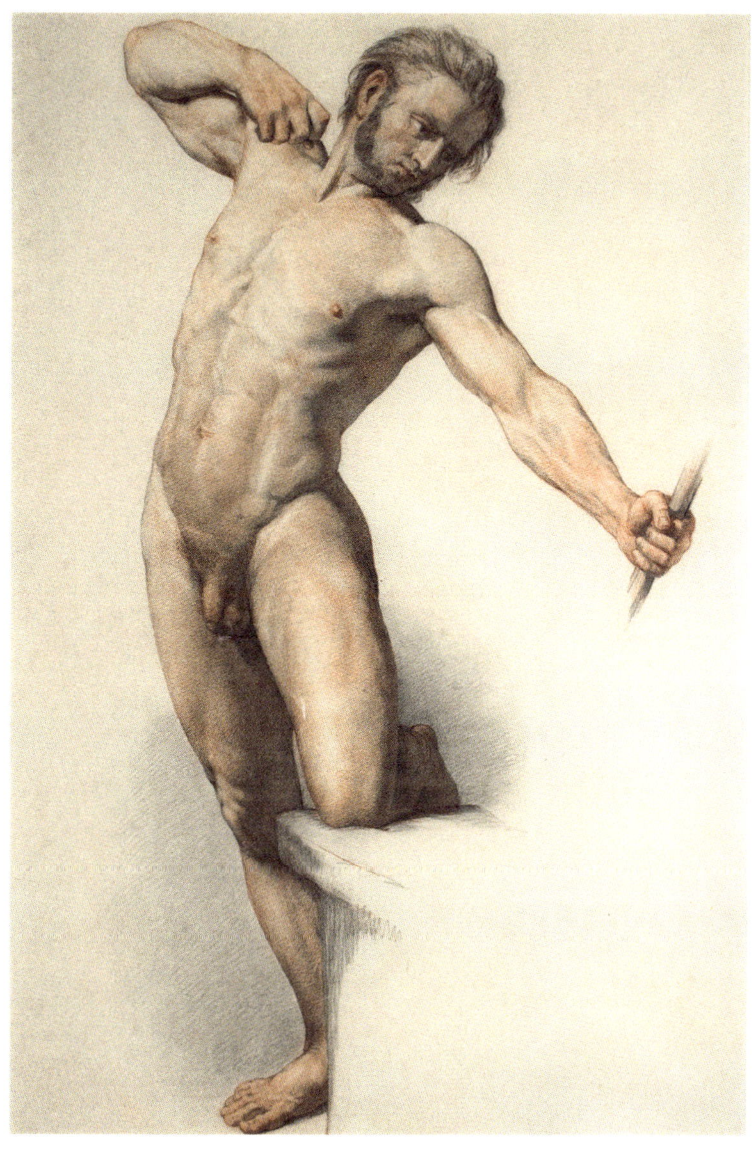

John Everett Millais, *Male Nude in the Attitude of an Archer*, circa 1847.
Towneley Hall Art Gallery and Museum, Burnley, U.K.

"who always looks over his shoulder and seems to be going away"; and the "patriarch" model, with "a great staff in his hand, which staff has been faithfully copied at the Exhibition in all its twists and knots at least once through the catalogue."[8] That was written with intent to amuse, of course, but with more than a grain of truth. The link that conventional nineteenth-century artists believed existed between the quality of the model and the quality of the work is not so bizarre if you consider today's search for authenticity in period films and TV adaptations.

In the art schools things continued as they always had. And while men reigned supreme, once the female nude was established as an artistic category in its own right, women were sought who could approximate the great nudes that followed Giorgione's Venus or Praxiteles's Aphrodite. In 1837 the British landscape painter John Constable reported a remark by the figure painter William Etty that (using a word associated with prostitution) he had "procured" a seventeen-year-old girl whom he described as "very like the Antigone and all in front memorably fine."[9] In 1871, the painter Edward Poynter hoped to employ the then much-admired Italian models for London's new Slade School of Art: their sandal-wearing habit, he said, meant that their feet had not been ruined by tight shoes. "The feet are always a most terrible stumbling block for beginners ... not only on account of the deformities contracted from various causes, but of the swollen veins and the purple colour which would not be found in so great an extent in a person in motion but which naturally results from the model being obliged to stand for hours together in one position."[10]

By the end of the nineteenth century, when models had never been more in demand, both by art schools and by professional painters, art changed and with it the demand for models. The subject matter and style of this new kind of art, introduced by the Impressionists in 1874 in Paris, did not require traditional models. Academies still needed them, as did the old-fashioned painters, but the avant-garde practitioners based their art on subjectivity and on formal explorations of marks, color, and the picture plane, and could manage very well without a model—or at least without those of the type that had ruled since the Renaissance.

In their place came the model we, until quite recently, thought of when the term "artist's model" came up: female, fun, and likely as much a mistress as a model. From the start of the twentieth century, the very same sexuality that the life class and respectable painters tried so hard to exclude became an exciting part of what "model" meant. The story of how this happened has a lot to do with the invention of bohemia, that French country within a country populated by creative artists and their mistresses, brought to popular attention in 1845 by Henri Murger's *Scenes of Bohemian Life*. Bohemia presented the artist as male (at a time, it should be said, when women were beginning to find their way into art education) and the model as female, a seductive image that was

8. Edgar Johnson, ed., *Letters from Charles Dickens to Angela Burdett-Coutts, 1841–1865* (London: Jonathan Cape, 1953), p. 66.

9. Peter Leslie, ed., *The Letters of John Constable, R.A., to C.R. Leslie, R.A., 1826–1837* (London: Constable & Co., 1931), pp. 164–65.

10. Edward J. Poynter, R.A., *Ten Lectures on Art* (London: Chapman & Hall, 1879), Lecture 3, p. 42.

exported around the Western world and still controls minds today. Like the man in a black beret at the easel, the female-model/male-artist pairing has become a kind of shorthand for art itself, despite the fact that artists are no longer exclusively male, despite the fact that sexual freedom is (we hope) allowed to all, and despite the fact that many artists do not use models at all. Its grip on the imagination has helped block out the history of modeling itself.

And what of the life class? It continued as always, of course. But the direction art had taken in the twentieth century was impossible to ignore, and by the 1960s, in some countries and in some academies, the life class was considered as outdated as grinding your own colors. Many who graduated from prestigious art schools after 1970 have never been taught to draw or expected to draw accurately in the traditional manner and have certainly never attended a life class. Nonetheless, there were always those who remained convinced of the validity of drawing from the living model, and in the last few decades even schools that succumbed to the "express yourself" form of art education have reintroduced life classes.

Into this history steps Iggy Pop. Like all models before him, he takes up a pose in front of a room of artists who set out to capture on paper what they see. He is male and well-built, and his revealing body shows the muscles beneath the skin. He is punctual, displays no temperament, and does not fidget. The instructor sets the model's position, and the time-honored process of pose, rest, pose again is followed. If he moves for any reason, to scratch, to cough, to drink a glass of water, he is able to return to the original pose, helped by a spot marked on the wall that Deller has directed him to look at. Though they find it hard to put into words, artists are convinced that good models exist. Everyone agrees: Iggy Pop is a good model.

As in earlier centuries the room is quiet, the pencils scrape, the instructor mumbles suggestions. If the model Thomas Bromhead were to walk in now he would feel at home. But there is a difference. Though Iggy Pop was chosen, as life class models always were, for his body, it is not because his body resembles some anonymous ideal of perfection, but because his body is a kind of map of a career in which his physique has played and still plays an important part. Rather than a generic "fine" body, it is a particular and personal body, and an artist's job is to catch that in their chosen medium. Says Jeremy Deller: "For me it makes perfect sense for Iggy Pop to be the subject of a life class; his body is central to an understanding of rock music and its place within American culture. His body has witnessed much and should be documented."

Substitute the words "this man" for "his body" and it could be a portrait painter speaking. You could make an argument that in a sense both are intended for public consumption: the body of Iggy Pop in performance is equivalent to the body of Iggy Pop in a painted portrait. But an Iggy Pop in the privacy of the studio—in repose, minus music, minus movement—is a completely different matter. Stripped of the Dionysian energy, it becomes a body laid out for study. Where better than in the silence of the life class, with its uncompromising link of eye to drawing implement, to try to catch the facts beneath its mystery?

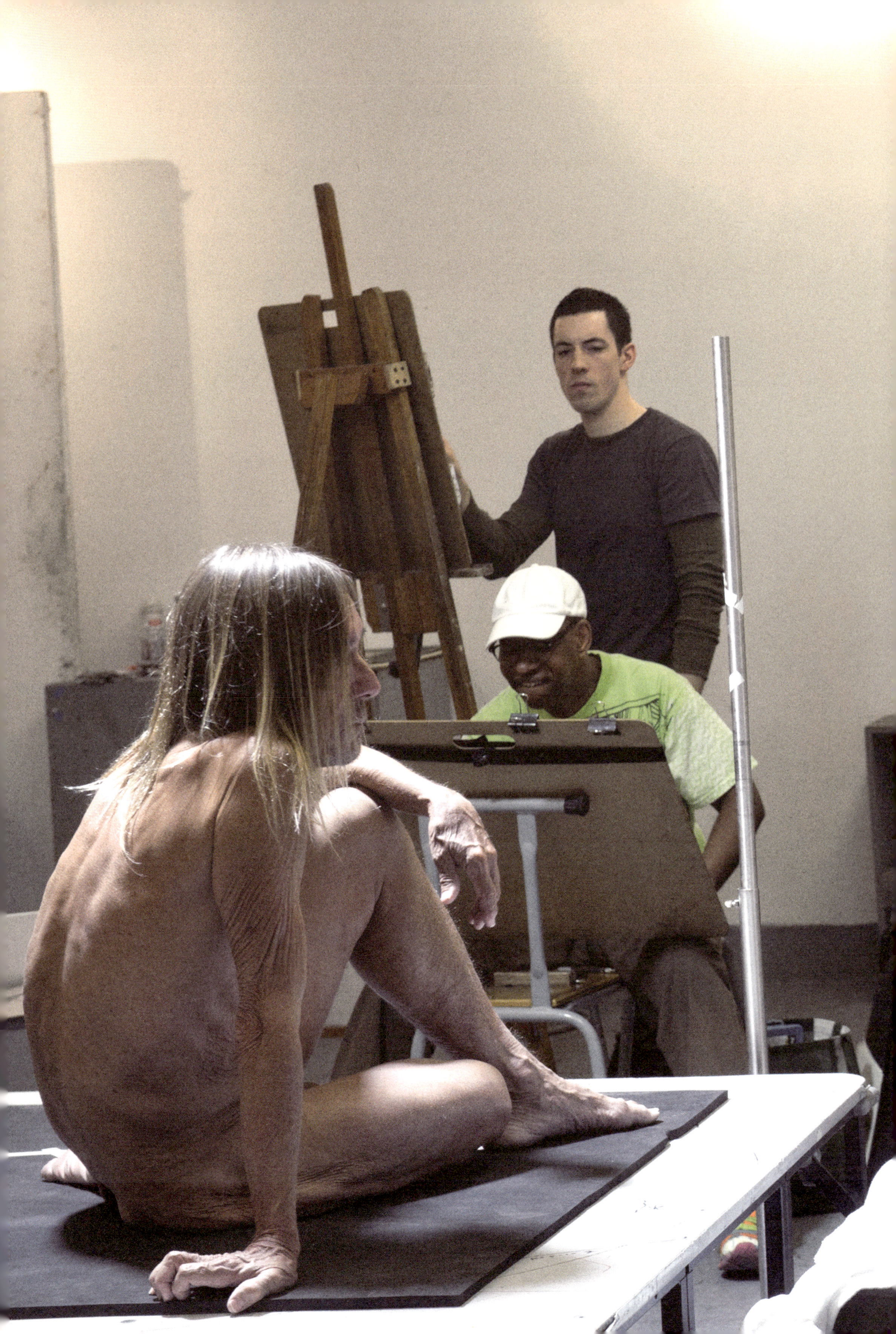

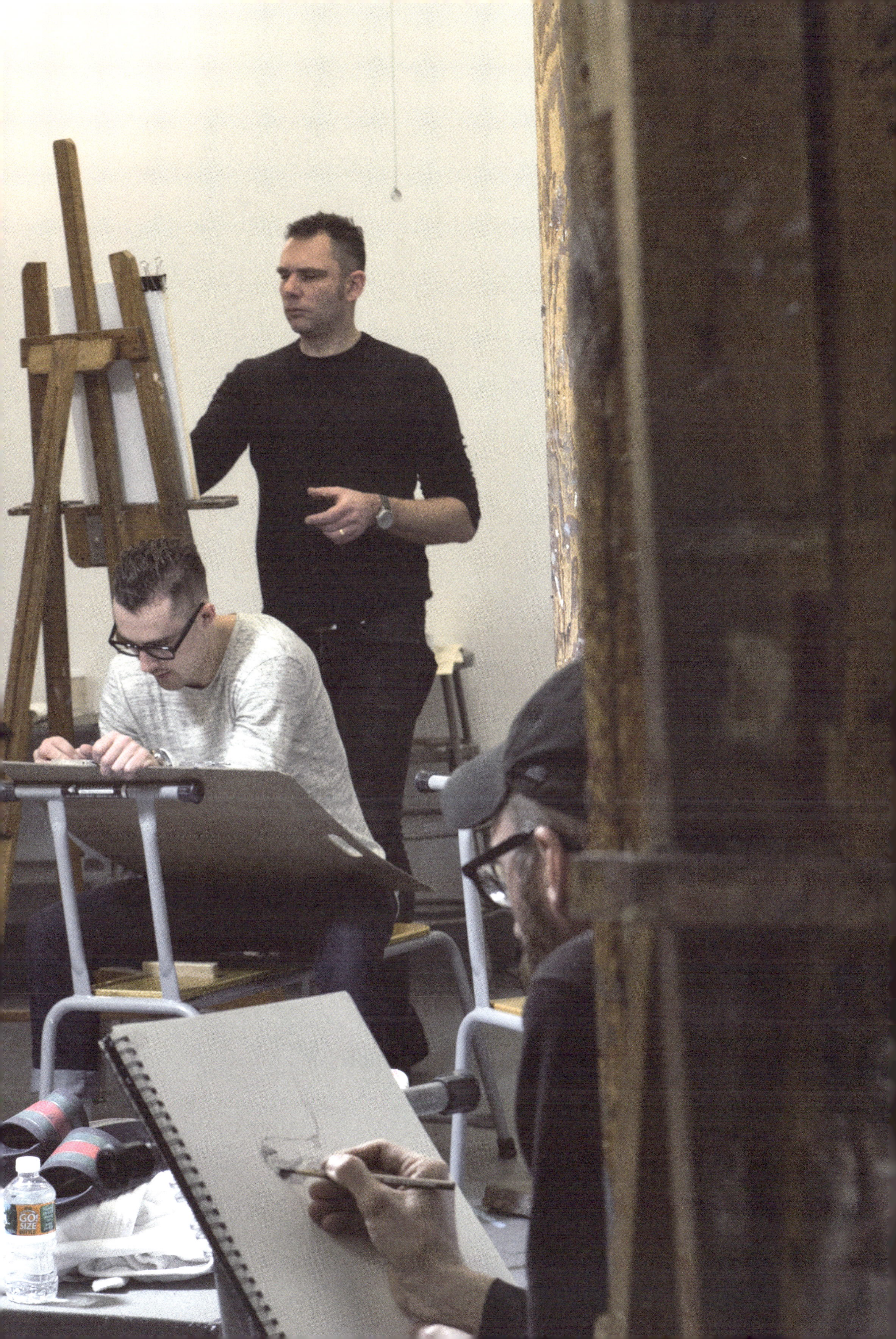
GO!
SIZE

Life Class Drawings

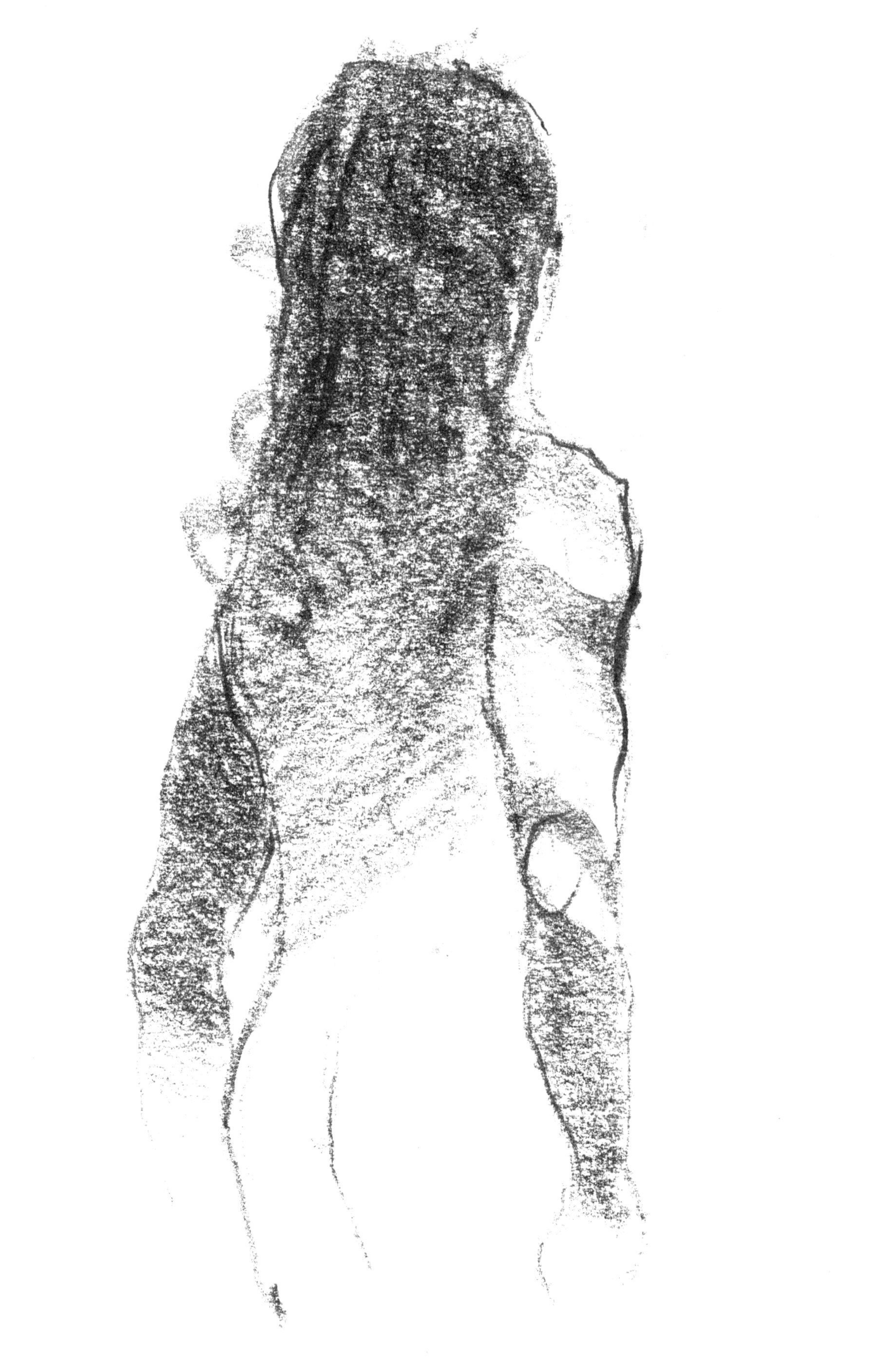

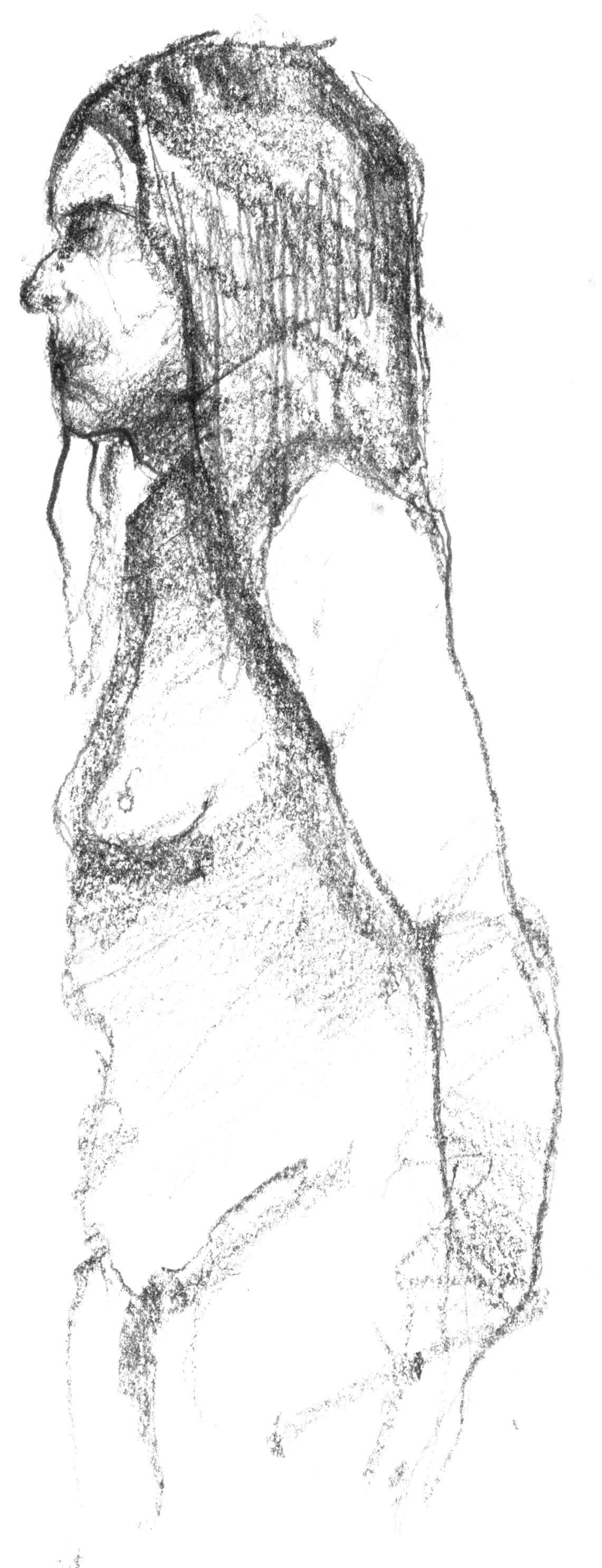

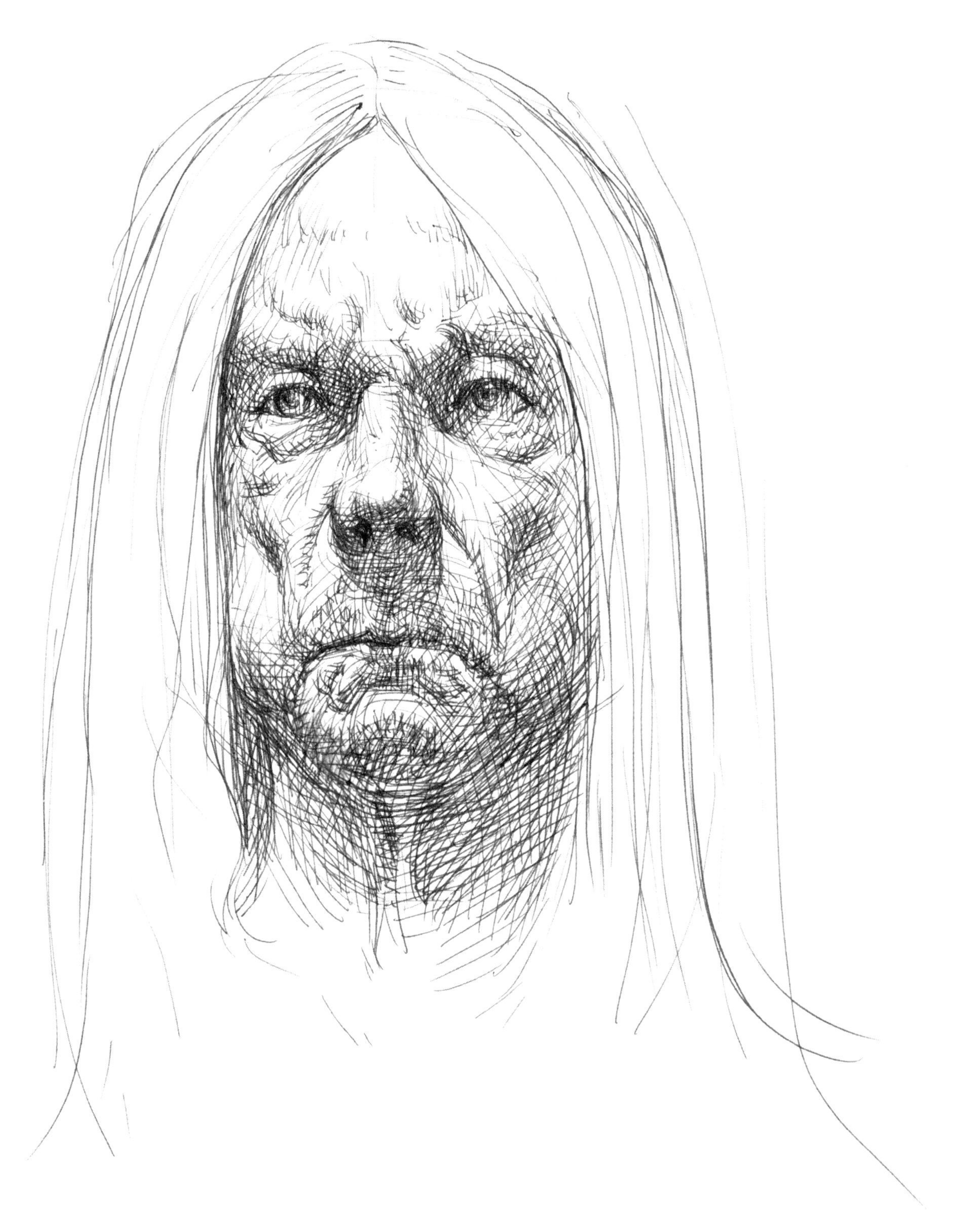

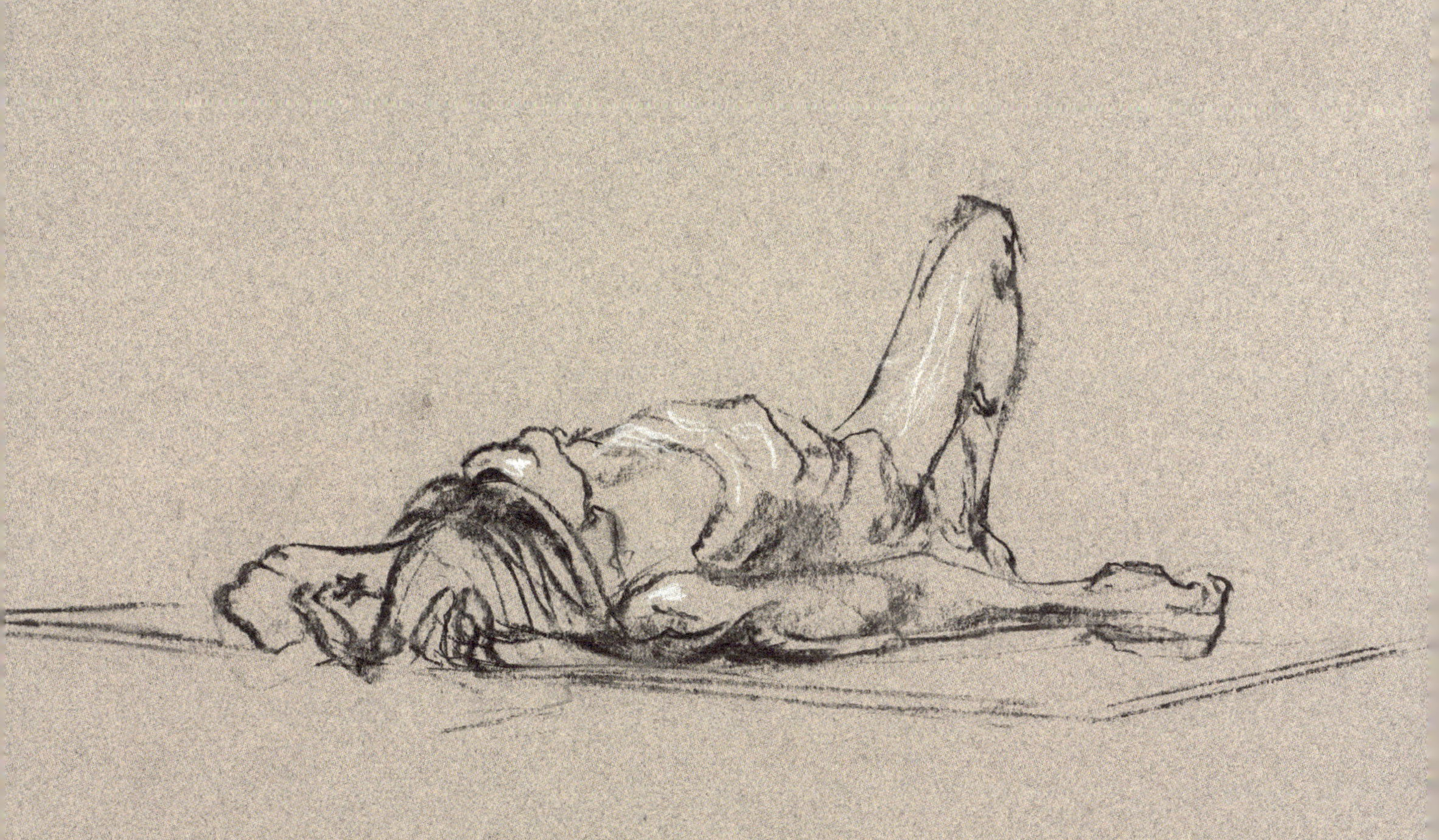

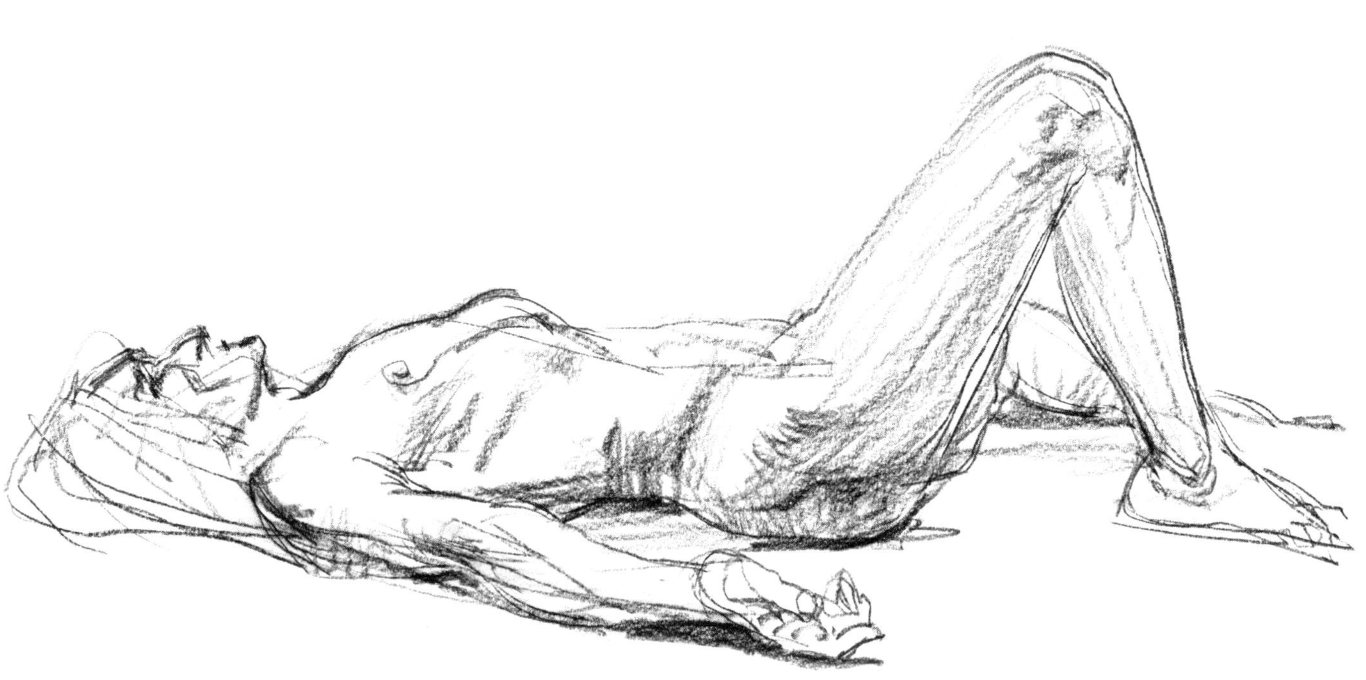

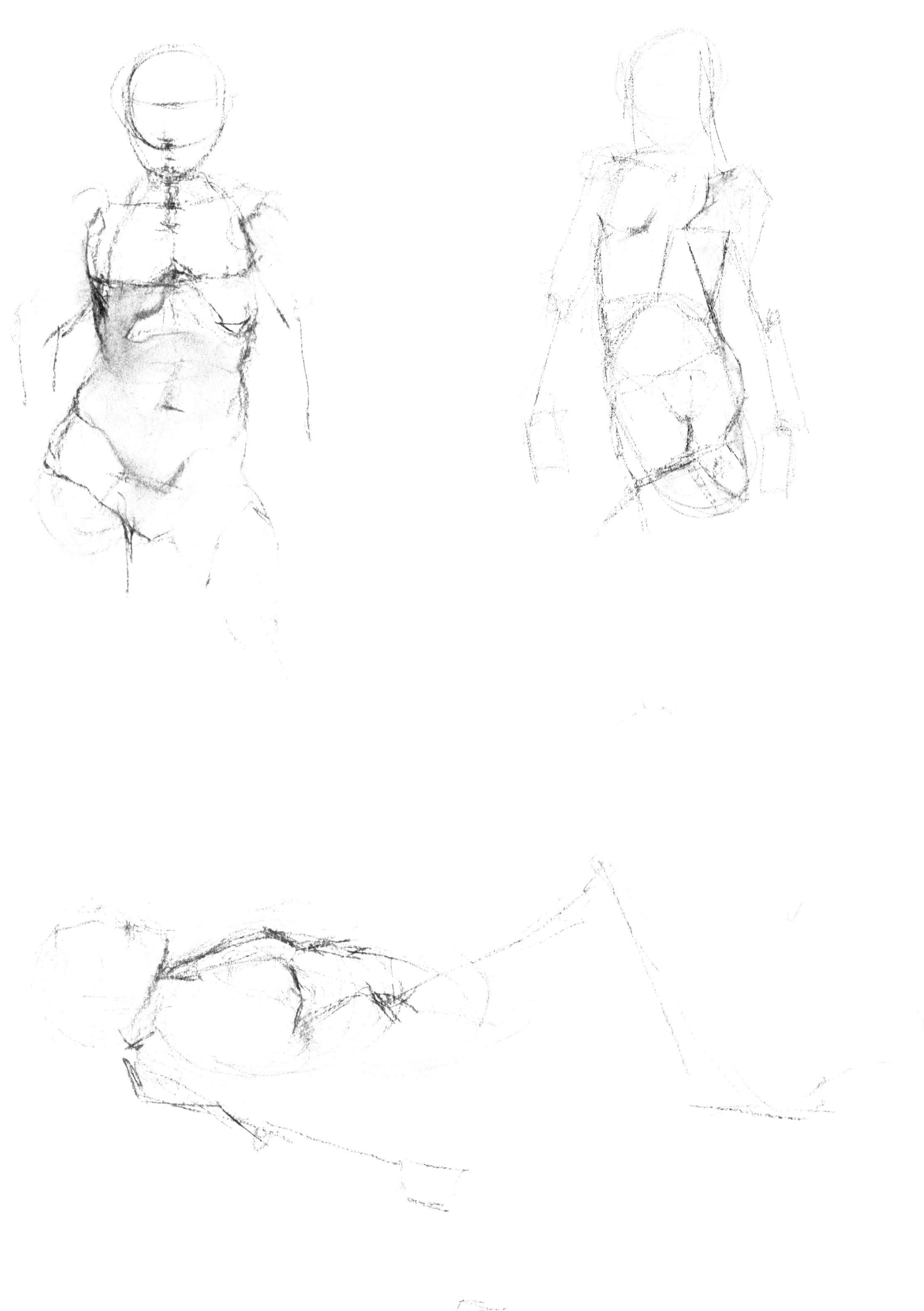

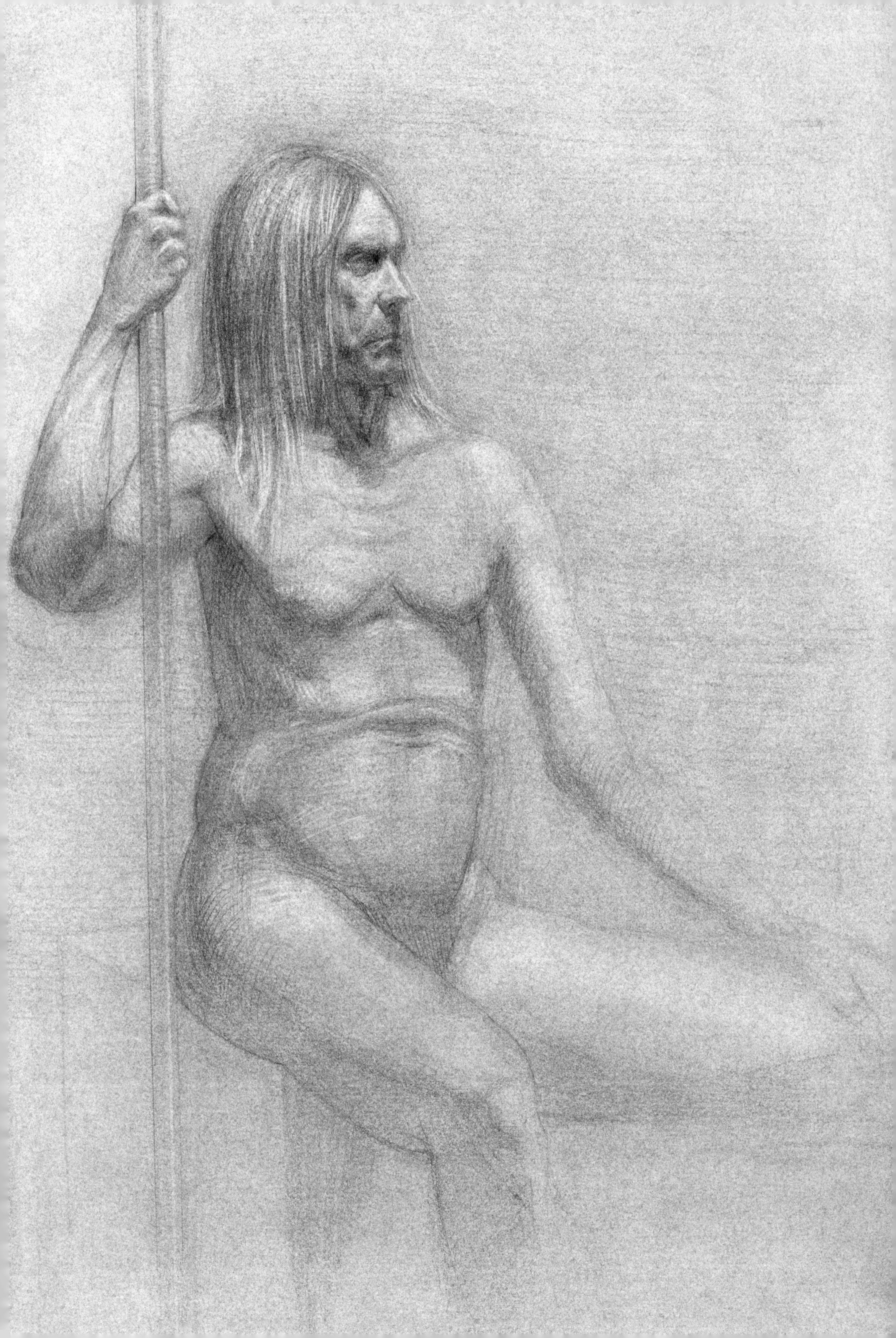

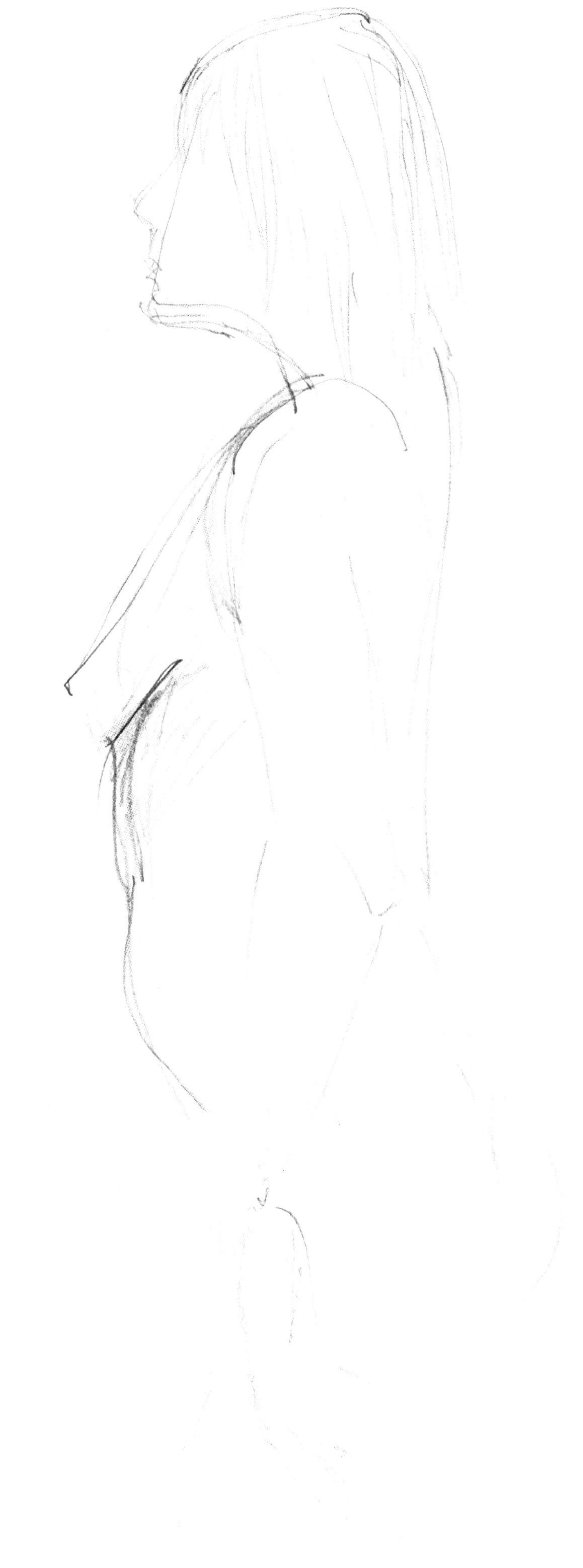

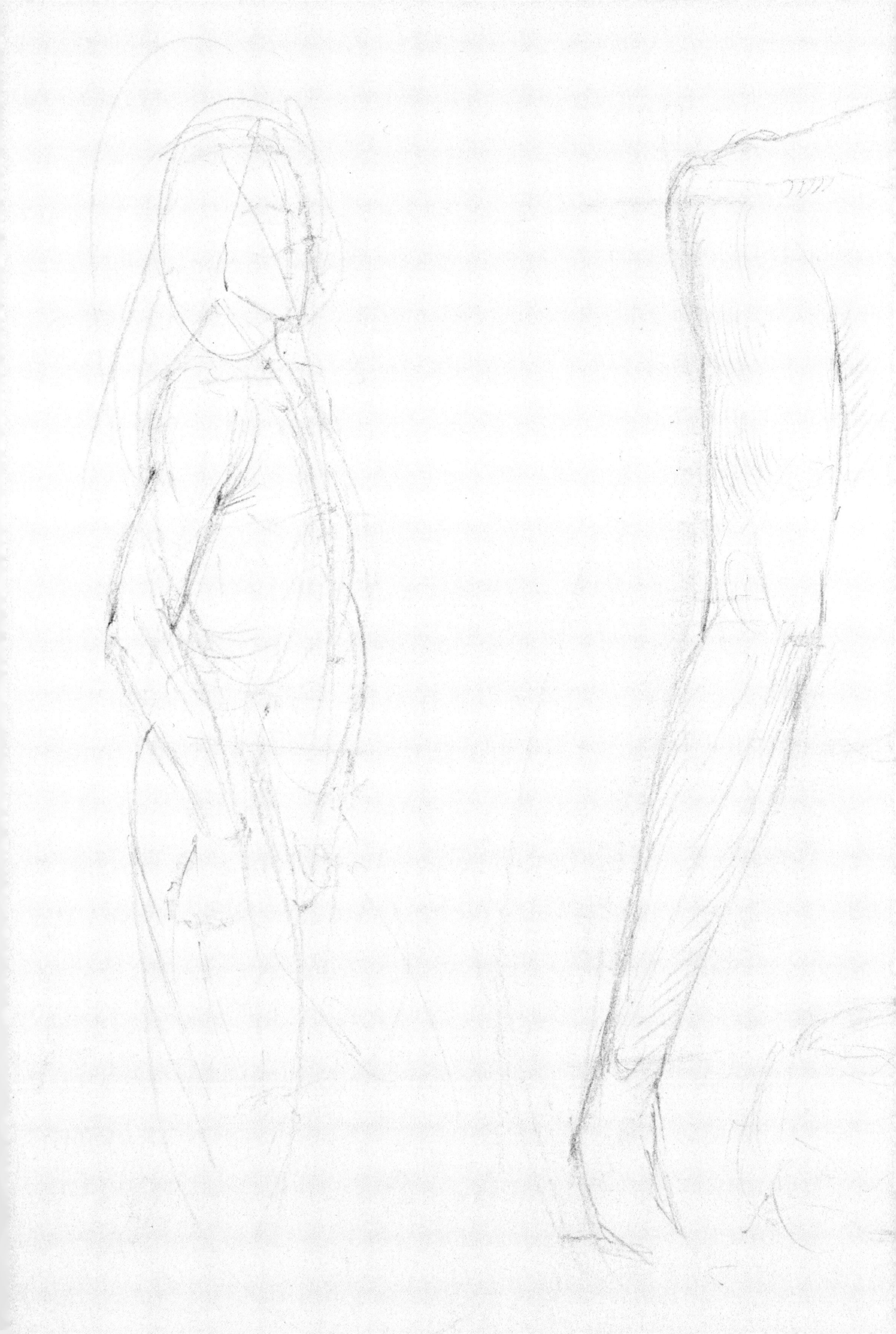

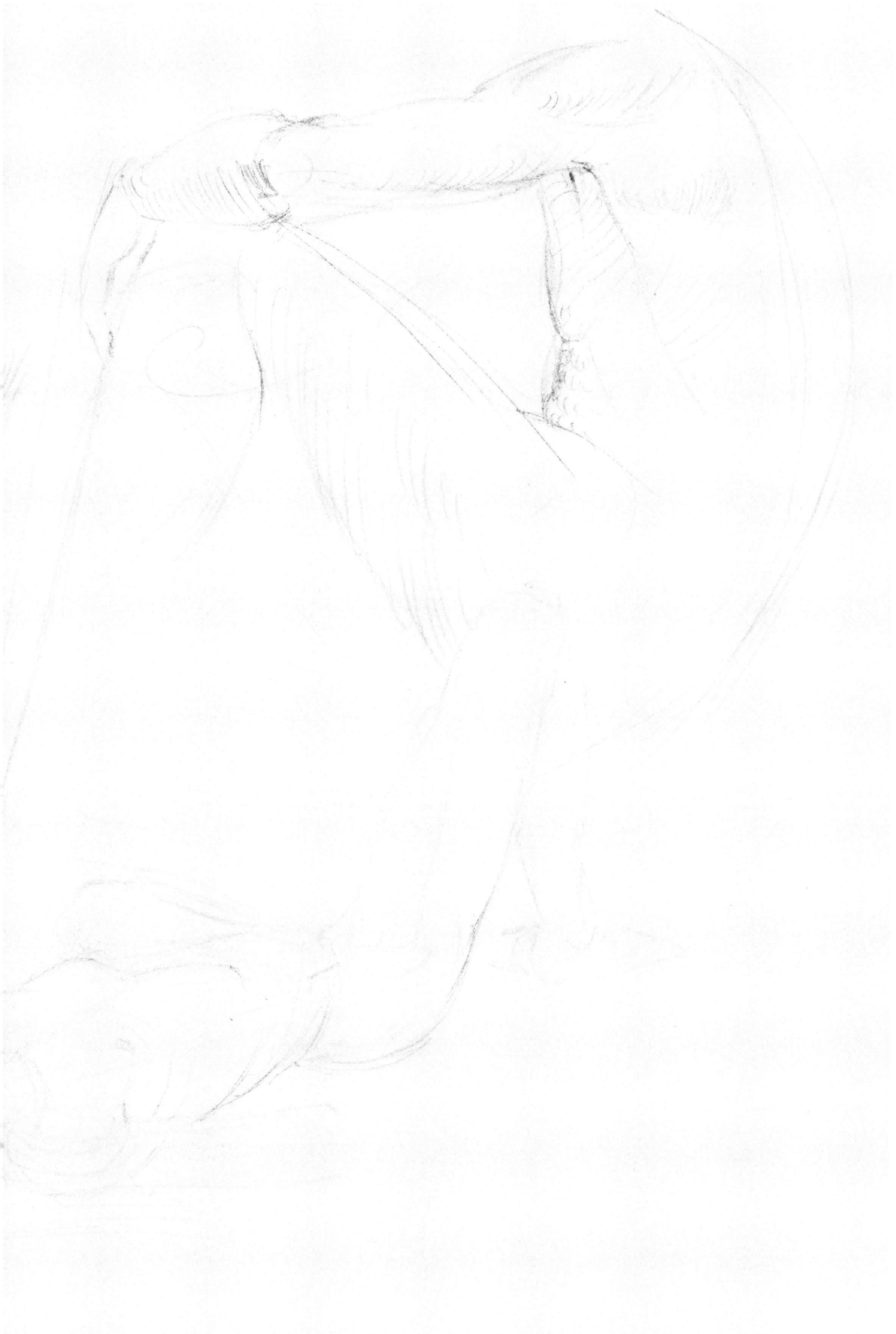

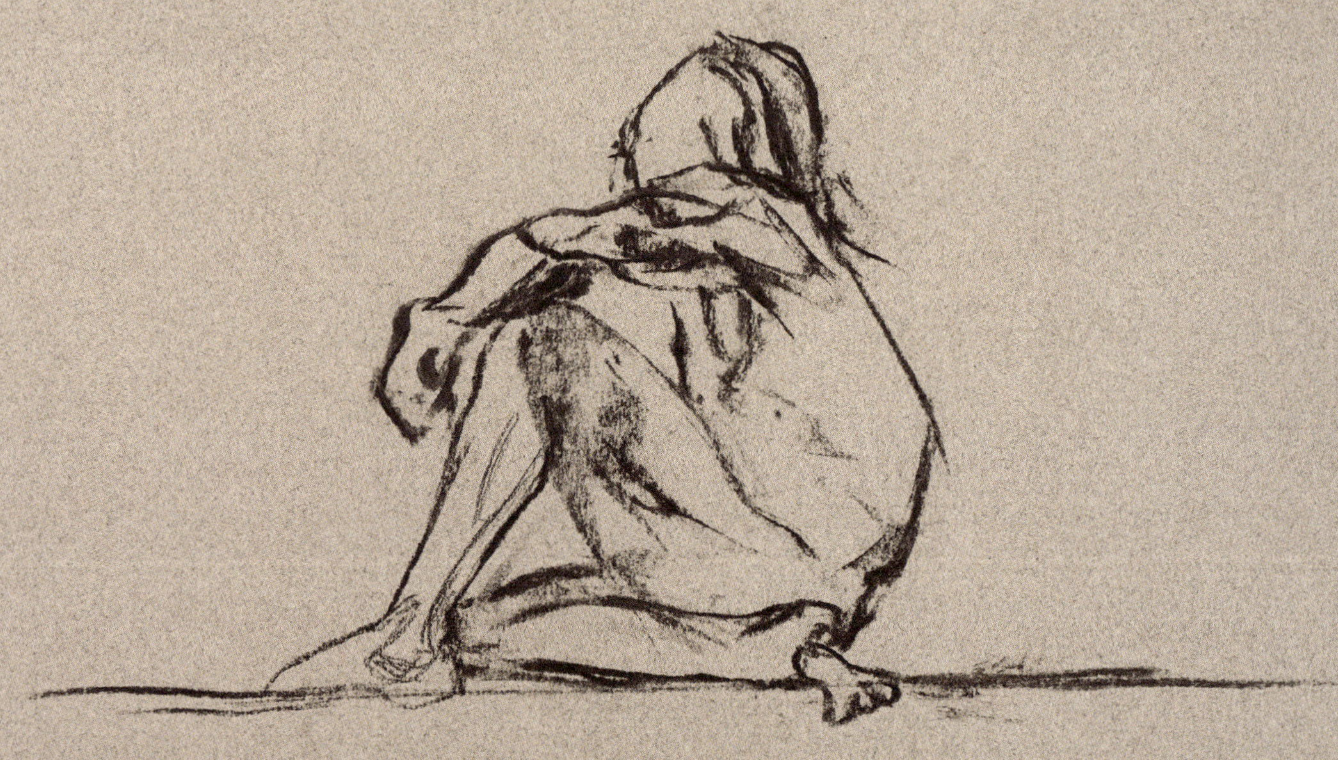

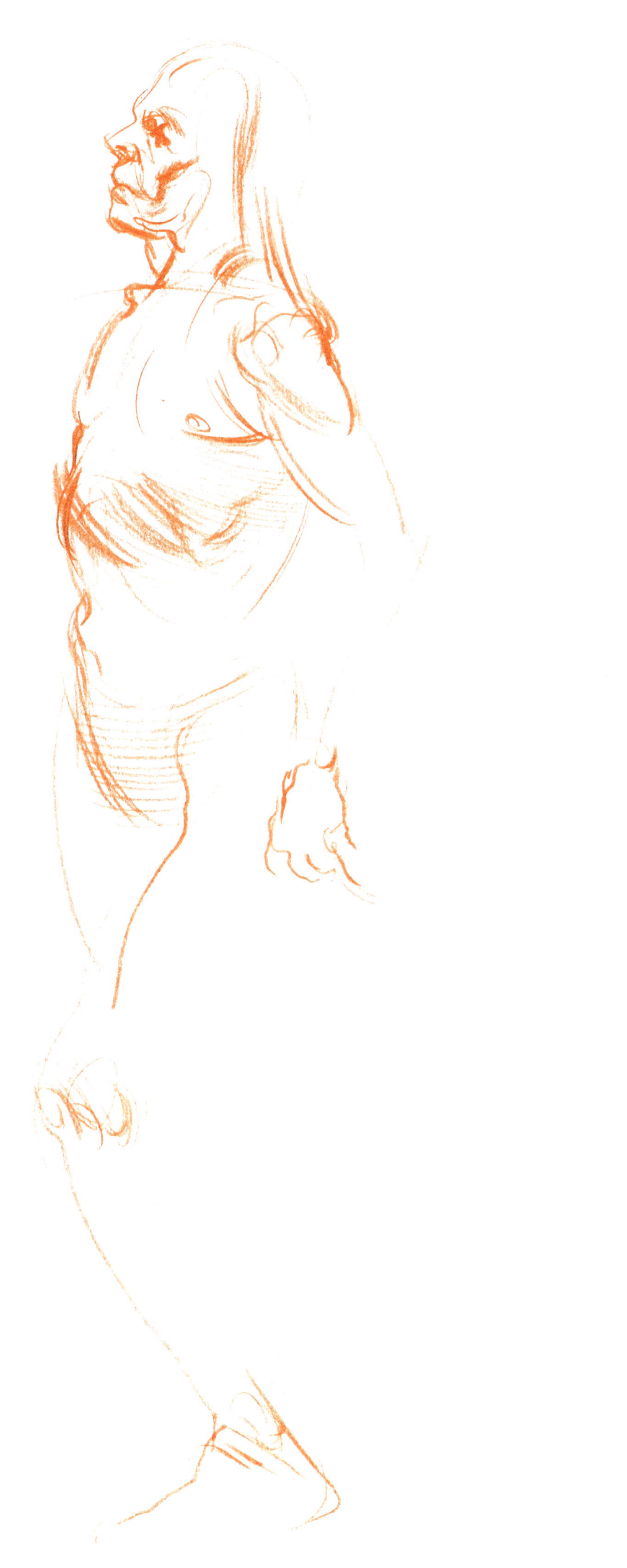

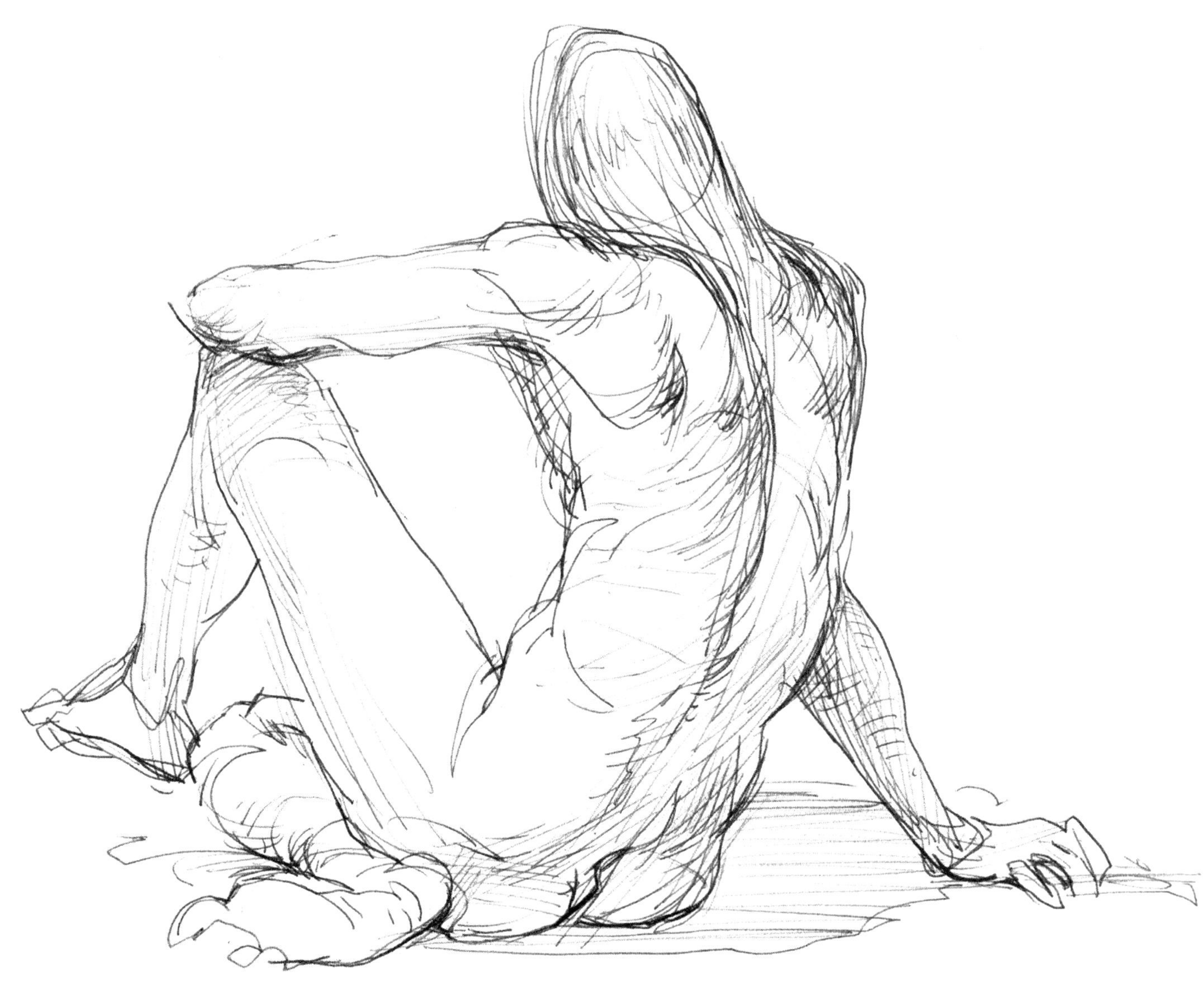

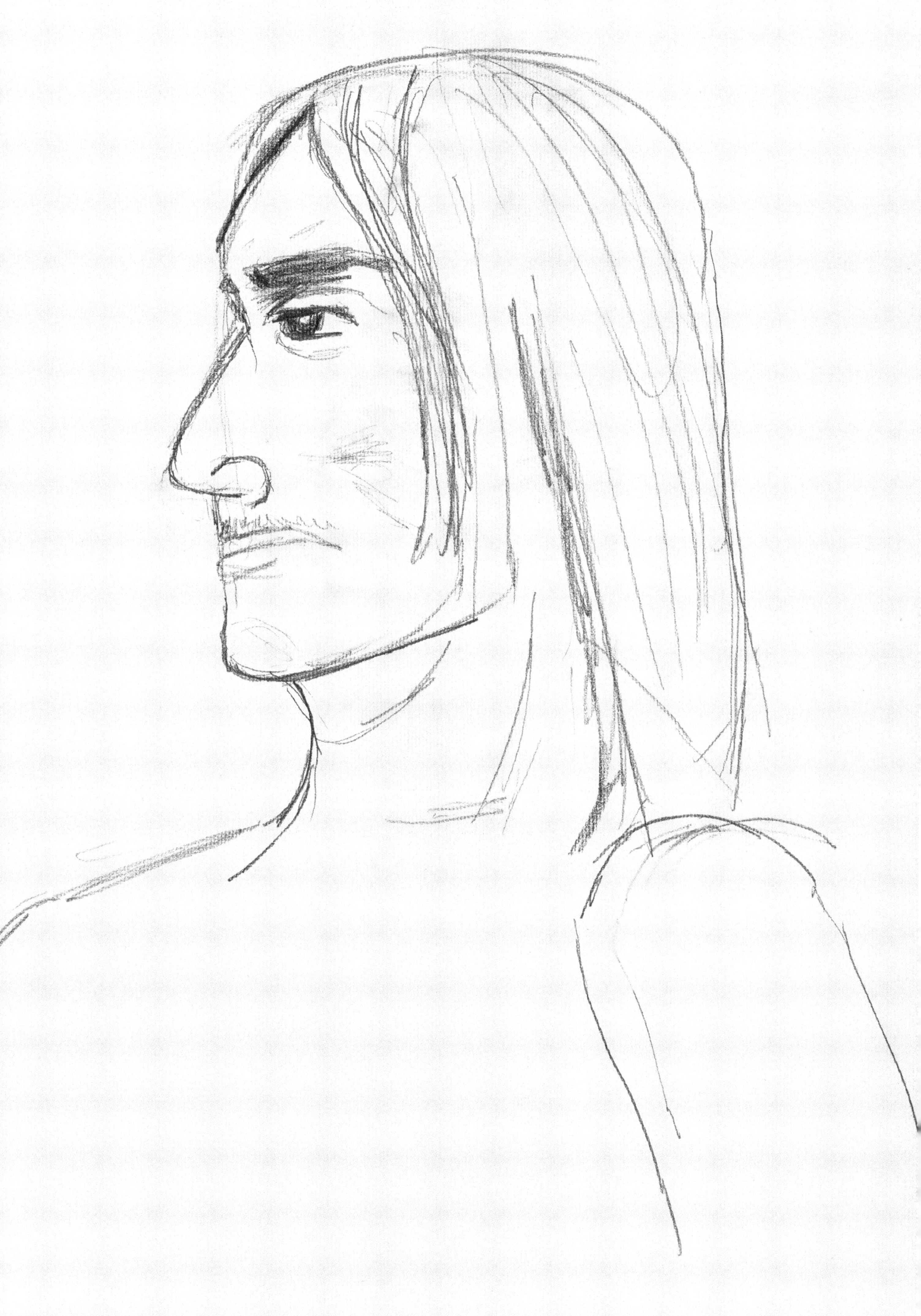

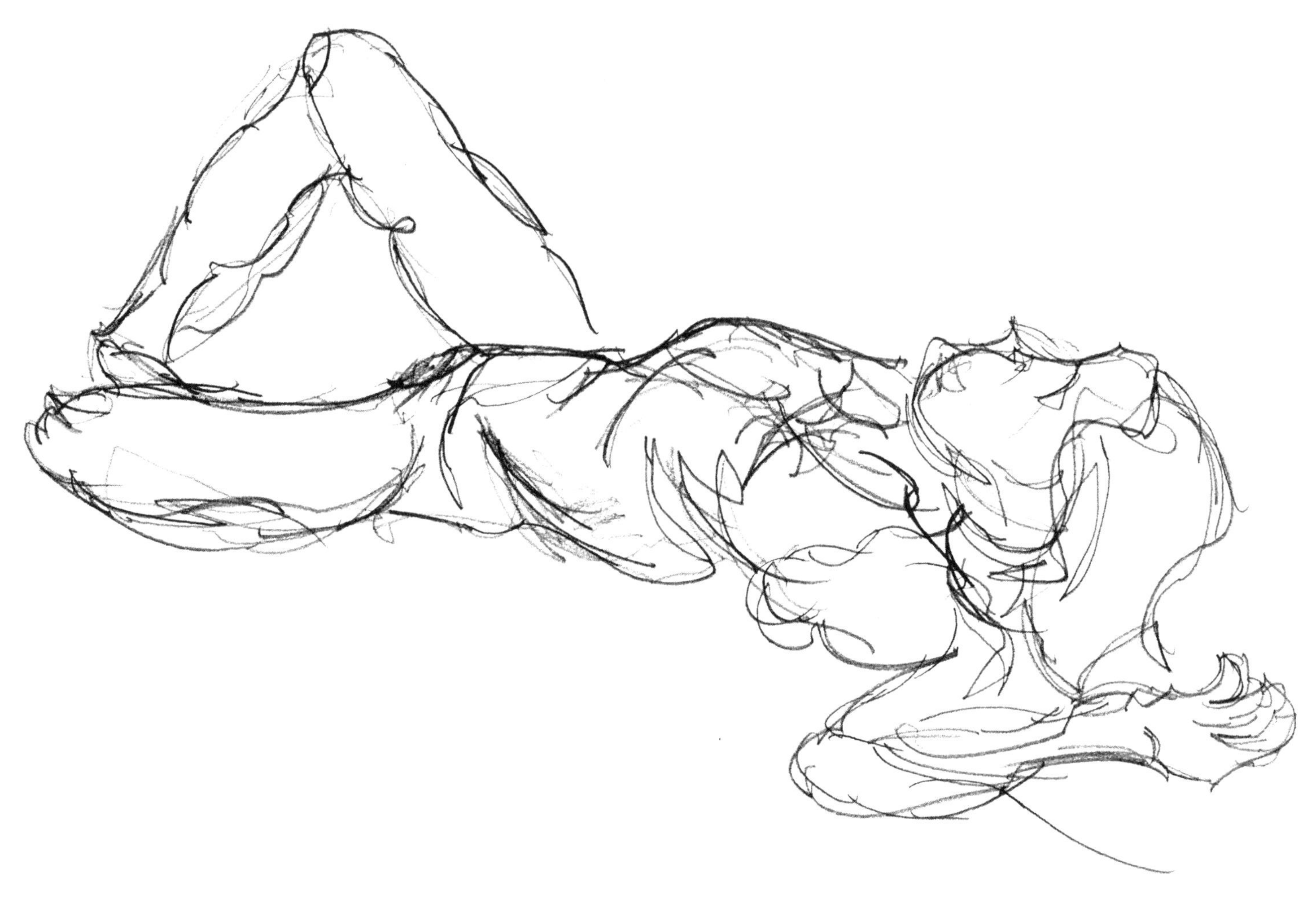

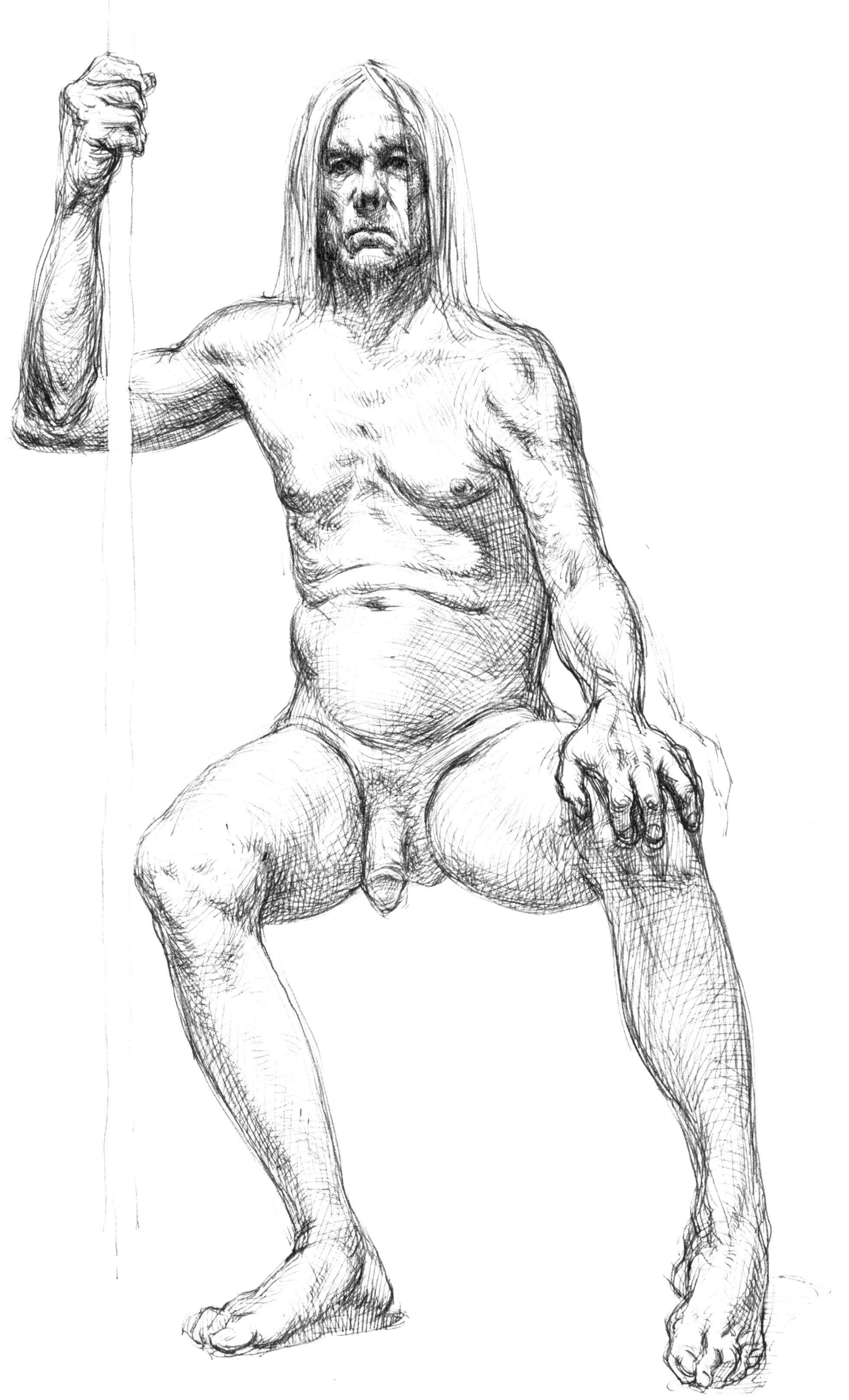

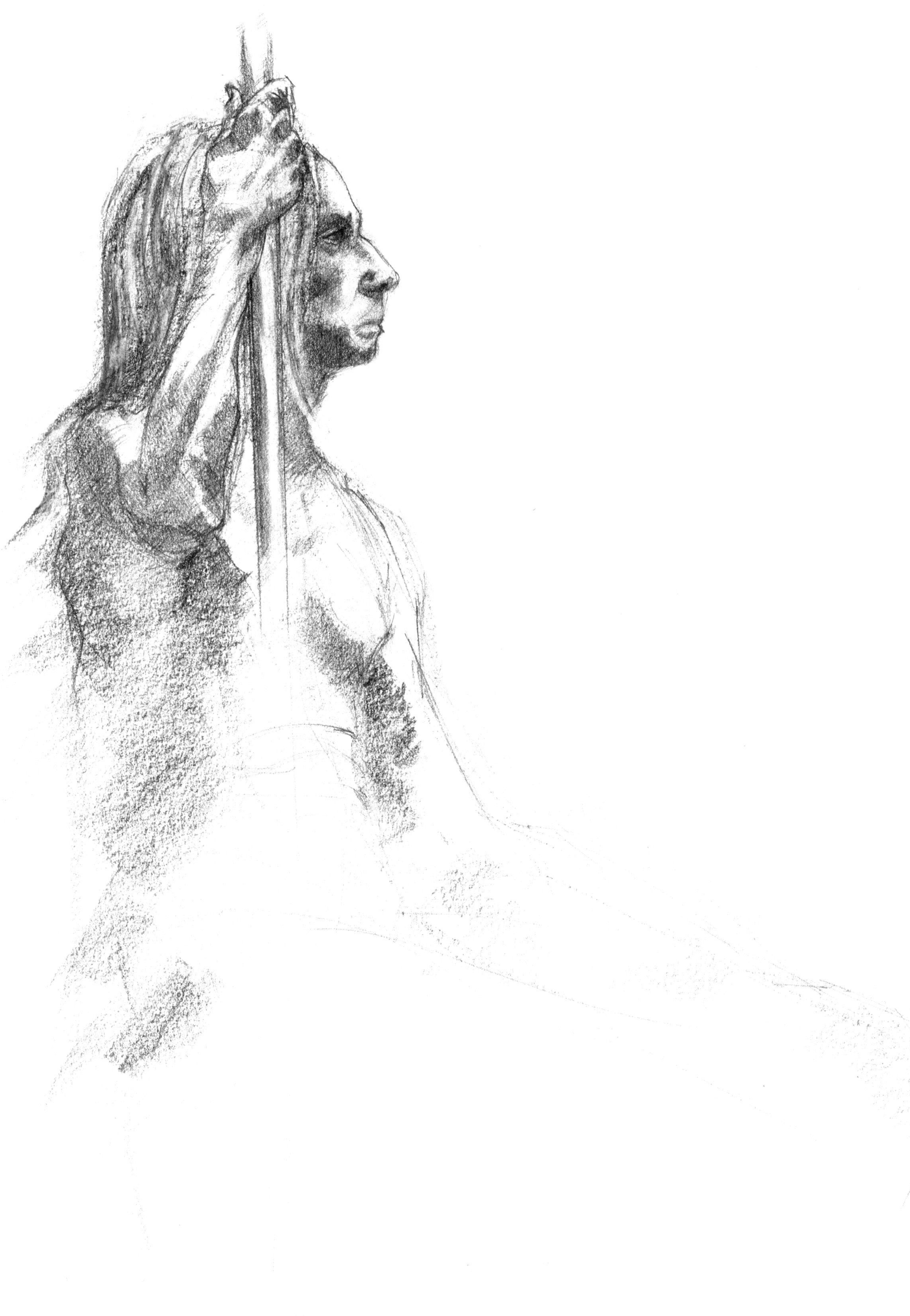

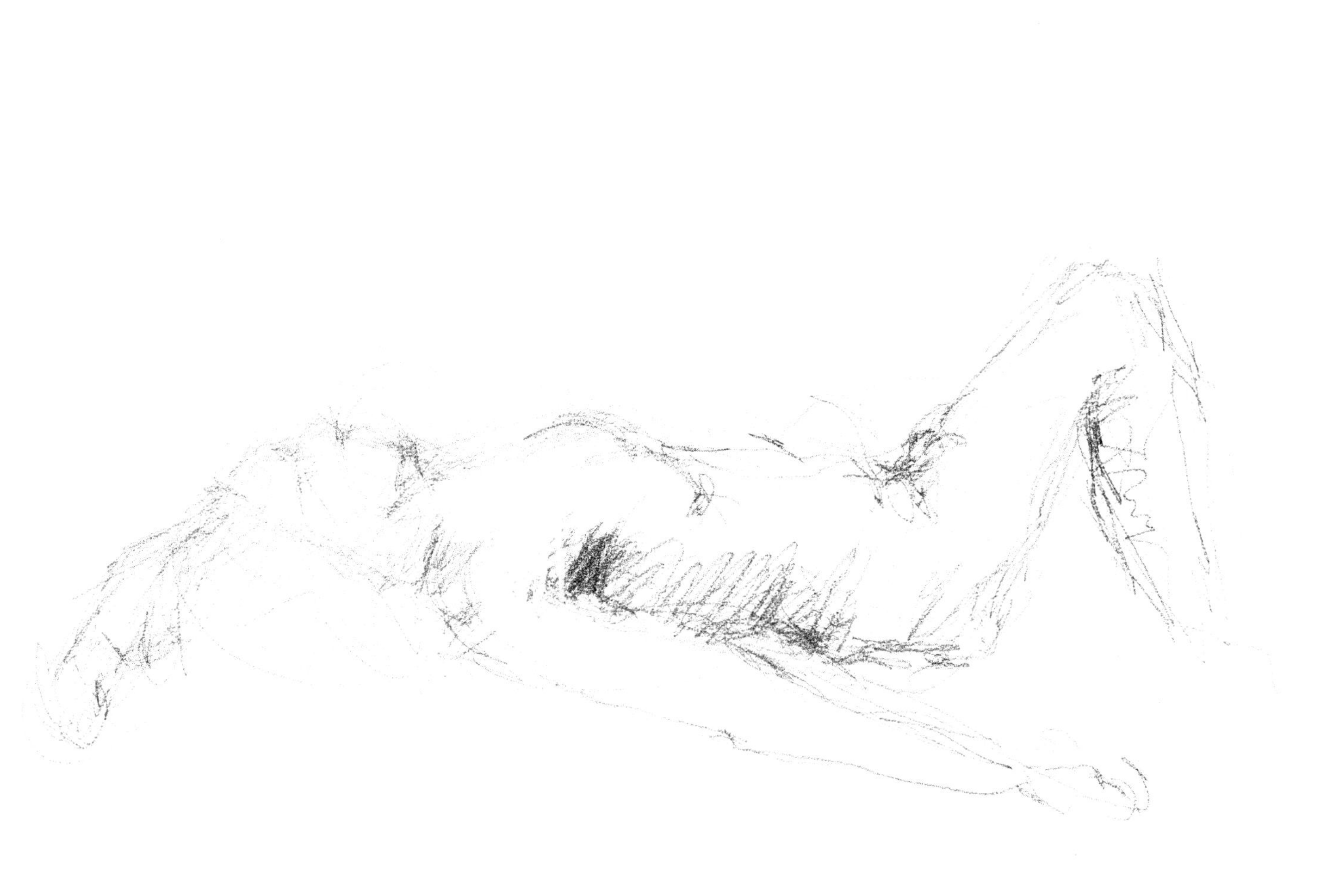

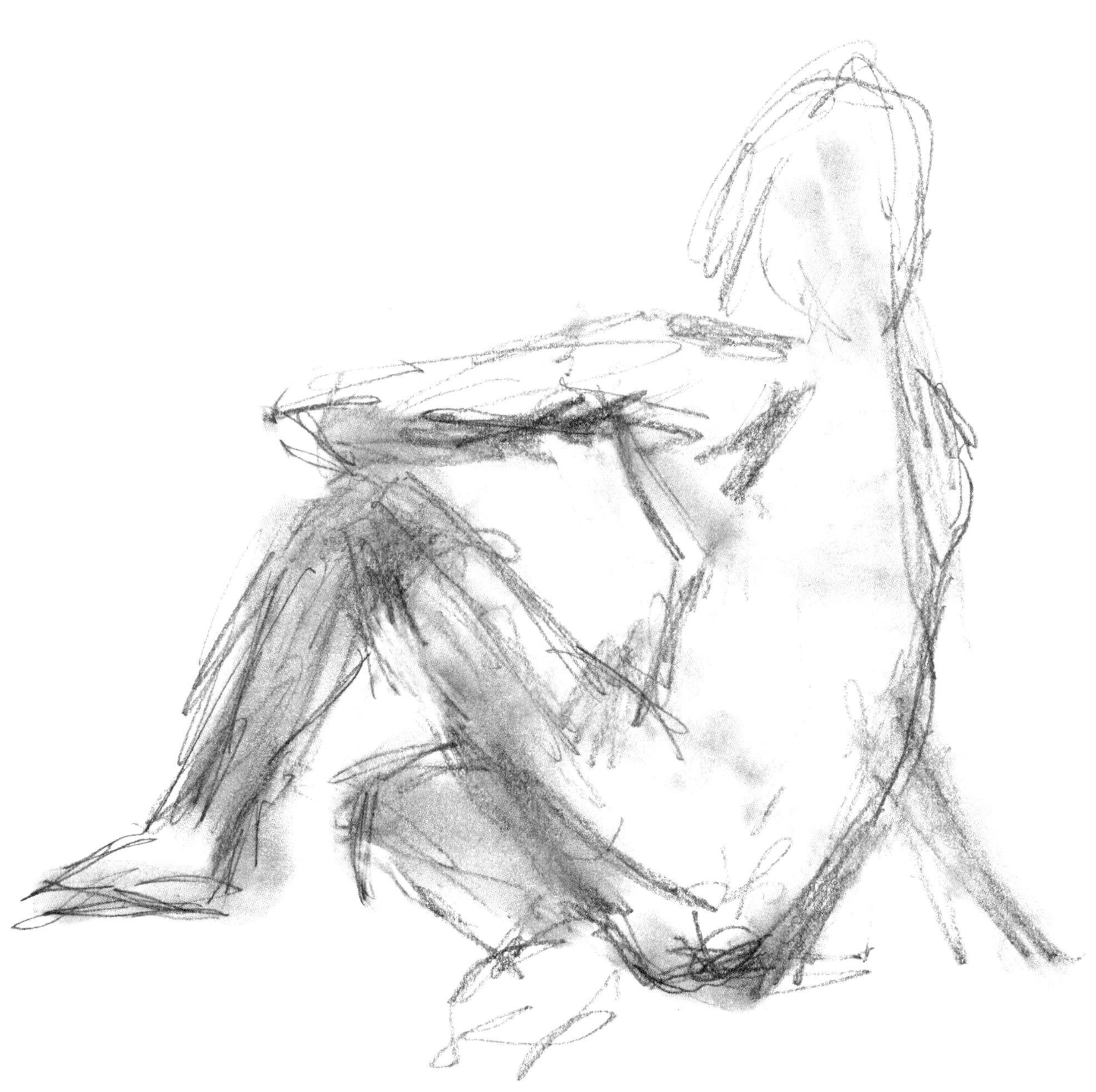

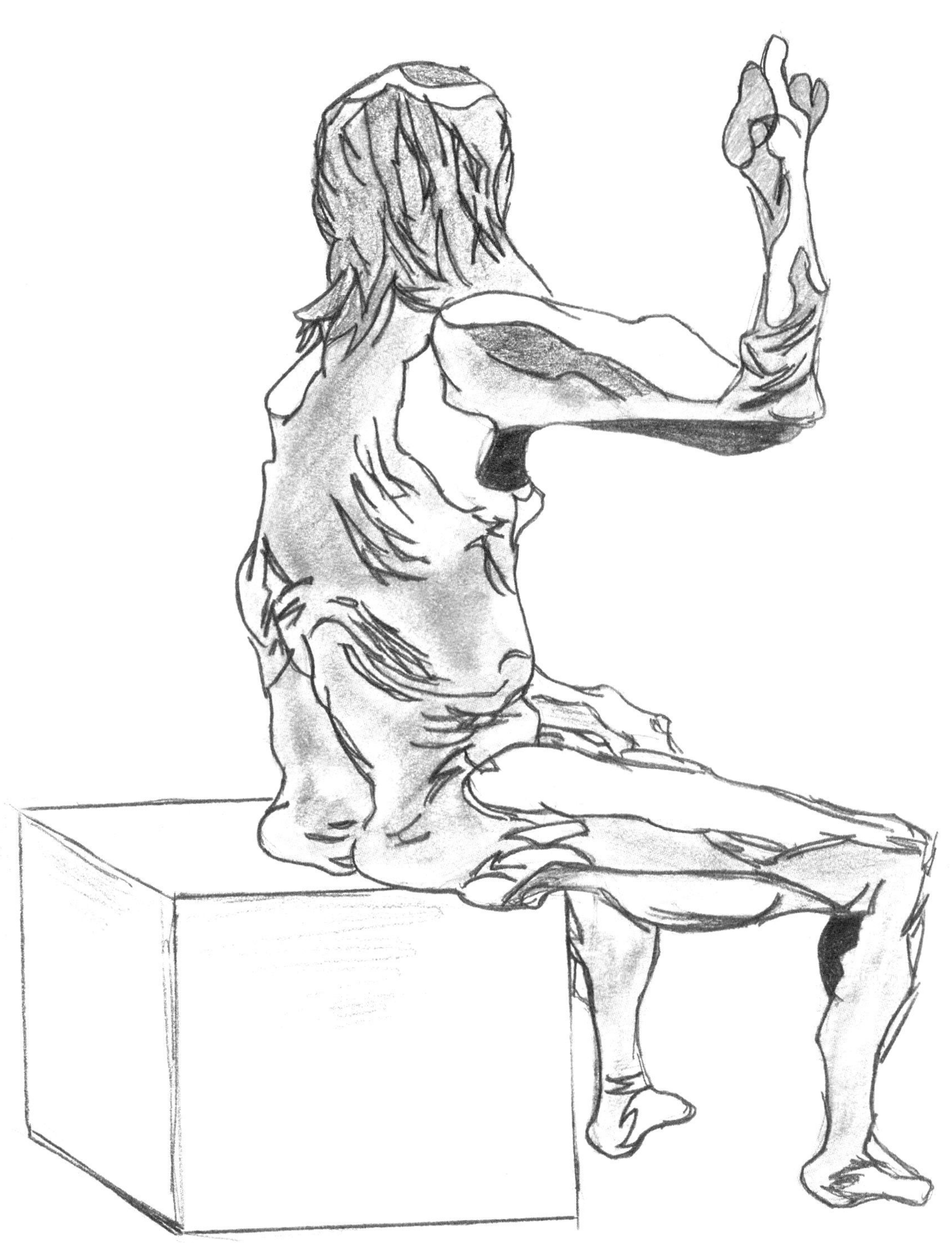

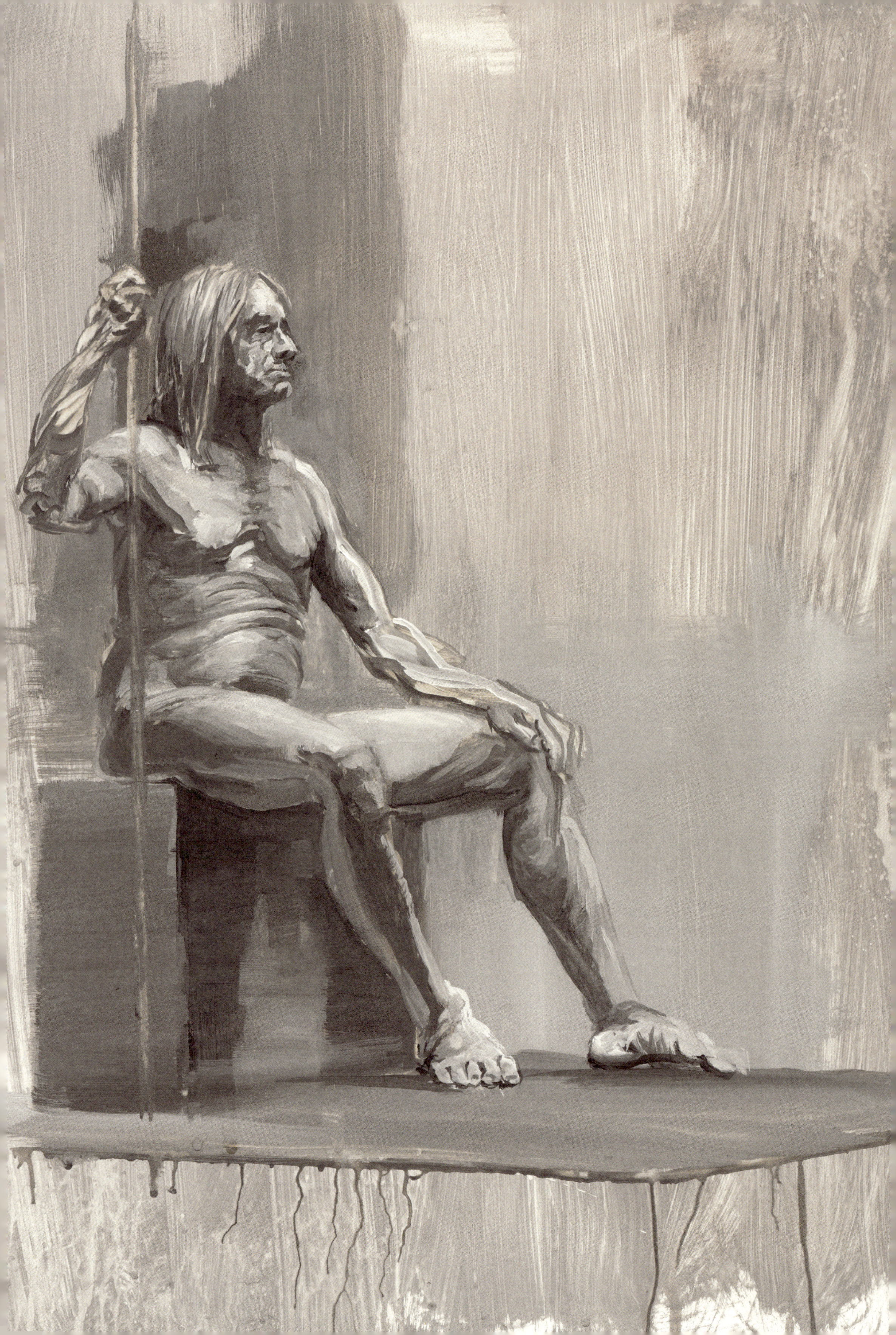

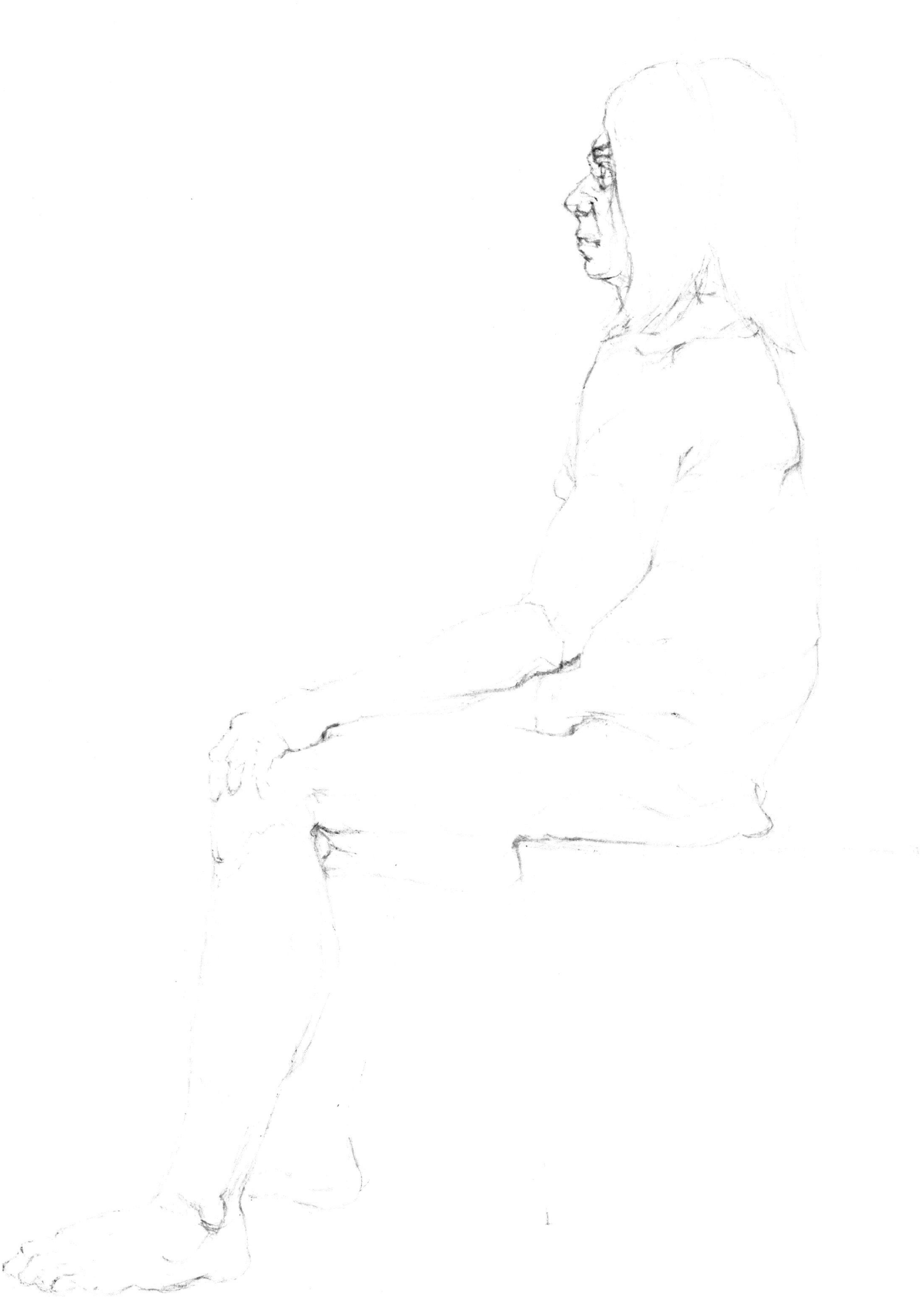

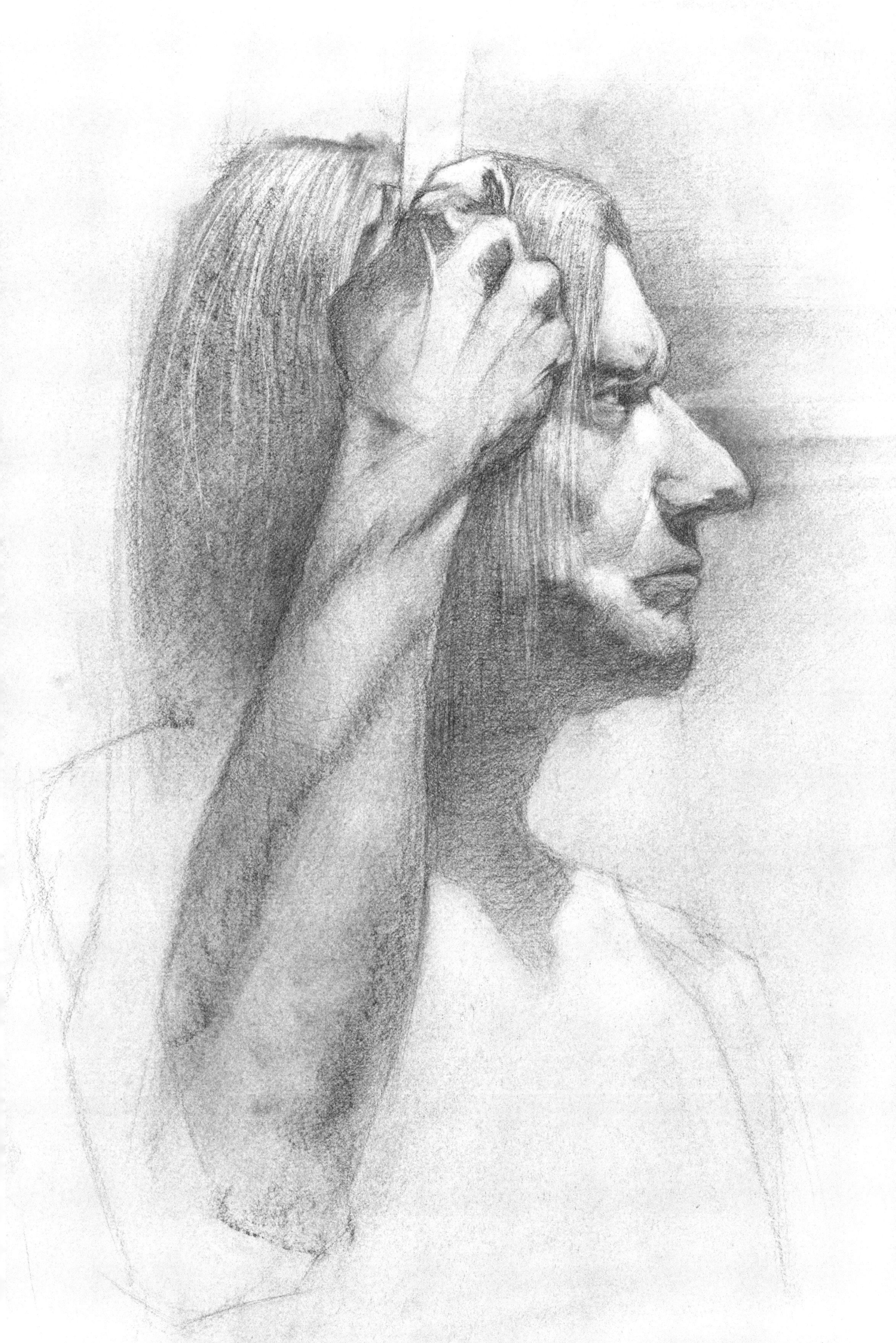

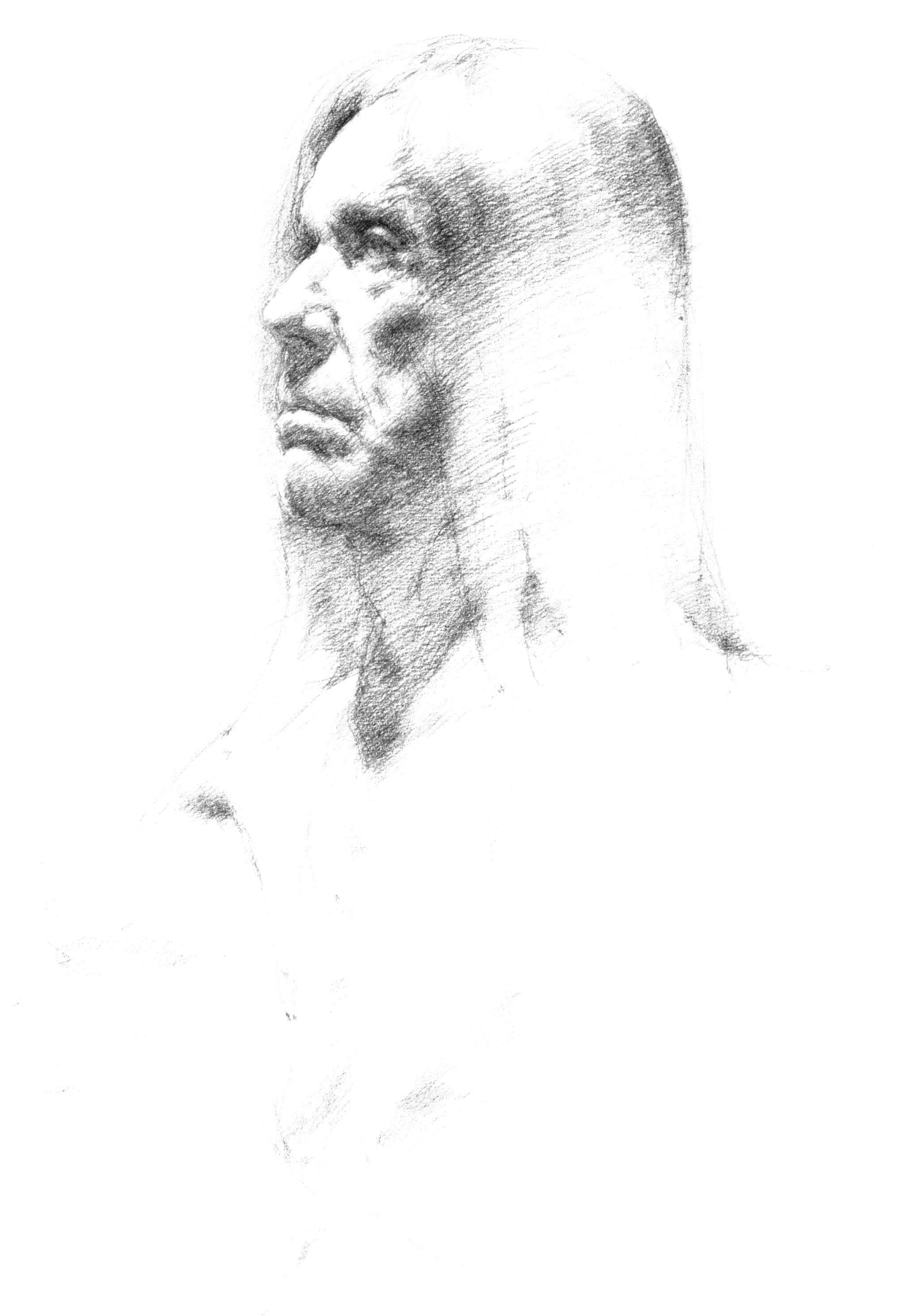

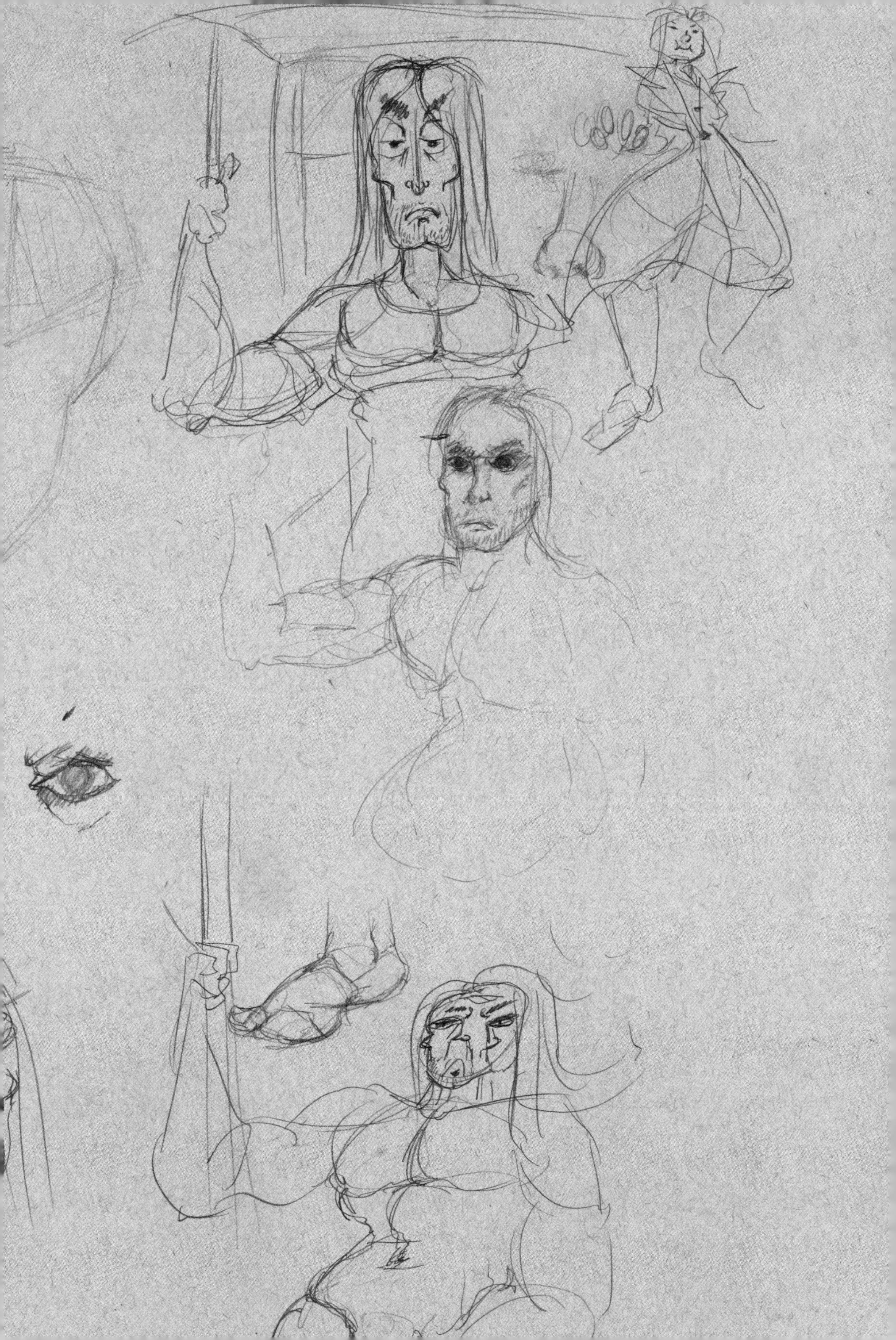

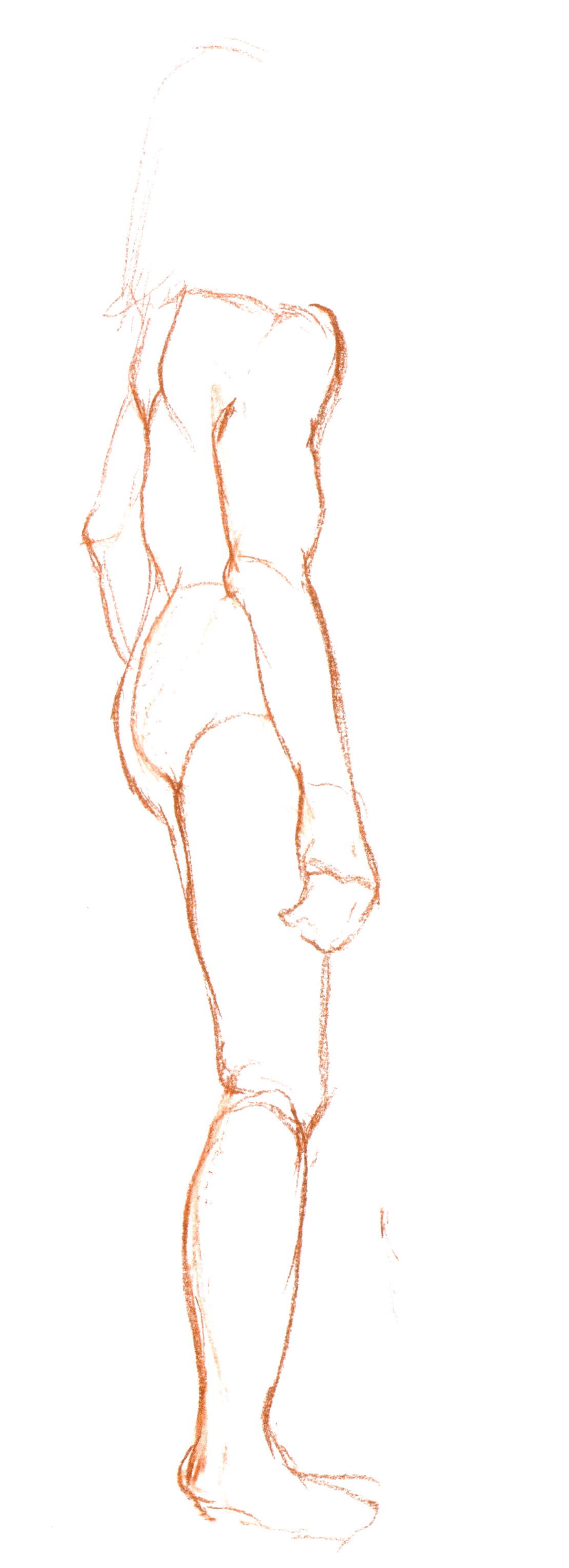

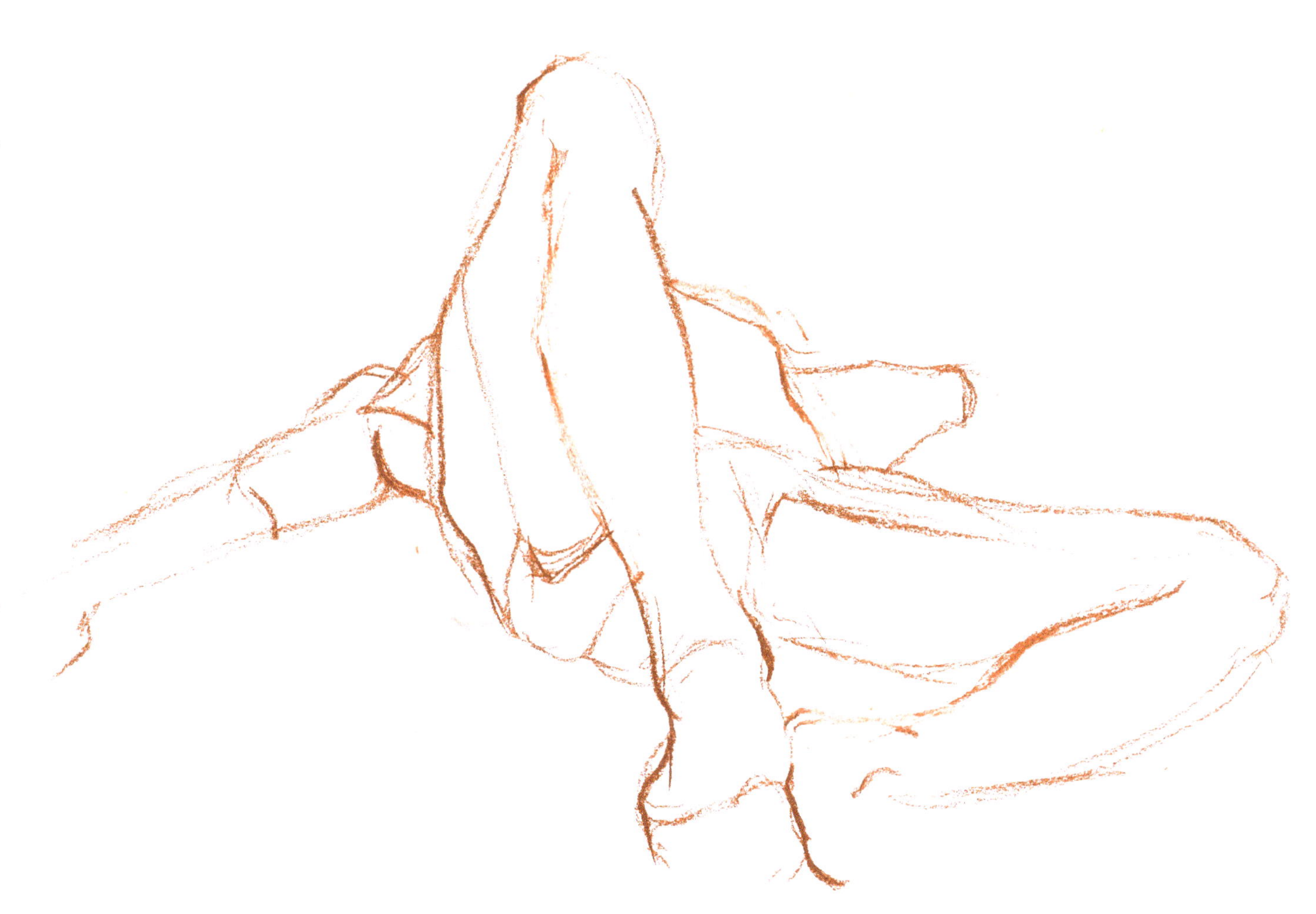

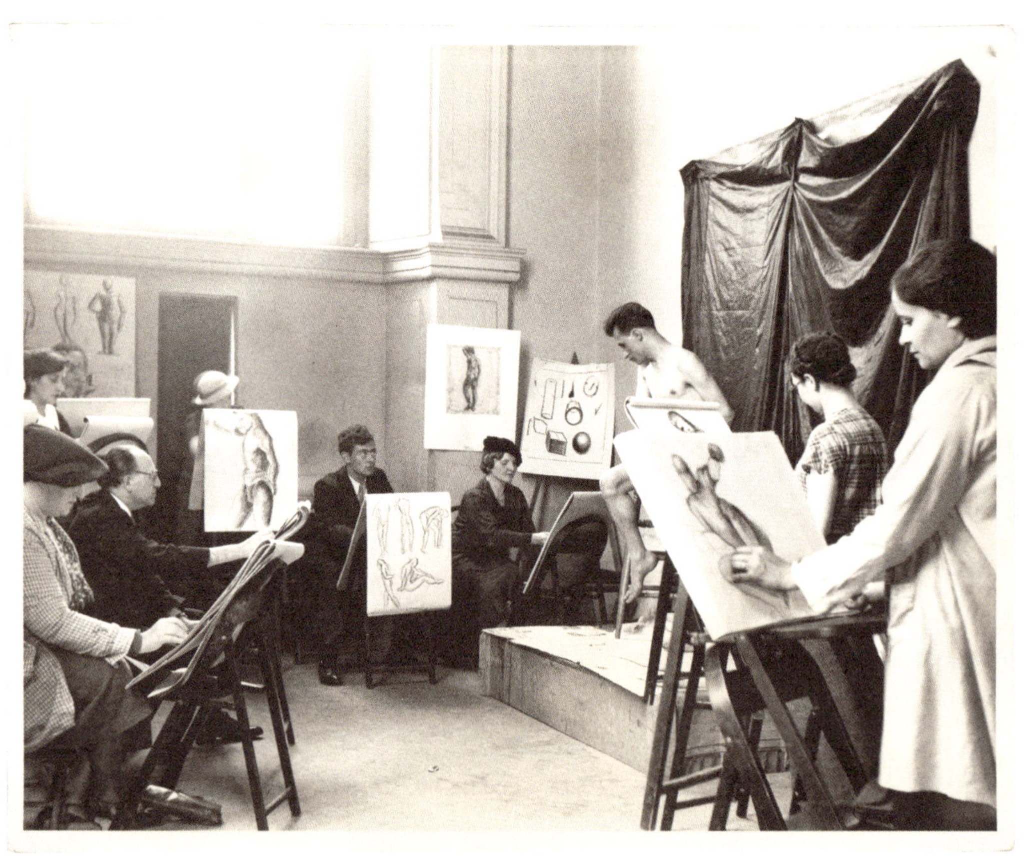

A life class for adults at the Brooklyn Museum, under the auspices of the New York City Works Progress Administration Art Project, circa 1935

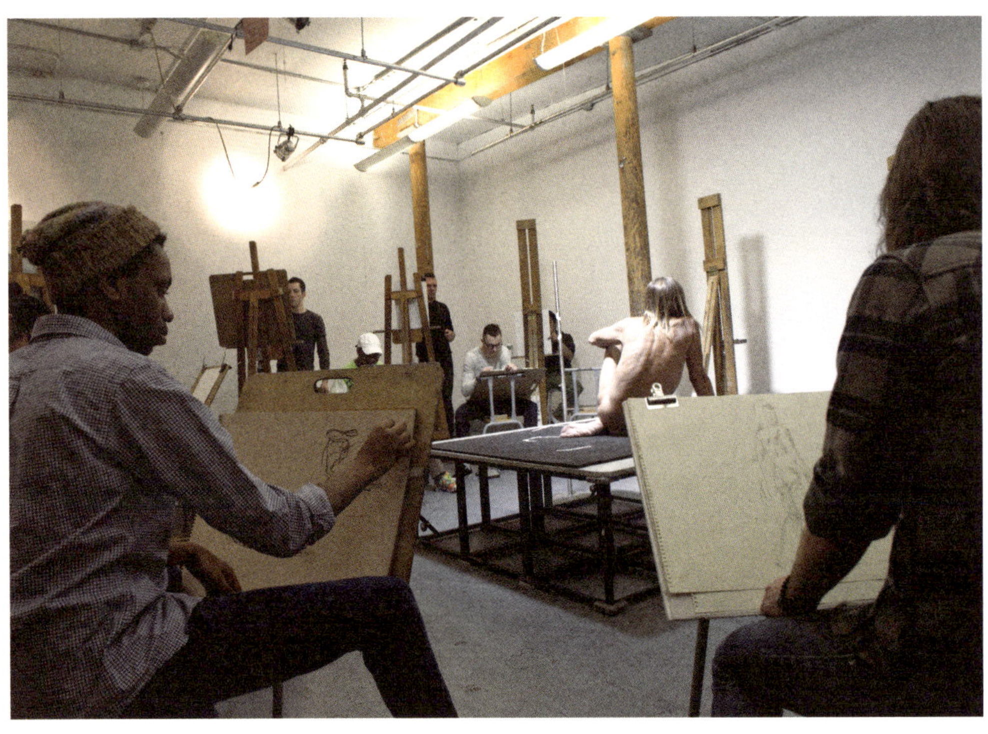

Iggy Pop Life Class in progress, February 21, 2016, New York Academy of Art

How to Organize an Iggy Pop Life Class

Sharon Matt Atkins

When Jeremy Deller approached us with his concept to organize a life drawing class with Iggy Pop as the model, it made complete sense for the Brooklyn Museum. Drawing from the live model has a long tradition not only in the history of art, as Frances Borzello's essay outlines, but also at the Museum. Dating back to 1841, the Brooklyn Museum has provided hands-on art education by organizing drawing classes. While records do not indicate whether or not life drawing was part of the program in the Museum's earliest years, when it was known as the Brooklyn Institute of Arts and Sciences, drawing was certainly among the offerings and likely included models. In the 1930s, life drawing classes for adults were held at the Museum under the auspices of the New York City WPA Art Project. A photograph from 1935 documents one class held in the Museum's third-floor galleries with a male model (opposite page). Later, in 1941, the Brooklyn Museum Art School opened as a non-degree professional school for artists. Drawing instruction from the model was central to the curriculum until the school closed in 1985 and was transferred to Pratt Institute. An advertising poster produced for the School in 1971 provided a humorous take on the dynamic between artists and model (page 124). Today, the Museum's Education Division continues to offer life drawing classes as part of its Gallery/Studio Program.

This history, along with the Museum's encyclopedic collections, encouraged Pop to partner with Jeremy and with the Brooklyn Museum to stage this one-of-a-kind life class.[1] (Most life drawing models remain anonymous, and rarely if ever is their identity widely known, let alone a celebrity.) Once he confirmed his participation, in December 2015, Jeremy and I set out to organize the logistics of the class, including its participants, instructor, and location.

Our first step was to select the participants and the instructor. We were keen to identify a group of artists who would reflect the diversity of New York City, as much as twenty-two people can. Rather than an open participation call, we contacted drawing instructors to solicit recommendations for students. With so many art schools in the greater New York City area to choose from, we focused on those with dedicated drawing programs, particularly ones with an interest in traditional, academic study from the nude model. We reached out to Michael Grimaldi, New York Academy of Art; Peter Cox, the Art Students League of New York; Frank Lind, Pratt Institute, Brooklyn; Jeanne Wilkinson, Kingsborough Community College, Brooklyn; and Zen Browne, Gallery/Studio Program, Brooklyn Museum. Each instructor provided us with the names and work samples of several of their students.

1. See the interview with Iggy Pop, pages 11–31.

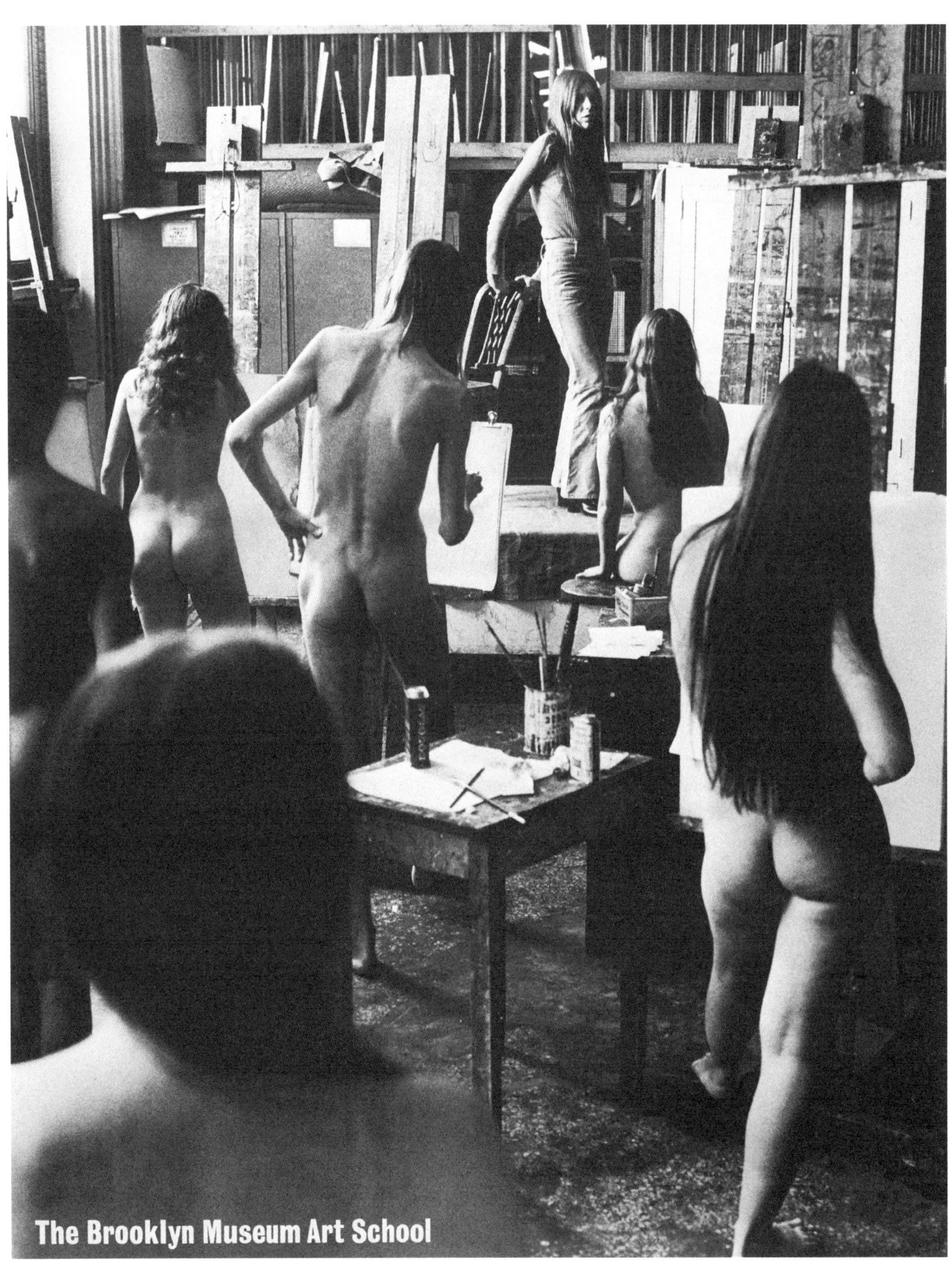

Richard Levy, *Poster for the Brooklyn Museum Art School*, circa 1971

As part of the selection process, we met with the instructors to discuss their students' drawings, which significantly shaped the organization and structure of the class. The most valuable part of our research was our visit to Peter Cox's "Anatomy and Drawing" class at the Art Students League of New York, the influential school founded by artists in 1875. Cox's invitation to attend his class (which had about fifty students and two models, male and female) offered a firsthand opportunity to consider what we would need for our own class. In the end, we also identified several artists from his class to participate.

After making the initial selection of candidates, I reached out to the artists and explained Jeremy's concept, but did not share the identity of the model. Jeremy wanted the artists to agree to participate based on an interest in working with the Brooklyn Museum rather than the identity of the model. The group of twenty-one class participants ranged from nineteen to eighty years of age with varying backgrounds, and included undergraduate and graduate students, practicing artists, and retirees.[2]

We also needed to hire an instructor to lead our class, a factor that became linked to our consideration of the best venue. The New York Academy of Art has roomy, classic drawing studios with everything needed to stage a life drawing class. After all, we wanted the class to be as typical as possible. Michael Grimaldi, Director of the Department of Drawing at the Academy, and an artist who often works from life, enthusiastically agreed to lead the class. Michael's role was equally critical to the success of the class itself. He helped direct and time the sequence of poses. The layout of the room also needed to be carefully considered. Some artists preferred to work standing, some liked to be seated, while others wanted specific angles or viewpoints of the model.

Before the class began, the artists settled into their assigned spots. After Pop arrived, we asked the participants to leave the room to allow Jeremy and Michael to work with the model to set what would be the "long pose." We knew in advance that Pop preferred a seated pose for the longest one, so we had already set up the stage with a block for him to sit on and a pole for him to hold onto. Once he found a comfortable pose, one he could sustain for the approximately three hours of the "long pose," Michael taped out the location of his hand on the pole and his feet on the platform, which would allow him to situate himself easily back into the same position after each break. The model then left the room, and the class reentered and got settled.

Finally, the start of the class. Our model made his entrance with great enthusiasm, making jokes with the artists. He began with a series of four poses, each held for five minutes. These quick poses offered the artists an opportunity to get warmed up and accustomed to drawing his body. The first pose was a standing one. Michael used a timer to mark the end of the pose, but Iggy mentioned that he was singing his songs to himself; since he knew the exact time of each song, he could tell when a pose was coming to an end.

2. For biographical information on the participating artists, as well as the complete list of their drawings, see pages 130–140.

Initially, we were only going to have three short poses, but Iggy wanted to rest after the first standing pose and quickly lay down on the stage, relaxing his legs casually on the platform. Jeremy immediately saw that it was a good pose, and we stuck with it for the next five minutes. Another standing pose followed, and then a coiled, seated position with one leg up and his arm resting on it.

The rest of the class focused on one long, seated pose that lasted approximately three hours. It was held for fifteen to twenty minutes at a time, with five-minute breaks in-between. The pose calls to mind the classical tradition of a seated figure of authority and power, often holding a scepter; one can imagine Pop as a naked, unidealized version of the Napoleon in Ingres's painting (opposite page).

The class resulted in 107 drawings. They range from subtly sinuous line sketches delineating the naked form to highly detailed portraits. The artists and sitter together created a corpus of work that will stand as documentation of this body—the iconic nature of which is analyzed in Mark Beasley's essay—and as a record of Jeremy Deller's vision. Accessioned into the Museum's collection, the drawings can inspire generations of visitors to contemplate Pop's "performed" body and, more broadly, the dynamic, still vital relationship between performance, drawing, and the male form.

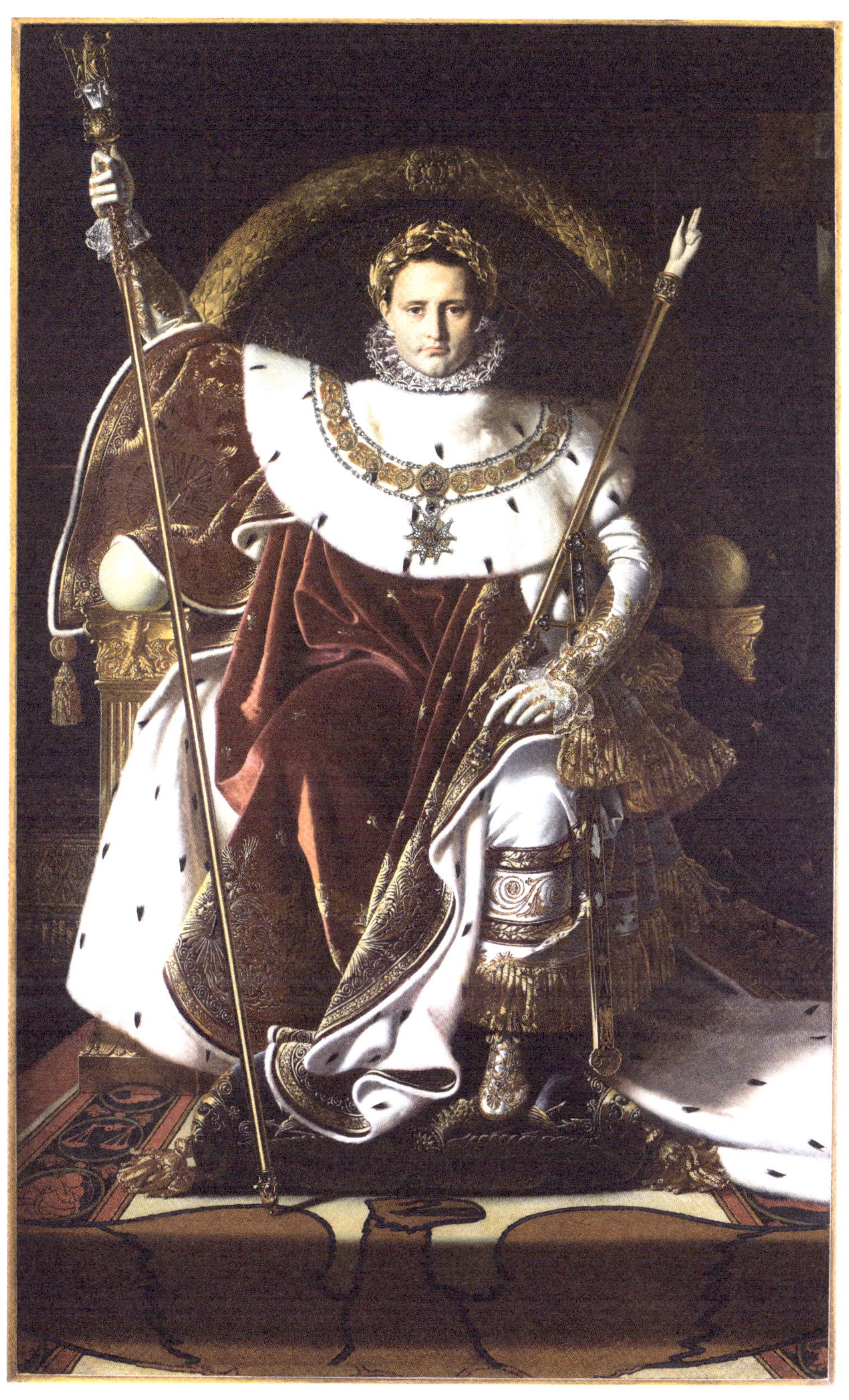

Jean-Auguste-Dominique Ingres, *Napoleon I on His Imperial Throne*, 1806.
Musée de l'Armée, Paris

Group portrait of the Iggy Pop Life Class participants,
February 21, 2016, New York Academy of Art →

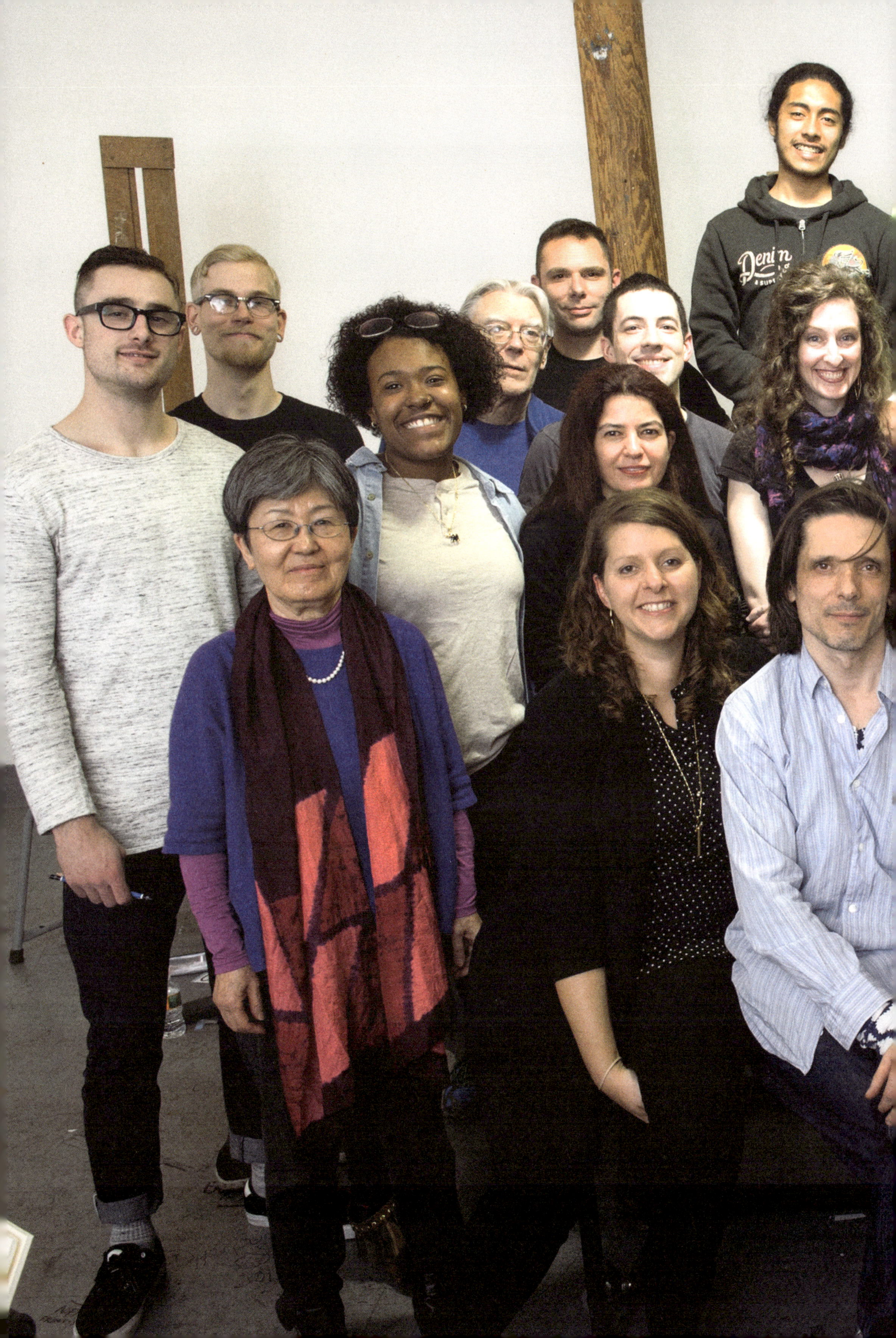
Denim

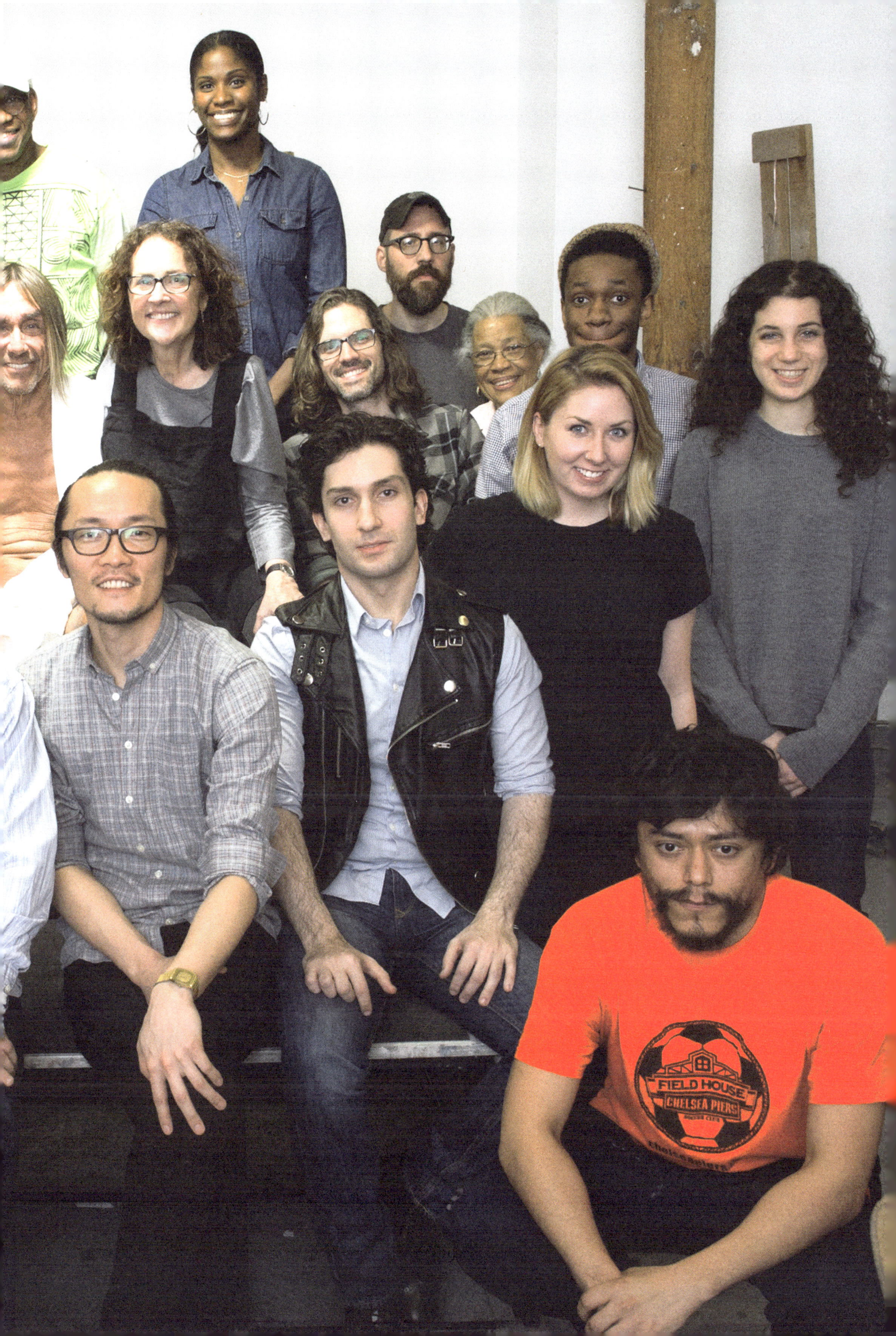
FIELD HOUSE
CHELSEA PIERS

Artists' Biographies and Life Class Drawings

Compiled by Emily Annis

All drawings are in the Brooklyn Museum Collection. An asterisk (*) denotes a drawing included in the exhibition and reproduced in the plates of this book. Plates represent details of the original drawings.

Jeremy Day
American, born 1976

Day was seventeen when he took his first life drawing class, at the Minneapolis College of Art and Design. In 2003, he enlisted in the United States Air Force and served for five years. During that time he continued to paint while stationed in Germany. Day has studied at the Art Students League of New York since moving to Brooklyn in 2013.

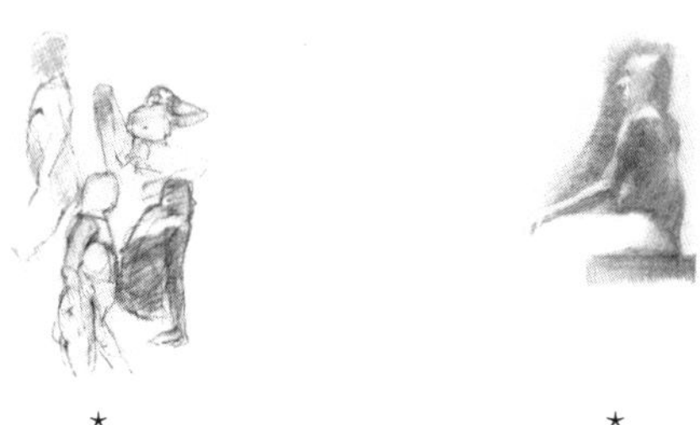

Jeanette Farrow

After studying computer animation and graphic arts at the Computer Arts Institute in San Francisco in the late 1990s, Farrow started her own web design business in 2002. Since relocating to New York, she has studied drawing and sculpture at the Art Students League of New York.

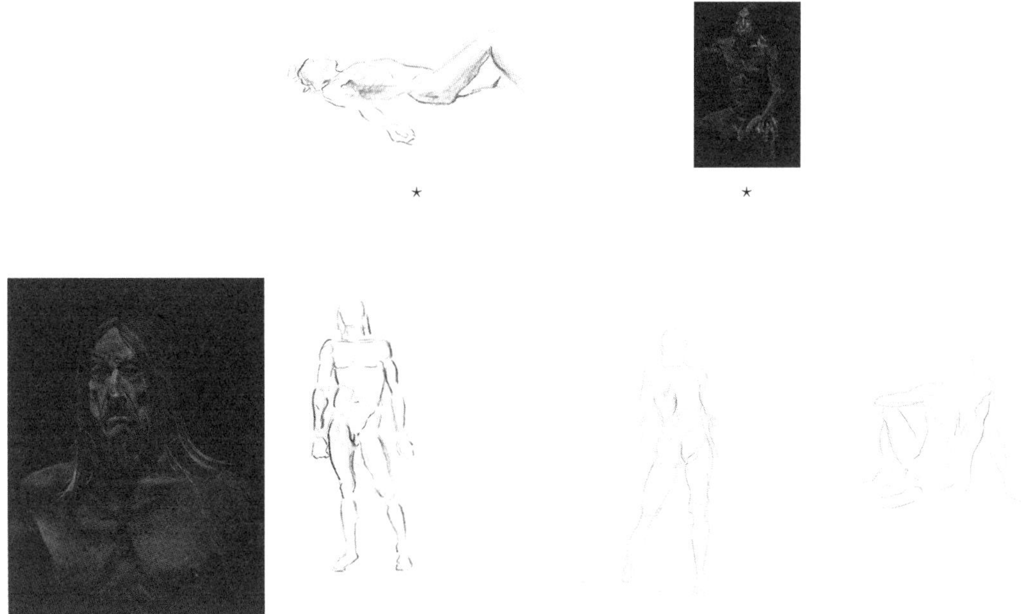

Margaret Fisher
American, born 1993

Fisher began making art as a teenager. She received an associate's degree from Pratt Institute, Brooklyn, in illustration and graphic design and is currently pursuing a BFA degree in painting at Pratt. She has won numerous awards in the Mid-Atlantic region and received a painting commission from the Massachusetts Institute of Technology, Cambridge.

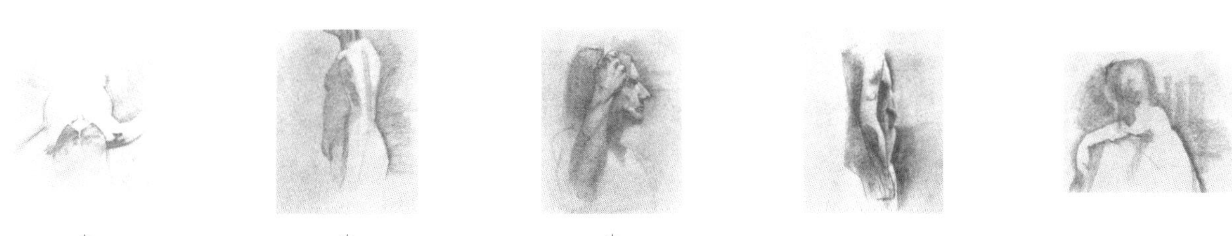

Seiji Gailey
American, born 1987

Hailing from Anchorage, Alaska, Gailey began studying painting and drawing at the Art Students League of New York in 2011. His work has been included in four group exhibitions at the League and has received both Honorable Mention and Best in Show multiple times in the annual student competitions.

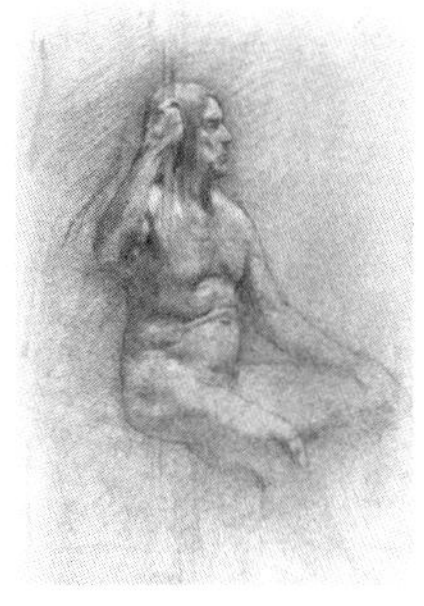
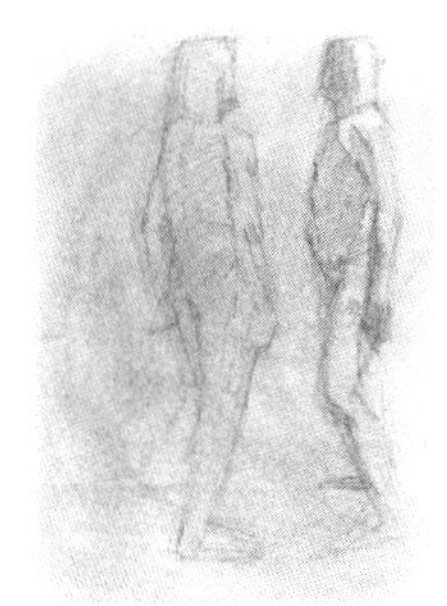
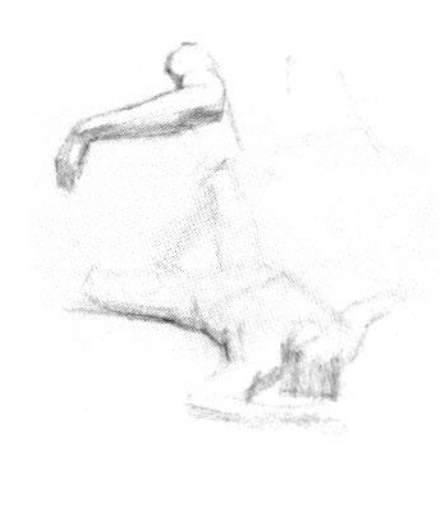

*

Michael Grimaldi
American, born 1971

Grimaldi has been the Director of the Department of Drawing at the New York Academy of Art since 2015. Prior to that, he taught at the National Academy of Design and the School of Visual Arts, both in New York; the Pennsylvania Academy of the Fine Arts, Philadelphia; the Art Students League of New York; and Drexel University College of Medicine, Philadelphia, where he founded the artistic anatomy program. He has received grants from the Stacey Foundation and the Elizabeth Greenshields Foundation, and has completed residencies with the Forbes Foundation in Balleroy, France, and the American Academy in Rome. His work has been included in national and international group exhibitions, and he has had solo exhibitions at the Musée Montaigue, France; the Art Students League of New York; the Studio Gallery, Washington; John Pence Gallery, San Francisco; Arcadia Gallery, New York; and Fontbonne University Gallery of Art, St. Louis.

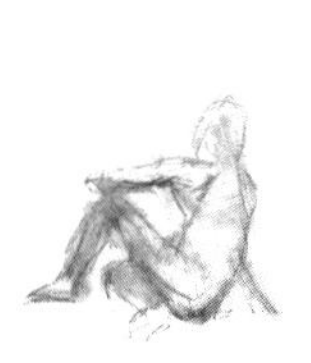
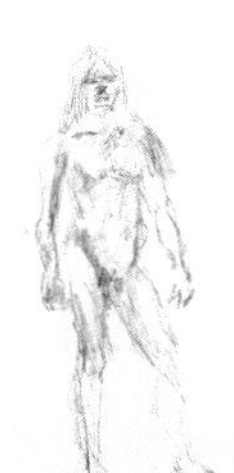
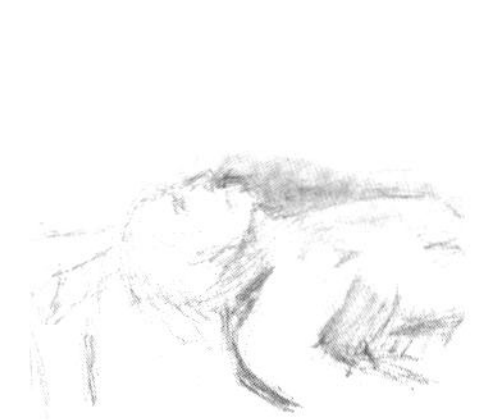
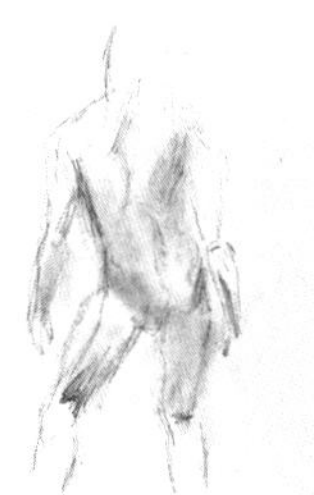
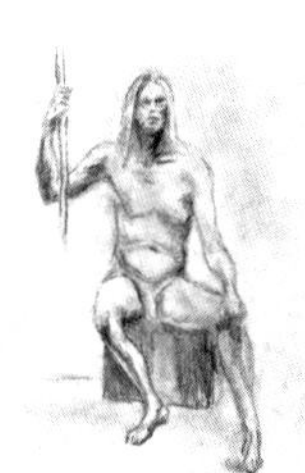
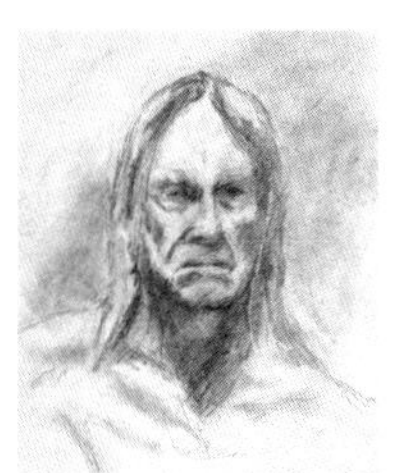

*

Robert Hagan
American, born 1943

Hagan received an MFA degree from the University of Wisconsin in 1968 and has continued to study art with the Brooklyn Museum's Gallery/Studio Program. His work has been included in numerous group exhibitions in the New York City area, including *Click! A Crowd-Curated Exhibition* (2008) at the Brooklyn Museum.

Tobias Hall
American, born 1981

After receiving his BFA degree from Arizona State University, Hall studied painting and drawing with various private instructors in Santa Fe, Seattle, Paris, and the Hague. His work has been included in numerous national exhibitions. He has received grants from the Studio Escalier, Paris, and the John F. and Anna Lee Stacey Foundation. Hall is currently pursuing an MFA degree at the New York Academy of Art.

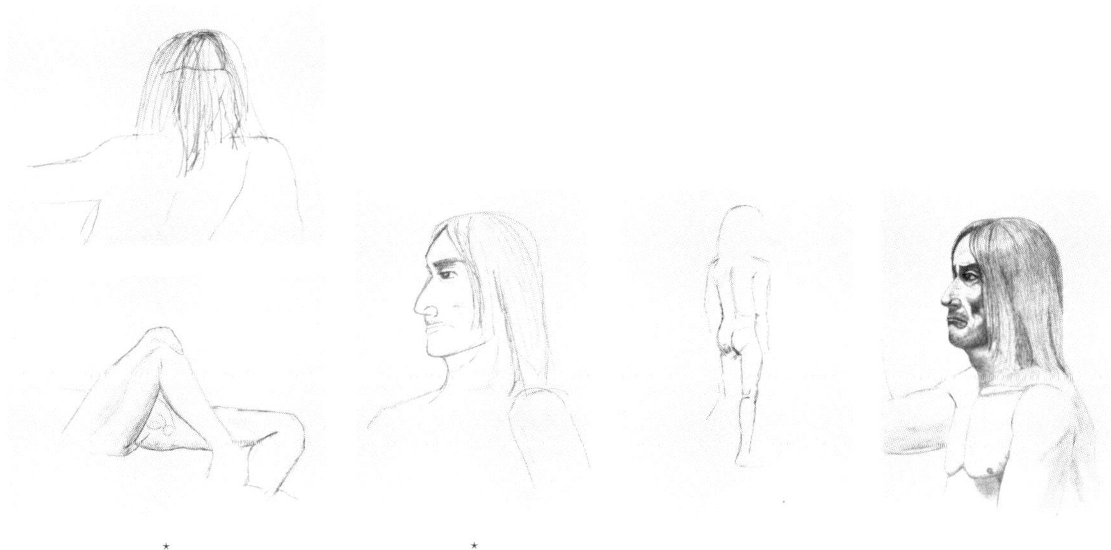

Deirdra Hazeley
American, born 1982

Following completion of a bachelor's degree in textiles and apparel at Cornell University, Hazeley went on to receive MA degrees in comparative sociology, from Florida International University, and in art and art education, from Columbia University, New York. Her work has been exhibited in galleries throughout Brooklyn, and she has completed residencies with the League Residency at Vytlacil, Sparkill, New York, and the Vermont Studio Center, Johnson. Hazeley continues to study drawing in the Brooklyn Museum's Gallery/Studio Program.

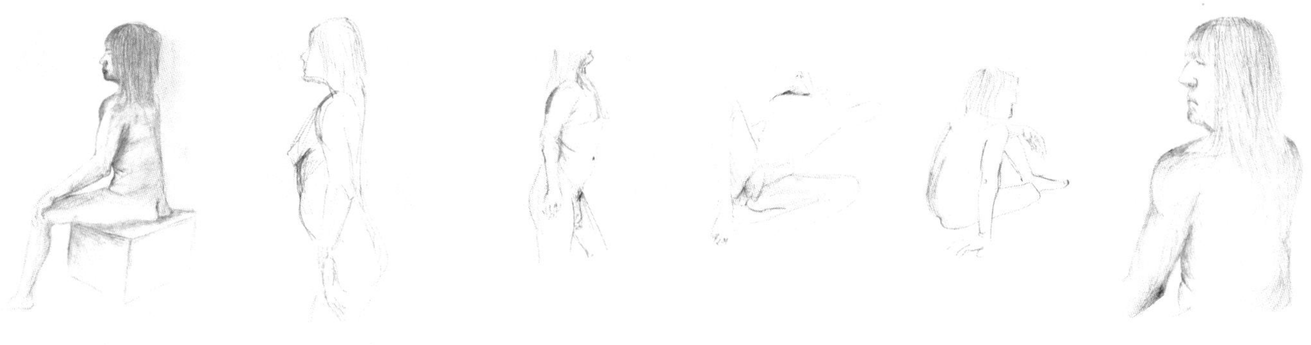

Patricia Hill
American, born 1936

Hill's interest in art began when she attended the High School of Music and Art (now the Fiorello H. LaGuardia High School of Music & Art and Performing Arts) from 1949 to 1953. After that, she went on to receive a master's degree in psychology from Brooklyn College and became a certified early-childhood teacher. Hill returned to art in her retirement and has studied in the Brooklyn Museum's Gallery/Studio Program for the past decade.

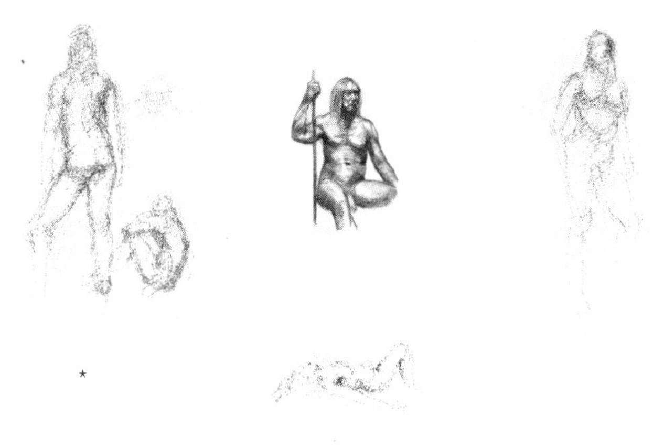

Okim Woo Kim
American, born Korea, 1942

While working in the health-care industry as a pharmacist for more than four decades, Okim Woo Kim has practiced drawing and painting. She has studied and exhibited with the Art Students League of New York since 2000 and has been recognized as Best in Show six times at the annual student competitions.

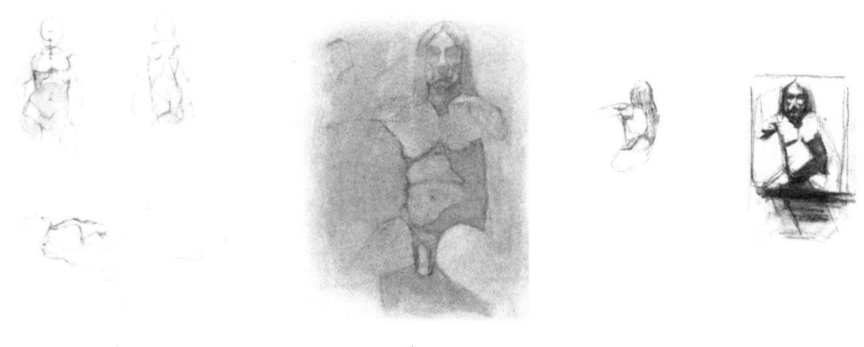

Maureen McAllister
American, born 1952

Prior to studying drawing, McAllister worked in the marketing industry for over three decades and taught at Parsons School of Design and the New School. She began her training as an artist first with the Park Slope Art School Atelier in 2013 and joined the Art Students League of New York in 2014.

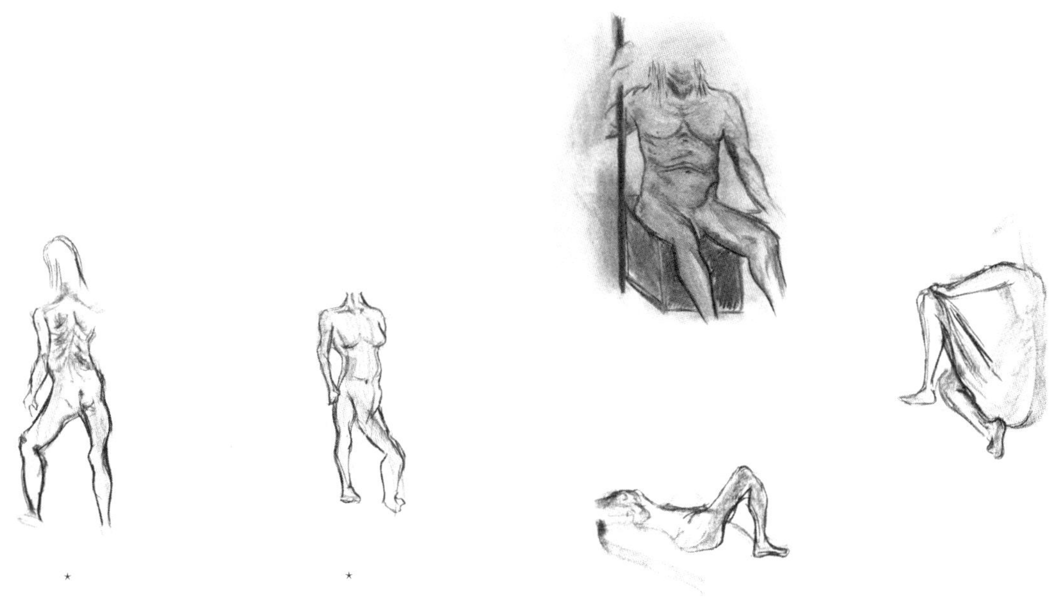

Kallyiah Merilus
American, born 1996

At the time when Merilus was selected to participate in the Iggy Pop Life Class, she was new to drawing, having begun her first drawing class just two weeks prior. She is currently pursuing an associate of arts degree at Kingsborough Community College, Brooklyn.

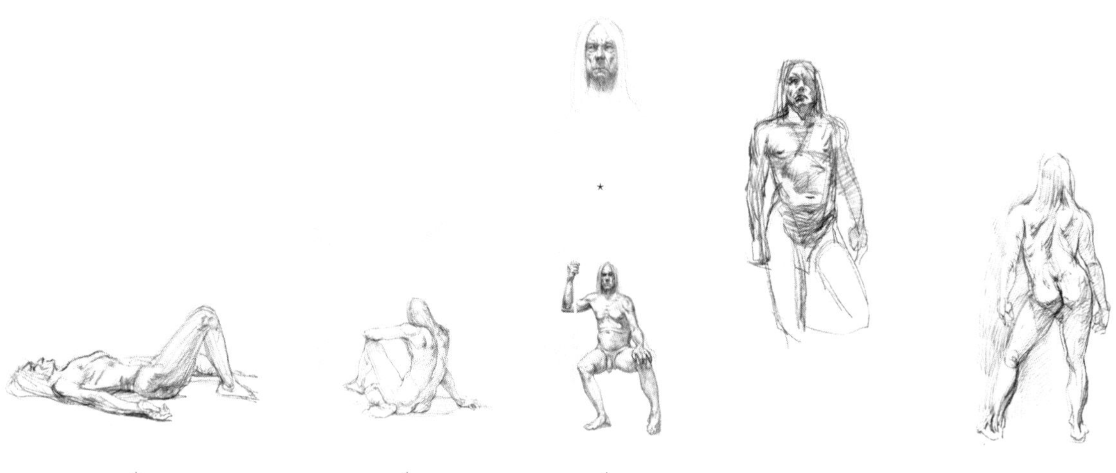

Guno Park
Canadian, born Korea, 1979

Since 2003, Park has taught figure, animal, and anatomical drawing and computer animation in art schools in Canada and the United States. His work has been exhibited throughout the New York City area and in Toronto, and has been published in numerous books, including *The Art of Ballpoint* (Rockport Publishers, 2016) and *The Sketchbook Project* (Princeton Architectural Press, 2015). Park has completed residencies in Giverny, France, and Macau, China. He holds an MFA degree from the New York Academy of Art.

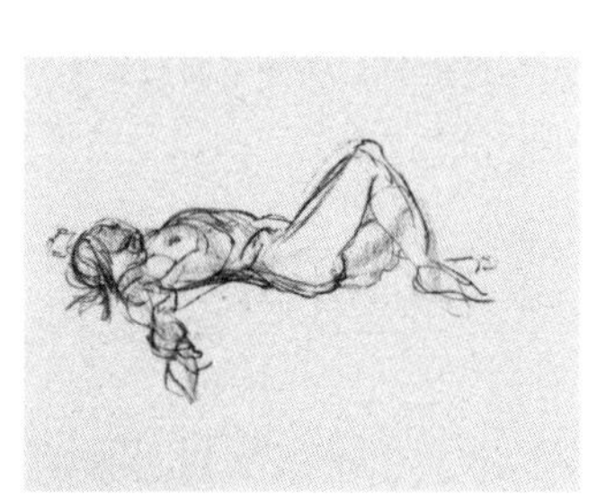
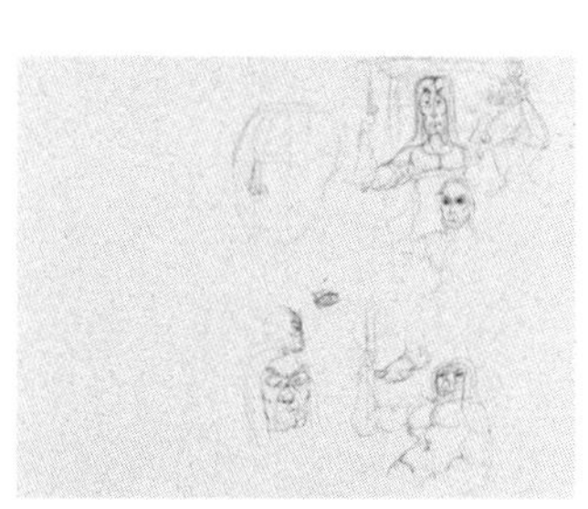
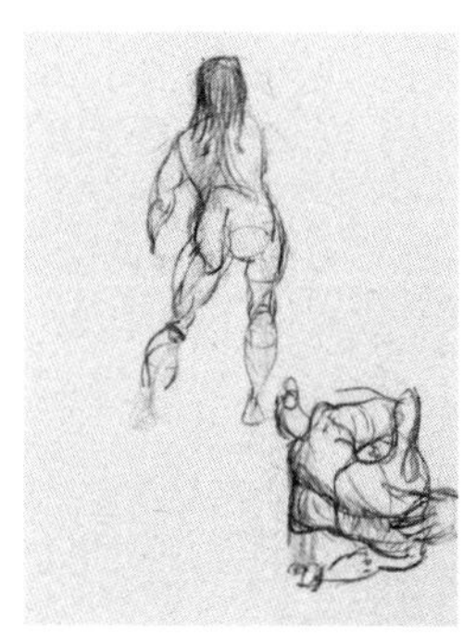
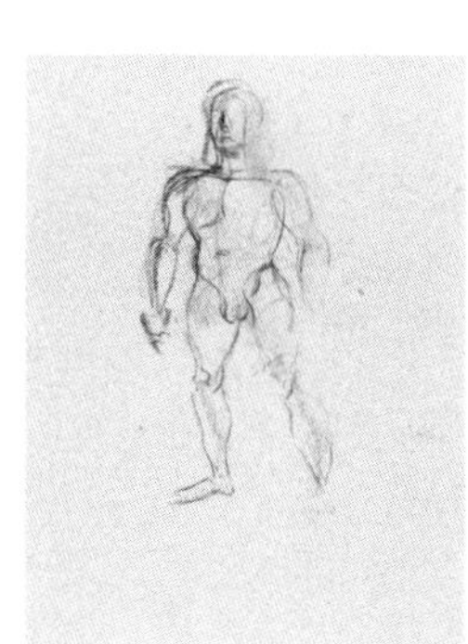
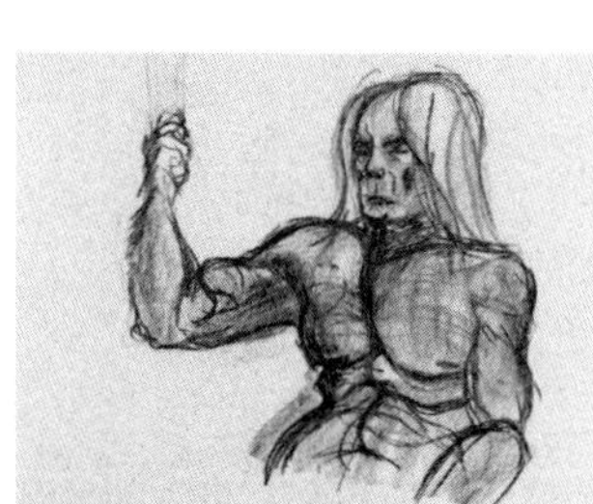
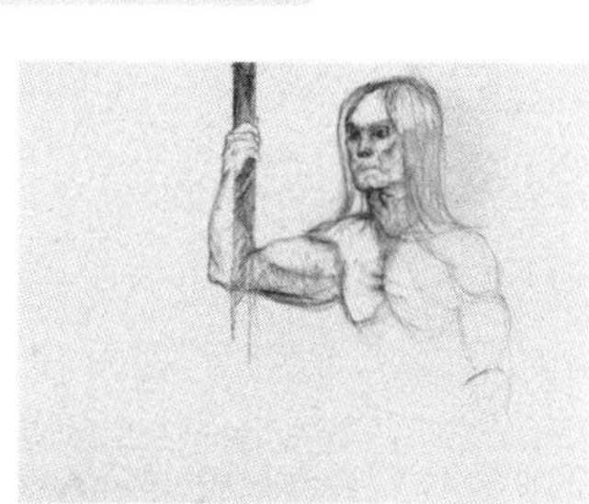

Kinley Pleteau
American, born 1994

Pleteau received a BFA degree in 2-D animation from Pratt Institute, Brooklyn, in 2016. His focus is on traditional and digital frame-by-frame animation, as well as stop-motion graphics-based animation.

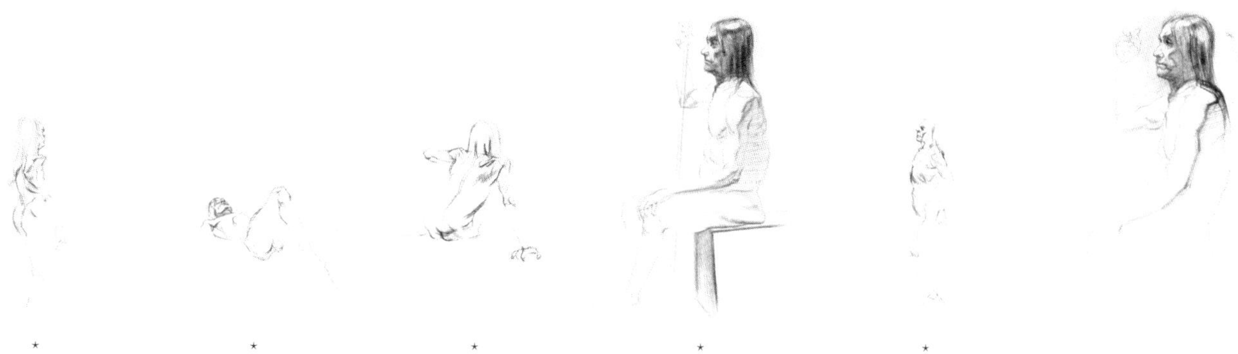

Angel Ramirez
American, born Peru, 1978

Ramirez graduated from the School of Visual Arts in 2001 with a BFA degree in illustration and cartooning. He has since continued his training by attending classes at the Art Students League of New York.

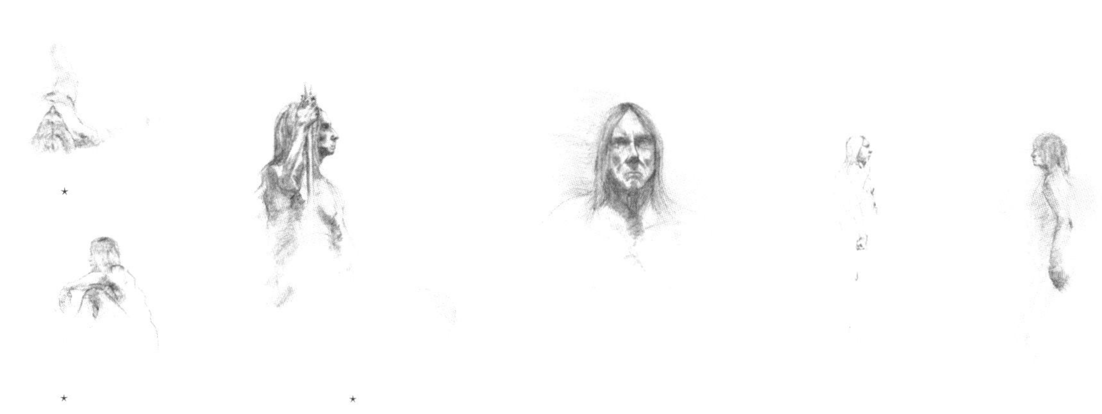

Robert Reid
Trinidadian, born 1960

Trained as an architectural draftsman, Reid pursued his passion for painting when he relocated to New York City in 1989 and began studying at the School of Visual Arts and the Art Students League of New York. Since the mid-1990s, his work has been included in gallery and museum exhibitions throughout the city, including *Black Romantic: The Figurative Impulse in Contemporary African-American Art* (2002) at the Studio Museum in Harlem.

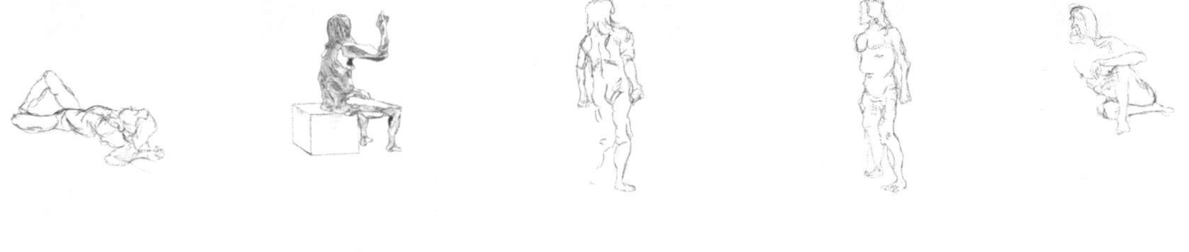

Mauricio Rodriguez
American, born 1996

Rodriguez joined his first drawing class in the fall of 2015, when he began studying at Kingsborough Community College, Brooklyn. He is pursuing an associate of arts degree in fine art.

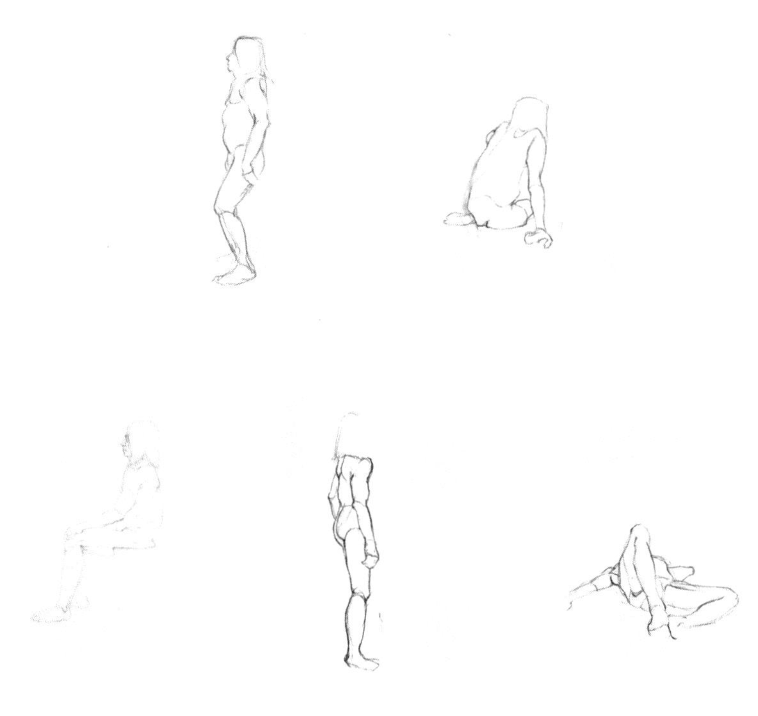

Danielle Rubin
American, born 1995

As a student at Pratt Institute, Brooklyn, pursuing a BFA degree in painting, Rubin has studied anatomical drawing and narrative illustration. Her work has been included in group exhibitions at Skidmore College, Saratoga Springs, New York, and at Pratt.

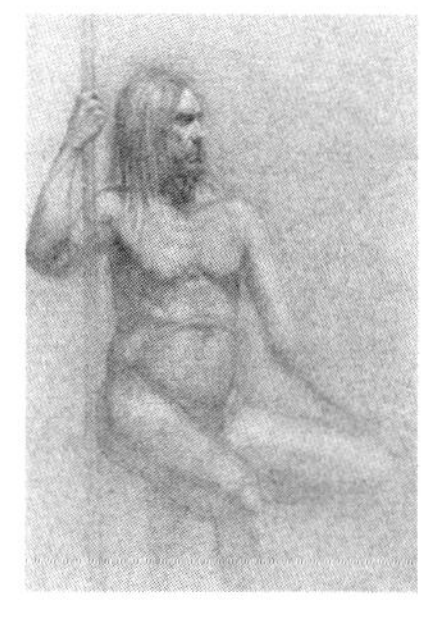

Taylor Schultek

American, born 1990

After completing his BFA degree at Minnesota State University Moorhead, Schultek received an MFA degree from the New York Academy of Art. His work has been included in numerous national and international exhibitions. He has also painted commissioned murals in Minnesota, North Dakota, and New York City.

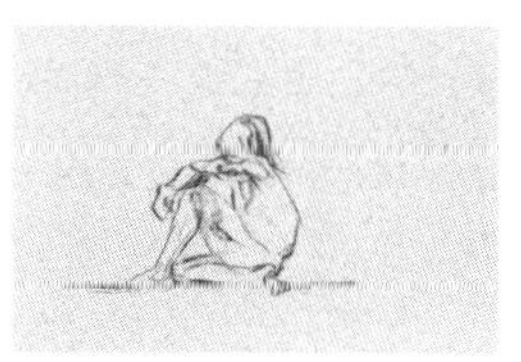

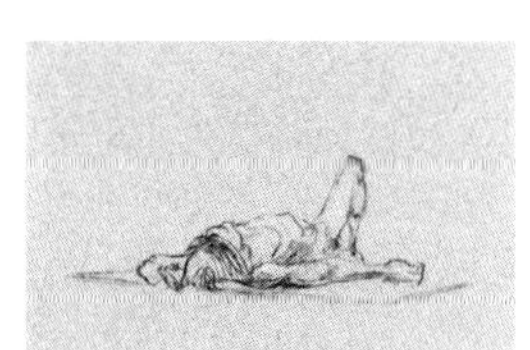

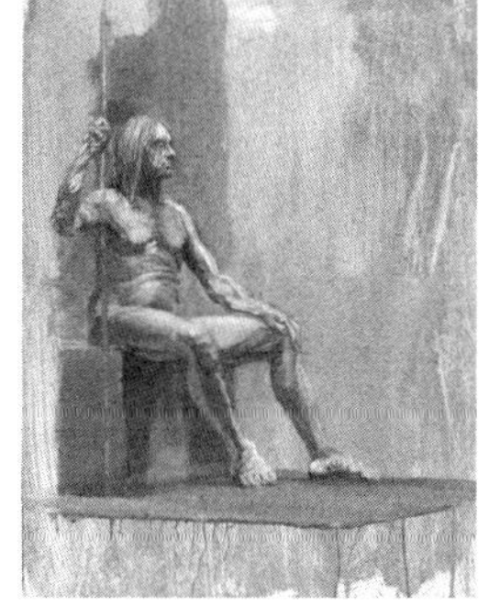

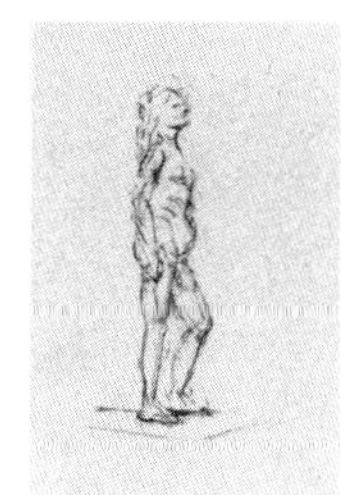

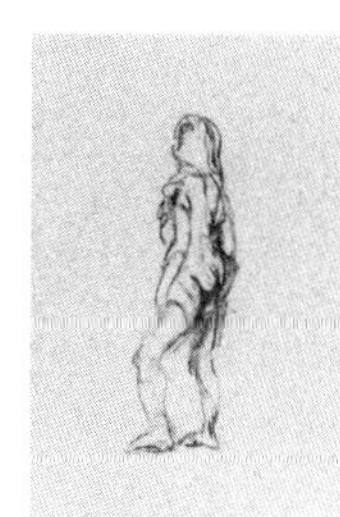

Charlotte Segall

American, born 1983

Segall's work has been included in many group exhibitions in New York, Georgia, New Mexico, and Leipzig, Germany, and is in the collections of Diane and Sandy Besser, Allouche Gallery, and Eileen Guggenheim. She holds a BFA degree from Savannah College of Art and Design, Georgia, and an MFA in painting from the New York Academy of Art.

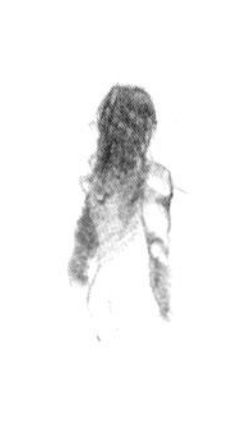
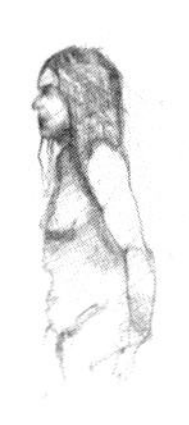
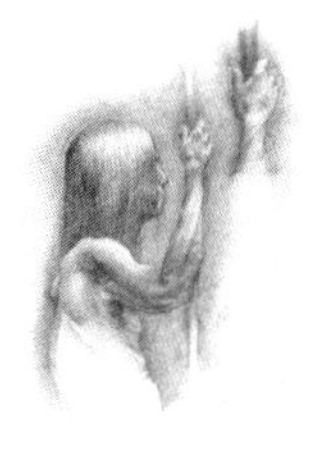
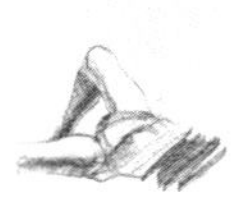

*   *   *

Andrew Shears
American, born 1990

Shears began studying journalism at Fort Lewis College in Colorado and transferred to Pratt Institute, Brooklyn, in 2014 to pursue a BFA degree in painting. He worked in France as a studio assistant and continues to paint in connection with private art commissions.

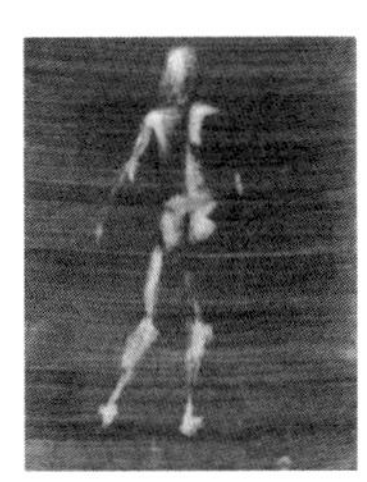
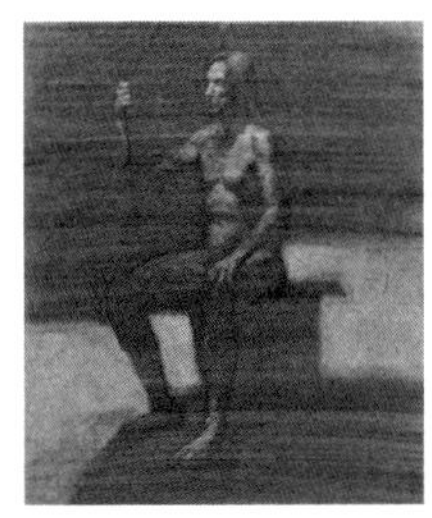
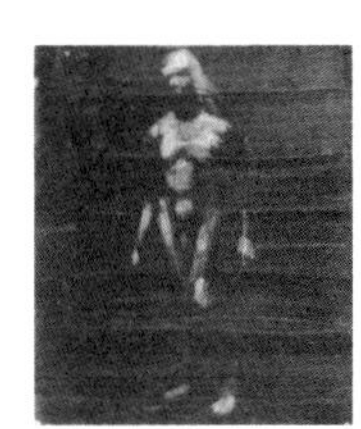
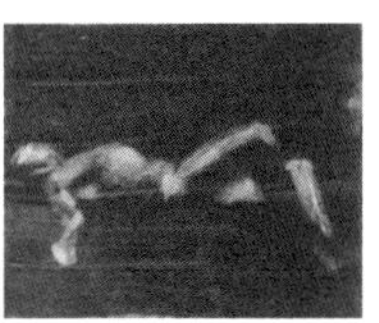

*   *

Levan Songulashvili
Georgian, born 1991

Originally from Tbilisi, Georgia, Songulashvili came to New York to study at the New York Academy of Art, where he recently received an MFA degree. He has received many awards, including the Prime Minister's Award from the International Education Center of Georgia.

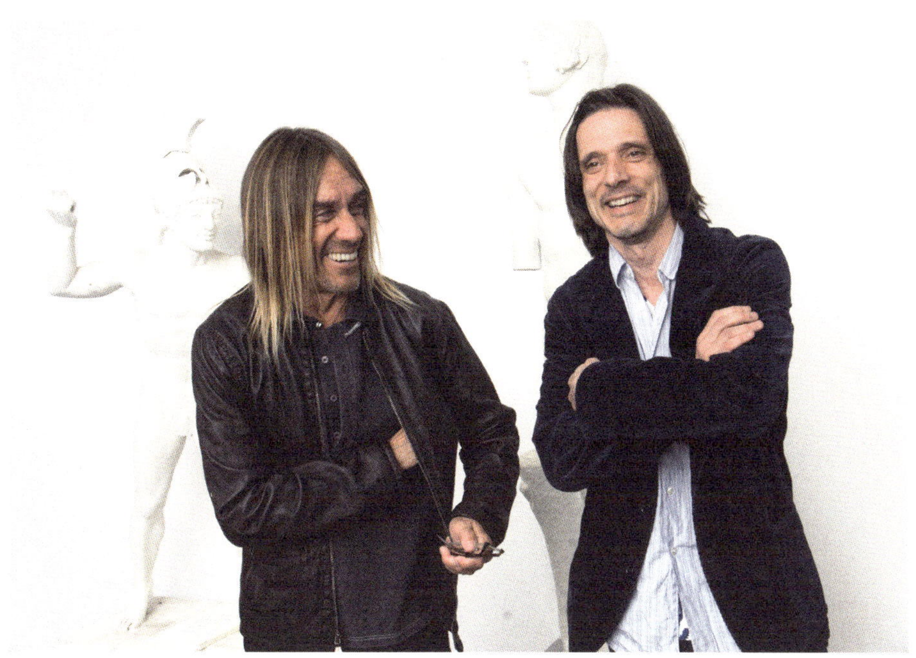

Iggy Pop (left), Jeremy Deller (right), New York, February 2016

Iggy Pop

A pioneer of rock music, Iggy Pop (American, born James Newell Osterberg, Jr., 1947) is a singer-songwriter, musician, and actor. Born and raised in Michigan, Pop began performing in the 1960s. In 1967, he formed The Stooges, a band that has significantly influenced the trajectory of rock music. Pop is known for dynamic and unpredictable stage performances, a trademark throughout his career. These highly physical events often left his body battered and cut. His music has encompassed a number of styles over the course of his career, with well-known albums such as *The Idiot* (1977) and *Lust for Life* (1977) (both co-written and produced by David Bowie), *Blah Blah Blah* (1986), *Brick by Brick* (1990), and *Skull Ring* (2003). In 2010, The Stooges were inducted into the Rock and Roll Hall of Fame. In 2016, Pop's seventeenth album, *Post Pop Depression*, a collaboration with Josh Homme of Queens of the Stone Age, was released to wide acclaim.

Jeremy Deller

London-based conceptual artist Jeremy Deller (English, born 1966) is known for orchestrating large-scale collaborative projects. In 2001, Deller worked with former miners and members of reenactment societies to restage a violent confrontation between the police and striking miners that had occurred in 1984, during the yearlong miners' strike in the United Kingdom. For *It Is What It Is*, commissioned by The Three M Project and Creative Time in 2009, Deller toured the United States with a car destroyed in a 2007 bomb attack in Baghdad, inviting journalists, Iraqi refugees, soldiers, and scholars to share their experiences. He has developed several music projects, including *Acid Brass* (1997), a brass-band performance of acid house music. Winner of the 2004 Turner Prize, Deller represented Great Britain at the 55th Venice Biennale in 2013.

Contributors

Sharon Matt Atkins is Vice Director, Exhibitions and Collections Management, Brooklyn Museum. At the Museum she has organized exhibitions such as *Stephen Powers: Coney Island Is Still Dreamland (To a Seagull)* and *FAILE: Savage/Sacred Young Minds*, both in 2015. In 2014, she organized the Brooklyn presentation of *Ai Weiwei: According to What?* and curated *Swoon: Submerged Motherlands*. She received her MA and PhD from Rutgers University.

Mark Beasley is a British curator, writer, and artist based in New York. He is currently a curator at Performa, New York, and curatorial advisor for the inaugural Okayama Art Summit triennial (2016). He is a faculty member and tutor in the MA program in curatorial practice at the School of Visual Arts, New York. His first LP with the group Big Legs is available on the London- and Amsterdam-based Junior Aspirin Records.

Frances Borzello has specialized in the social history of art since obtaining her doctorate at the University of London. She has published many books, including *The Naked Nude* (Thames & Hudson, 2012) and *The Artist's Model* (Faber reprint, 2013). Her most recent book is *Seeing Ourselves: Women's Self-Portraits* (Thames & Hudson, revised edition, 2016). She lives in England.

Image Credits

Photographs of Brooklyn Museum collection objects are by Sarah DeSantis. Photographs of the Iggy Pop Life Class in progress are by Elena Olivo (inside cover by Jeremy Deller). All life class drawings of Iggy Pop © the individual artists. The following list includes additional photo credits required by the owners of the images.

p. 6: Mick Rock (British, born 1948). *Iggy Pop Backbend*, 1972. Photographic print. Mick Rock/Feral Cat Productions. © Mick Rock 1972, 2016

p. 10: Diego Velázquez (Spanish, 1599–1660). *Mars*, circa 1638. Oil on canvas, 70 × 37 in. (179 × 95 cm). Museo del Prado, Madrid, PO1208. © Madrid, Museo Nacional del Prado

p. 13: Gerald Malanga (American, born 1943). *Iggy Pop*, 1971. Photographic print. Archives Malanga, 0026. © Gerard Malanga. All Rights Reserved

p. 14: Richard Bernstein (American, 1939–2002). *Iggy Pop*, 1972. Silkscreen, 33 × 42½ in. (83.8 × 108 cm). © Richard Bernstein Estate

p. 15: Peter Hujar (American, 1934–1987). *Iggy Pop Lying Down*, 1969. Photographic print. Courtesy Pace/MacGill Gallery, New York and Fraenkel Gallery, San Francisco. © 1987 The Peter Hujar Archive LLC

p. 18: Douglas R. Gilbert (American, born 1942). *Iggy Pop in Soldier's Field, Chicago*, 1970. Photographic print. Premium Archives. (Photo: Douglas R. Gilbert/Premium Archives/Getty Images)

pp. 20–21: Eadweard Muybridge (British, 1830–1904). *Animal Locomotion*, 1884–87. Photographic prints; full sheet, 19¼ × 24 in. (48.9 × 61 cm). Brooklyn Museum; Anonymous gift in memory of Jack Boulton, 1989.30.28

p. 23: *Satyr Holding a Jar*, circa 30 B.C.E.–395 C.E. Egypt; Roman Period. Terracotta, painted, 7³⁄₁₆ × 3¹⁄₁₆ × 1¹¹⁄₁₆ in. (18.2 × 7.8 × 4.3 cm). Brooklyn Museum, Charles Edwin Wilbour Fund, 37.1634E

p. 23: *Ithyphallic Man with a Harp*, 3rd–4th century C.E. Egypt; Roman Period. Terracotta, slipped and painted, 5¹¹⁄₁₆ × 3⅞ × 2³⁄₁₆ in. (14.4 × 9.8 × 5.6 cm). Brooklyn Museum; Gift of Evangeline Wilbour Blashfield, Theodora Wilbour, and Victor Wilbour honoring the wishes of their mother, Charlotte Beebe Wilbour, as a memorial to their father, Charles Edwin Wilbour, 16.271

p. 23: Leni Sinclair (American, born Germany, 1940). *Iggy Pop*, 1968. Scan from a photographic print. Collection of Leni Sinclair, Detroit. © Leni Sinclair

p. 24: *Torso of Dionysus*, 2nd–3rd century C.E. Roman copy of a Hellenistic statue. Basalt, 11⁷⁄₁₆ × 5½ × 2¹⁵⁄₁₆ in. (29 × 14 × 7.5 cm). Brooklyn Museum; Anonymous gift, 80.249

p. 25: Erich Heckel (German, 1883–1970). *Figure Sketch*, 1927. Color lithograph in black, green, and violet on laid paper, 27⅛ × 20¹⁵⁄₁₆ in. (68.9 × 53.2 cm). Brooklyn Museum; Henry L. Batterman Fund, 58.166.2. © 2016 Artists Rights Society (ARS), New York/VG Bild-Kunst, Bonn

p. 27: Egon Schiele (Austrian, 1890–1918). *Male Nude (Self-Portrait)*, 1912. Lithograph on paper, 17⅝ × 15¹¹⁄₁₆ in. (44.8 × 39.8 cm). Brooklyn Museum; Brooklyn Museum Collection, X625.3

p. 31: *Standing Male Figure*, early 20th century. Chamba. Adamawa State, Nigeria. Wood, organic materials, 24⅜ × 6 × 5 in. (61.9 × 15.2 × 12.7 cm). Brooklyn Museum; Gift in honor of William C. Siegmann in recognition of his contributions to the study and understanding of African Arts, 2011.31.1

p. 64: James Fortune (American, born England, 1947). *Iggy Pop at the Whisky à Go-Go*, 1974. Photographic print. James Fortune Archives, Ashland, Virginia. © James Fortune

pp. 68–69: Mike Kelley (American, 1954–2012). *Confusion: A Play in Seven Sets, Each Set More Spectacular and Elaborate than the Last*, 1983. Pilot Theater, Los Angeles. (Photo: Courtesy of the Mike Kelley Foundation for the Arts)

p. 70: Mike Kelley (American, 1954–2012). *The Oracle at Delphi*, 1978. Performance at CalArts. (Photo: Courtesy of the Mike Kelley Foundation for the Arts)

pp. 72–73: Thomas Copi (American, born 1945). *Iggy Pop*, 1970. Photographic print. Michael Ochs Archives. (Photo: Tom Copi/Michael Ochs Archive/Getty Images)

p. 75: Chris Burden (American, 1946–2015). Production still from the film *Through the Night Softly*, 1973. Gagosian Gallery. © Chris Burden courtesy of the Burden/Rubins Revocable Trust and Gagosian Gallery. (Photo: Charles Hill)

p. 80: Luis Meléndez (Spanish, 1716–1780). *Self-Portrait Holding an Academic Study*, 1746. Oil on canvas, 39³⁄₁₆ × 32⁵⁄₁₆ (99.5 × 82 cm). Musée du Louvre, Paris. © RMN–Grand Palais/Art Resource, NY. (Photo: Jean-Giles Berizzi)

p. 84: Sandro Botticelli (Florentine, circa 1444–1510). *The Birth of Venus*, 1486. Tempera on canvas, 68 × 109½ in. (172.5 × 278.9 cm). Galleria degli Uffizi, Florence. (Photo: Scala/Art Resource)

p. 84: Johann Zoffany (German, 1733–1810). *Life Class of the Royal Academy (The Academicians of the Royal Academy)*, 1771–72. Oil on canvas, 39¾ × 58 in. (101.1 × 147.5 cm). Royal Collection Trust, U.K. / © Her Majesty Queen Elizabeth II, 2016

p. 86: George du Maurier (British, born France, 1834–1896). "Female School of Art: Useful Occupation for Idle and Ornamental Young Men." *Punch*, May 30, 1874. © Punch Limited

p. 87: John Everett Millais (British, 1829–1896). *Male Nude in the Attitude of an Archer*, circa 1847. Pencil and chalk, 28 × 19 in. (71 × 50 cm). Towneley Hall Art Gallery and Museum, Burnley Borough Council, Lancashire, U.K.

p. 122: *A Life Class for Adults at the Brooklyn Museum, Under the Auspices of the New York City Works Progress Administration (WPA) Art Project*, circa 1935. Archives of American Art, Smithsonian Institution; Federal Art Project, Photographic Division collection, circa 1920–1965, bulk 1935–1942

p. 124: Richard Levy (American, born 1940). *Poster for the Brooklyn Museum Art School*, circa 1971. Brooklyn Museum Archives, Records of the Brooklyn Museum Art School. © Richard Levy, poster concept, design, and photograph

p. 127: Jean-Auguste-Dominique Ingres (French, 1780–1867). *Napoleon I on His Imperial Throne*, 1806. Oil on canvas, 102 × 64 in. (259 × 162 cm). Musée de l'Armée/Dist. RMN–Grand Palais/Art Resource, NY. (Photo: Pascal Segrette)

Acknowledgments

We first began discussing this project for the Brooklyn Museum in late 2015, which means that this publication and its related exhibition were organized in record time, at least by normal art museum standards. All involved responded to the concept with genuine excitement, making it possible to complete all aspects of the project successfully on our accelerated schedule.

Both the Brooklyn Museum and Jeremy Deller extend our deepest gratitude to Iggy Pop. Without his openness to being the model, none of this would have come to fruition. His dynamic career inspired the concept, but more than that, it was his generous spirit, humor, and warmth that made us all feel connected to the life class experience.

Many people deserve our thanks in helping to realize this project. Henry McGroggan helped us to coordinate myriad details with Iggy's busy touring schedule and offered important guidance for related matters. We are thankful to the drawing professors who recommended students as candidates for the class: Zen Browne, Brooklyn Museum Gallery/Studio Program; Peter Cox, the Art Students League of New York; Frank Lind, Pratt Institute; Jeanne Wilkinson, Kingsborough Community College; and Michael Grimaldi, the New York Academy of Art. We also extend our appreciation to Peter Drake, Dean of Academic Affairs at the New York Academy of Art, for helping us secure a drawing studio there to host the class. Grimaldi also eagerly signed on to lead the class and help us with the studio set-up.

The participating artists are at the core of the project, and we thank them for joining the project and making such memorable contributions, all of which are reproduced in "Artists' Biographies and Life Class Drawings" (beginning on page 130). We were thrilled that art historian Frances Borzello and curator, writer, and artist Mark Beasley signed on to contribute to the publication. Their broad perspectives are the perfect complement to the drawing project.

At the Brooklyn Museum, Anne Pasternak, Shelby White and Leon Levy Director, championed the project from the beginning. Kevin Stayton, former Deputy Director and Director of Collections and History, and Nancy Spector, Deputy Director and Chief Curator, provided valuable guidance on the exhibition. Brooklyn Museum curators Rich Aste, Edward Bleiberg, Connie Choi, Joan Cummins, Kevin Dumouchelle, Nancy Rosoff, and Eugenie Tsai devoted time to sharing their expertise with us on the related collection objects in the show. The exhibition team nimbly coordinated all aspects of this complex undertaking. Emily Annis, Curatorial Assistant, Exhibitions, enthusiastically assisted in organizing the life drawing class and the exhibition in addition to compiling the artists' biographies printed here. Dolores Farrell, Lisa Small, Cora Michael, Lisa Genna, Gwen Arriaga, Sara Devine, and Holly Harmon provided their valuable support. Lisa Bruno, Beatriz Centeno, Elyse Driscoll, Elaine Komorowski, Liz Reynolds, Walter Andersons, and their staff members helped plan the life drawing class and the exhibition. The elegant installation design was created by Matthew Yokobosky.

James Leggio, Head of Publications and Editorial Services, guided the progress of the publication with great appreciation of the topic. His colleague Anya Szykitka assisted with the editing; Sallie Stutz managed the Museum's merchandising plan for the book; and our Digital Lab team—Deborah Wythe, Sarah DeSantis, Jonathan Dorado, and Jessica Palinski—oversaw photography and image rights with expertise and good cheer. We are most pleased to partner with Daniel Scott and his colleagues at Heni Publishing, London, on the production of the book, and we are fortunate to have had Fraser Muggeridge and Rachel Treliving as the graphic design team.

Jeremy wishes to extend special thanks and appreciation: "To Anne Pasternak for saying yes, and to Sharon Matt Atkins for her patience with me." He also thanks Jarvis Cocker and Adam Dineen.

S.M.A. / J.D.